D1188131

Debates in Economic History

Edited by Peter Mathias

The Classical Economists and Economic Policy

The Classical Economists and Economic Policy

edited with an introduction by
A. W. COATS

METHUEN & CO LTD
11 NEW FETTER LANE LONDON EC4

First published 1971 by Methuen & Co Ltd
Introduction © 1971 by A. W. Coats
Printed in Great Britain by
Richard Clay (The Chaucer Press), Ltd,
Bungay, Suffolk

SBN 416 17660 7 hardback
SBN 416 18470 7 paperback

Distributed in the U.S.A.
by Barnes & Noble Inc.

Contents

Preface

The history of economic thought, as the history of any other branch of intellectual life such as the history of philosophy, theology, science or aesthetics, can be pursued in two quite different ways. The first may be described as 'internal'. In this mode, the history of economic thought becomes a study of the evolution of the different concepts involved, tracing their intellectual pedigrees, plotting the modifications introduced by different thinkers, identifying new ideas as they join the evolutionary stream of thought flowing towards the present. The tendency of such an approach (which itself makes a major methodological assumption about the nature of the subject) is to emphasize a smooth, logical evolution – usually a teleological evolution – of the corpus of thought, moving down from precedent to precedent, never going back on its tracks (though sometimes stopping in them). The internal coherence of the related system of ideas at any one time tends to be maximized; inconsistencies and conflicts of opinion (more particularly about the practical conclusions to be drawn from the ideas as signals for action and policy) minimized. In the philosophy of history generally such 'historicism' has for long been a target for the heavy guns of Professor Popper and others. Its parochial manifestation in British political history was tackled many years ago by Professor Butterfield as the 'Whig view of history', after generations when, it was sometimes said, the Historical Tripos at Cambridge was an exercise to keep the Whigs of Trinity in the true faith. These are battles long ago. But, in some more specialized branches of history, the same heresy quietly continues.

The other mode of study of the history of economic thought is to seek to equate the evolution of a conceptual apparatus to its external context. This is not so much to establish the relationships with neighbouring intellectual disciplines, such as philosophy, but to relate intellectual history to its historical context more widely. When this is done, at once, the clarity given by logical coherence gives place to much greater complexity in inter-relationships. At the more abstract level, for example, classical economic theory is often identified simply as the intellectual baggage of a bourgeoisie rising to dominance – the ideology of a laissez-faire industrial capitalism. As an explanatory device this has a certain crude utility, of course, but it obfuscates as much as it illumines when the focus is narrowed. There were passionate battles among economists and their followers, 'classical' in intellectual allegiance by any standards, over virtually every major policy issue of the early nineteenth century (agreed that what was kept out of the policy arena owed much to a residual consensus linked to the intellectual assumptions current at the time). The motivations of businessmen were also as suspect to the classical economists as they were to the landed classes and free competition was seen, in practice, as much as a protection against capitalists as it was a secret weapon which belonged in their own armoury.

Professor Coats's introduction, and this volume as a whole, raise fundamental questions of the relations between theory and practice. If more problems than answers result, with greater complexity than simplicity, that has its value, for the study of present-day connections between these entities no less than for appreciating the subtleties of their connection in the past.

Peter Mathias

All Souls College, Oxford
7 January 1971

Acknowledgements

I am most grateful to Professors R. D. Collision Black of Queen's University, Belfast, and T. W. Hutchison of the University of Birmingham for their critical comments on an earlier draft of the Introduction.

The editor and publishers wish to thank the following for permission to reproduce the articles listed below:

Allen & Unwin, Ltd and Farrar, Straus & Giroux, Inc for 'Nassau Senior and Classical Economics' by Marian Bowley (*Nassau Senior and Classical Economics*, 1937); Edward Arnold, Ltd for 'The Classical Economists and the Labourer' by A. W. Coats (*Land, Labour and Population in the Industrial Revolution*, 1967); Cambridge University Press for 'The Classical View of Ireland's Economy' by R. D. Collison Black (*Economic Thought and the Irish Question, 1817–1870*, 1960); The *Quarterly Journal of Economics* for 'The Classical Economists and the Factory Acts – A re-examination' by M. Blaug (vol. 72, May 1958); The *Quarterly Journal of Economics* and The Clarendon Press for 'Ricardo's Views on Monetary Questions' by R. S. Sayers (*Quarterly Journal of Economics*, 1953, and *Papers in English Monetary History*, 1953); The University of Chicago Press for 'Private versus Public Education, A Classical Economic Dispute' by E. G. West (*Journal of Political Economy*, vol. 72, October 1964).

Editor's Introduction

I

One has to be on one's guard against the temptation to believe that a man's importance has to be measured by his noisiness or his verbosity or even by his talents. A comparatively commonplace man or a man whose thought was for the most part commonplace (as Palmerston's was) may easily have had a greater influence upon a given society than a man who lived deeply and intensely but remote from common experience. So one is torn between the lure of the 'typical', the 'representative', and that of the eccentric and exotic.
W. L. *Burn*, The Age of Equipoise, A Study of the MidVictorian Generation (*London, 1964*) *p. 19*.

Never before has the economist exerted so great an influence on public policy as he does today. Medieval and early modern governments frequently consulted experts on financial and trading matters, and the nineteenth-century 'revolution' in government brought in its train a marked increase in the corps of permanent officials engaged in collecting information and dispensing advice on economic problems. But since the Second World War, the situation has been transformed under the combined influence of the growth of government activity and the Keynesian revolution in economic thought. Ministers of state, increasing numbers of whom have been formally trained in economics, nowadays rely heavily on their economic advisory councils and committees; and most sizeable private institutions and business firms utilize the services of economic and statistical experts. Doubtless the growth of the economist's importance in public affairs is less obvious and alarming than the parallel growth in the influence of scientists and technologists. Yet the two movements pose similar questions, and both have provoked widespread discussion among scholars and laymen.

This discussion has inspired several studies of the economist's role as official adviser and the theoretical and practical relationships between economic 'science' and public policy,[1] and these works provide a useful background for any historical investigation of the interaction of economic ideas and policy. In the present instance this background is especially relevant, for there are striking, if superficial, similarities between the current situation and the position of the English classical economists in the decades following Waterloo. Then, as now, members of the public were exposed to a barrage of analysis and opinion on economic affairs – on questions of money and banking, the foreign exchanges, taxation, the national debt, the corn laws and free trade, population growth and poverty, trade unions and factory legislation. And in addition to the usual pronouncements by politicians, journalists, and interested laymen, there were contributions from a small, but effective group of political economists who, for the first time in our history, demanded recognition as authoritative spokesmen of an established science. Then, as now, the economists drew on a coherent, systematic body of knowledge which they claimed was directly applicable to current affairs. And their importance was generally recognized, both by their numerous opponents and by their friends and disciples.

Needless to say, the differences between the early nineteenth-century classical economists and the mid twentieth-century Keynesians are greater than the similarities. The intellectual training, doctrines, professional status, and opportunities of the two groups were quite different,[2] and they functioned in

[1] For example, W. A. Jöhr and H. W. Singer, *The Role of the Economist as Adviser* (London, 1955); T. W. Hutchison, *'Positive' Economics and Policy Objectives* (London, 1964); idem., *Economics and Economic Policy in Britain, 1946–66: Some Aspects of their Interrelations* (London, 1968); and Donald Winch, *Economics and Policy, A Historical Study* (London, 1969).

[2] However, the classical economists were not unduly modest. In 1823 J. R. McCulloch believed 'the time cannot be far distant when a knowledge, or at least some little attention to Political Economy will be considered as necessary for legislators, as knowledge of Greek'. Cf. Mrs Alicia Pryme Bayne (ed.), *Autobiographic Recollections of George Pryme* (Cambridge, 1870), p. 127. Three years later, Robert Torrens maintained that an economist should be appointed to the Board of Trade because 'it partakes of the nature of a professional appoint-

quite different social and political environments. Nevertheless, the comparison is instructive, for knowing the complexities of the present situation, we are less likely to oversimplify and exaggerate the classical economists' influence, a common practice which has by no means been confined to their sympathizers. Vague and sweeping generalizations on the subject abound in the literature on nineteenth-century England, and it is only in recent times that serious efforts have been made to estimate the precise nature and significance of this influence. In the following pages we shall review the current state of knowledge on the matter and provide some representative examples of this reappraisal.

The first task is to define 'classical economics', an expression originally coined by Karl Marx. Here it will be taken to refer to the corpus of economic analysis and policy recommendations produced by the following writers: Adam Smith (1723–90), Jeremy Bentham (1748–1832), Thomas Robert Malthus (1766–1834), David Ricardo (1772–1823), James Mill (1773–1836), Robert Torrens (1780–1864), John Ramsay McCulloch (1789–1864), Nassau William Senior (1790–1864), and John Stuart Mill (1806–73). The list could easily be extended, but the foregoing individuals are usually regarded as comprising a genuine doctrinal 'school'.[1] Despite their frequent and sometimes significant differences of opinion, 'there was one master, one doctrine, personal coherence; there was a core; there were zones of influence; there were fringe ends'. Moreover, although these economists were still, strictly speaking, in a pre-professional stage, they constituted a sociological group, somewhat akin to modern professional scientists. That is, they 'developed

---

ment, requiring a peculiar course of study, and knowledge of an almost technical nature. . . . Though the time may not have actually arrived, yet it is rapidly approaching when it will be deemed as necessary to select the members of the Board of Trade from the Economists as it is to take the Bishops from the Church, or the Law Officers from the Bar.' Cf. Denis O'Brien, 'The Transition in Torrens's Monetary Thought', *Economica*, vol. 32 (August 1965), p. 272. Torrens was overoptimistic; but his opinion is especially interesting in view of the economists' behind-the-scenes influence on trade policy in the 1830s. Cf. Lucy Brown, *The Board of Trade and the Free Trade Movement 1830–42* (Oxford, 1958); also *infra*, p. 30.

[1] Bentham is the most controversial. Cf. *infra*, p. 10 n. 1.

attitudes to social and political questions that *were similar also
for reasons other than similar scientific views*. This similarity of
conditions of life and of social location produced similar
philosophies of life, and similar judgments about social
phenomena.'[1]

The importance of these common characteristics can hardly
be exaggerated, for the classical economists' approach to
economic policy was the direct outcome of a comprehensive
liberal philosophy which extended far beyond the conventional
boundaries of economic 'science'. Nor is this in any way
surprising. Nowadays, when strenuous efforts are made to
distinguish between the 'science' of economics and its 'application' to practical problems, even the most uncompromising
advocates of 'positive' economics accept that value judgements,
social prejudices, and political beliefs directly influence policy
recommendations. As Lord Robbins has remarked, 'A theory
of economic policy, in the sense of a body of precepts for action, must take its ultimate criterion from outside economics',[2]
and the classical economists, apart from Senior,[3] took this for
granted. Their views on current policy followed directly from,
and were entirely consistent with, their fundamental philosophical preconceptions. As is well known, Adam Smith's
Wealth of Nations (1776) was as much a tract for the times as a
treatise on economics, and the same is true of many of his
followers' writings. They 'were pre-eminently concerned with

[1] Joseph A. Schumpeter, *History of Economic Analysis* (New York, 1954), pp.
47, 470. Italics in original. Schumpeter was actually referring to the Ricardians –
that is, the last six economists named above, and their followers – rather than the
entire group of classical economists, and there is some risk of underestimating
their differences of opinion. Nevertheless his comments also apply *mutatis
mutandis* to the larger body, for he subsequently remarked that 'from about 1790
on, Smith became the teacher not of the beginner or of the public but of the
professionals, especially the professors. The thought of most of them, including
Ricardo, started from him, and most of them never got beyond him.' Ibid., p.
194.

[2] *The Theory of Economic Policy in Classical Political Economy* (London, 1952),
p. 177. The *locus classicus* of recent 'positive' economics is in Milton Friedman,
Essays in Positive Economics (Chicago, 1953), chap. I.

[3] Senior carefully considered the relationship between the 'science' and the
'art' of political economy, changing his mind more than once on the matter. Cf.
Marian Bowley, *Nassau Senior and Classical Economics* (London, 1937), part II,
chap. I.

policy, to a much greater degree indeed than any of their modern successors';[1] yet they made no serious effort to formulate a systematic theory of economic policy until 1848, when John Stuart Mill published his *Principles of Political Economy*. Consequently many of their ideas were implicit rather than explicit, and in order to comprehend their meaning it is often necessary to read between the lines.

THE CLASSICAL APPROACH TO ECONOMIC POLICY

Before embarking upon this hazardous undertaking, we may usefully draw upon recent discussions of the theory of economic policy as a foundation for our analysis of the classical position. Nowadays it is usually held that a scientific economist takes the 'ends' (or objectives) of policy as given and concentrates his attention on the allocation of the available 'means' (or scarce resources) to achieve those ends.[2] Such a statement is, however, simply a first approximation. In practice, the distinction between ends and means is rarely clear cut; what appear as ends from one viewpoint may turn out to be means to some higher or more ultimate objective. Nor are ends themselves impervious to analysis. Indeed, one of the important functions of economic reasoning is to examine the relations between various ends – which may prove to be competing rather than complementary[3] – and as a result, the initial order of

[1] Lord Robbins, *Politics and Economics* (London, 1963), pp. 12–13.

[2] This view was explicitly enunciated by James Mill in writing to Ricardo: 'Legislation is essentially a science, the effects of which may be computed with an extraordinary degree of certainty. . . . The ends are there, in the first place, known – they are clear and definite. What you have after that to determine is the choice of the means. . . .' Quoted from *Works and Correspondence of David Ricardo*, ed. P. Sraffa (Cambridge, 1952), vol. VII, pp. 211, 234–5, in T. W. Hutchison, *'Positive' Economics and Policy Objectives*, pp. 135–6. I have drawn freely on this valuable discussion of the relations between economic science and public policy.

[3] An obvious example is the conflict between 'wealth' and 'power' as ends of economic policy. Adam Smith's famous remark that: 'As defence, however, is of much more importance than opulence, the act of navigation is, perhaps, the wisest of all the commercial regulations of England', does not indicate *how much* opulence should be foregone for the sake of defence. Cf. *The Wealth of Nations*, ed. Cannan (London, 1904), vol. I, p. 429; and William D. Grampp, 'On the History of Thought and Policy', *American Economic Review*, vol. LV (May 1965), p. 131.

priorities may be substantially revised. In addition to the distinction between intermediate and ultimate ends, we can also distinguish between economic and non-economic ends, or between what may be called 'Ordnungspolitik' and 'Prozesspolitik'. 'Ordnungspolitik' refers to 'policy objectives concerned with setting up and maintaining a constitutional framework, or economic order for society, leaving the economic process within this framework to find its own objectives', whereas 'prozesspolitik' refers to more exclusively economic objectives, such as the maintenance of full employment or a high rate of economic growth.[1] Though not always easy to sustain in practice, this dichotomy is especially useful for our purpose since it helps to dispel the most widely held of all the many misconceptions about the classical economists.

Contrary to the view expressed by innumerable commentators, they did not advocate laissez-faire, if that expression is taken to mean an essentially negative conception of the economic and social role of government. Unquestionably they were suspicious of governmental activity, believing it to be often partisan, corrupt, or inefficient; but they did not regard the reduction of state intervention as an end in itself. It was a means to a higher end, namely, the attainment of individual freedom in economic, social, political, and religious life. Not only did the classical economists admit many exceptions to the general rule of government non-intervention, they also recognized that the law was supplemented by a variety of 'non-legal social controls',[2] which were essential components of the institutional framework of what Adam Smith termed the 'commercial society'. Smith's successors focused their attention on 'prozesspolitik' because they were fundamentally in agreement about 'ordnungspolitik'. And they tended to take the institutional framework for granted as they were addressing an audience which shared their liberal democratic social and political preconceptions.

The classical conception of 'ordnungspolitik' is clearly displayed in Adam Smith's *Wealth of Nations*, the principal source from which his followers derived their conception of

[1] Hutchison, op. cit., p. 125.   [2] See *infra*, p. 9.

a liberal socio-economic order. Ideally, Smith's *magnum opus* should be examined in conjunction with his *Theory of Moral Sentiments* (1759) and the writings of other members of the Scottish school of moral philosophy, such as David Hume, John Millar, and Adam Ferguson; but such an excursion would take us too far afield.[1] Yet it is important not to be misled by the metaphorical language in which Smith expressed his most penetrating contribution to the social sciences: the idea of a mechanism that co-ordinates the unintended consequences of individual decisions into an overall pattern of social action. As is well known, Smith described how an individual who 'intends only his own gain' is 'led by an invisible hand to promote an end which was no part of his intention'; but this should not blind us to the fact that his argument is 'built up by detailed inference from specific data and by examination of specific problems, and is not deduced from wide-sweeping generalizations concerning the universe in general'. Like his Scottish contemporaries, Smith endeavoured to explain social phenomena in naturalistic terms rather than by reference to divine ordination, and by the time he wrote the *Wealth of Nations* he was sufficiently independent of theology to be able 'to find defects in the order of nature without casting reflections on the workmanship of its Author'.[2]

To Smith, the fundamental objective of economic and social policy was the maximization of individual freedom within a framework of law and order. This meant far more to him than merely freedom from petty restrictions on industry and trade; it also meant freedom from absolute civil and spiritual power; and although he regarded benevolence as the 'supreme virtue', he attached greater practical significance to

[1] This and the next three paragraphs are based on my article, 'Adam Smith: The Modern Re-Appraisal', *Renaissance and Modern Studies*, vol. VI (1962), pp. 25–48. See also Gladys Bryson, *Man and Society: The Scottish Inquiry of the 18th Century* (Oxford, 1945), and A. L. Macfie, *The Individual and Society, Papers on Adam Smith* (London, 1967), esp. chaps. III and IV.

[2] Jacob Viner, 'Adam Smith and Laissez-Faire', a lecture originally delivered in 1926 and reprinted in *The Long View and the Short* (Glencoe, Ill., 1958), pp. 224, 222. The 'invisible hand' passage is from the *Wealth of Nations*, vol. I, p. 421. See also Macfie, op. cit., chap. VI.

the 'inferior' virtues of prudence, self-command, and justice. Of these, justice was

> the main pillar that upholds the whole edifice. If it is re-moved, the great, the immense fabric of human society . . . must in a moment crumble into atoms. . . . Society may subsist, though not in the most comfortable state, without beneficence; but the prevalence of injustice must utterly destroy it . . . [indeed], the peace and order of society is of much more importance than even the relief of the miserable.[1]

Liberalism was an antidote to authoritarianism and paternal-ism in all spheres of life, and there was a direct connection between commerce and civilization. According to Smith's 'conjectural history', as Dugald Stewart termed it, there were four main stages of economic and social life: hunting, pastur-age, farming, and commerce. At each stage there were appro-priate institutions, habits, and psychological traits, and there were concomitant variations in the accepted codes of behaviour and the prevailing moral standards. Commercial society was the highest stage, not simply in terms of economic growth but also because it afforded the maximum scope for individual freedom. Smith was not a vulgar exponent of capitalist apolo-getics; he welcomed commercial society because he believed that men's desire for gain would lead them to defend commer-cial freedom and thereby, indirectly and unintentionally, promote general freedom and civilization.[2] In a commercial society men continually came into close contact with one another and in the process they developed strong social sympathies and a more refined sense of justice and probity. In

[1] The quotations are from the *Wealth of Nations*, vol. I, p. 383, and *The Theory of Moral Sentiments*, ed. E. G. West (New York, 1969), pt. II, sect. II, chap. 3, p. 125, and pt. VI, sect. II, chap. 1, p. 331. Smith's conception of justice was very broad; it included 'religious freedom, freedom of speech, the free use of property, and representative government'. Cf. William D. Grampp, *Economic Liberalism*, vol. II: *The Classical View* (New York, 1965), p. 49.

[2] Joseph Cropsey, *Polity and Economy, An Interpretation of the Principles of Adam Smith* (The Hague, 1957), p. 95. On p. x he remarks that 'Smith advocated capitalism because it makes freedom possible – not because it *is* freedom'.

For Smith's 'stages' theory see his *Lectures on Justice, Police, Revenue, Arms*, ed. E. Cannan (Oxford, 1896), pp. 14 ff., 107 ff., 155–6, 253 ff.; also *Theory of Moral Sentiments*, pt. V, chap. 2.

the course of European history, Smith contended, the progress of commerce 'gradually introduced order and good government, and with them the liberty and security of individuals'. His belief in the fundamental mutuality of individual interests, notwithstanding the existence of numerous specific conflicts of interest between certain persons and groups, underlay the classical economists' conviction that the pursuit of individual self-interest was, on the whole, compatible with the general welfare of society. This compatibility was demonstrable on two distinct, but interrelated levels. In his economic analysis, chiefly in the *Wealth of Nations*, Smith explained how conflicts of interest between consumers and producers were resolved in a manner beneficial to the community at large, through the impersonal mechanism of the competitive price mechanism.[1] Yet his argument presupposed the social analysis of the *Theory of Moral Sentiments* in which he had demonstrated how men acquired a highly developed sense of social sympathy and mutual dependency in a commercial society.[2] They could safely be trusted to pursue their own self-interest without undue harm to the community not only because of the restrictions imposed by the law, but also because they were subject to built-in restraints derived from morals, religion, custom, and education. These 'non-legal social controls'[3] figured more prominently in the *Theory of Moral Sentiments* than in the *Wealth of Nations*, because the focus of Smith's interest was quite different

[1] See, for example, Robbins, *Theory of Economic Policy*, pp. 7–19.

[2] According to Gladys Bryson, in Smith's account 'there sometimes seem to be no individuals at all, so organic is the relation of person to person conceived to be'. Op. cit., p. 160. Smith frequently explained individual behaviour in social terms. Thus the division of labour resulted from man's 'propensity to truck, barter, and exchange', i.e. his natural desire to enter into economic relations with others. His desire to save stemmed less from the attractions of wealth *per se* than from his desire to be the object of admiration, envy, and emulation. Cf. *Wealth of Nations*, p. 15; *Theory of Moral Sentiments*, pt. I, sect. III, chap. 2, p. 71.

[3] Cf. the lengthy discussion in Warren J. Samuels, *The Classical Theory of Economic Policy* (New York, 1966), chap. 2. The precise relationship between the *Theory of Moral Sentiments* and the *Wealth of Nations* has been debated endlessly. Some authorities hold that, according to Smith, in market relationships 'one is dealing with strangers; . . . The social sentiments, therefore, are not aroused into action and man behaves in response to calculating, rational self-interest.' Jacob Viner, 'The Intellectual History of Laissez-Faire', *Journal of Law and Economics*, vol. III (October 1960), p. 60.

in the two works. Yet both aspects were essential to his system, and were recognized as such by his followers. In Ricardo's writings, it is true, social and institutional matters were treated only incidentally, but this is not the case with Bentham and the two Mills. And it is surely obvious that when the classical economists advocated individualism in preference to paternalism or authoritarianism, they had no fear that it would lead to social anarchy.

Jeremy Bentham, like Adam Smith, was much more than a mere economist;[1] and he was also a far more systematic thinker. After defining the ultimate objective of economic and social policy as 'the greatest happiness of the greatest number', he prescribed four particular and subordinate ends: 'subsistence, abundance, security, and equality'. Of these, the provision of subsistence was the *sine qua non* of all government – whereas abundance and security were the principal desiderata of *good* government. Equality was less important, for it was not in itself 'an instrument of felicity'; moreover, the pursuit of equality might conflict with the security of property.[2] However, Bentham's order of priorities does not mean that he defended property for its own sake. On the contrary, like Smith and other eighteenth-century liberals, he believed that a prosperous property-owning community was the best safeguard against arbitrary government.

[1] T. W. Hutchison has argued that although Bentham started out as a disciple of Adam Smith, his later economic theory and policy recommendations diverged so markedly from the Smith–Ricardo tradition that it is virtually meaningless to classify him as a 'classical' economist. Cf. 'Bentham as an Economist', *Economic Journal*, vol. LXVI (June 1956), pp. 288–306. Lord Robbins, on the other hand, unhesitatingly places Bentham in this category (op. cit., p. 2) and, at the risk of some oversimplification, I have followed his example. The personal and doctrinal links between Benthamism and classical economics are far too intricate to be dealt with adequately in this introduction; but the connections in the field of policy-making are too strong to be neglected. For further comments on this matter see *infra*, pp. 21, 24 ff.

[2] Cited from Bentham's *Constitutional Code* by Wesley C. Mitchell, *Types of Economic Theory from Mercantilism to Institutionalism*, ed. Joseph Dorfman, vol. I (New York, 1967), p. 225. Cf. Hutchison, '*Positive' Economics and Policy Objectives*, pp. 132–4. Bentham, like J. S. Mill, recognized the difference between good government and free government, and sometimes expressed a preference for the former. Mill, however, distinctly preferred free government. Cf. Robbins, op. cit., pp. 185–6.

J. S. Mill apart, the classical economists who succeeded Bentham paid comparatively little attention to 'ordnungs-politik', largely because they accepted the orthodox liberal values and were preoccupied with the development of economic theory and its application to practical problems. They failed to recognize the basic inconsistency between their belief in individual freedom, which predisposed them in favour of non-intervention, and their general acceptance of the principle of utility, which was neutral as between intervention and non-intervention. The 'greatest happiness' principle logically entailed support for government action in every case where it could be shown that intervention would do more good than harm; and it is now generally accepted that their conception of the functions of government was neither doctrinaire nor inflexible.[1] Consequently, with the passage of time, they recognized that in an expanding urban-industrial society there was a need for an increasing number of state regulations; and it is therefore hardly surprising that late nineteenth-century Fabian socialists owed much to their utilitarian predecessors, from whom they inherited 'a legislative doctrine, a legislative instrument, and a legislative tendency pre-eminently suited for the carrying out of socialistic experiments'.[2]

In his *Principles of Political Economy with Some of their Applications to Social Philosophy* (1848), John Stuart Mill undertook a more systematic analysis of the general principles of economic and social policy than any of his predecessors.

His subtitle reflected his strong conviction that

for practical purposes, Political Economy is inseparably intertwined with many other branches of social philosophy. Except on matters of mere detail, there are perhaps no

[1] See, for example, H. Scott Gordon, 'Laissez-Faire', *International Encyclopedia of the Social Sciences* (New York, Macmillan, 1968), vol. VIII, pp. 546–9. Also the works by Robbins, Samuels, and Viner quoted elsewhere in this introduction.

[2] A. V. Dicey, *Law and Opinion in England* (London, 1940), p. 310. Dicey was one of several influential late nineteenth-century scholars who erroneously attributed to the classical economists a simplistic conception of laissez-faire which contrasts sharply with their often cautious and moderate attitude towards state intervention. For further discussion of this complex problem see *infra*, p. 14 ff.

practical questions, even among those which approach nearest to the character of purely economical questions, which admit of being decided on economical premises alone.[1]

Mill's approach involved a rejection of the narrower Ricardian focus on 'prozesspolitik'[2] in favour of the Smithian conception of 'ordnungspolitik', for he aimed to bring the *Wealth of Nations* up to date by taking account of subsequent theoretical advances and 'the best social ideas of the present time'. Although he declared that 'laissez-faire . . . should be the general practice: every departure from it, unless required by some great good, is a certain evil', he nevertheless approved of numerous exceptions to that general rule on the grounds of expediency.[3] Distinguishing between the 'necessary' and the 'optional' functions of government, Mill remarked that the former species was 'considerably more multifarious than most people are at first aware of'. In addition, he contrasted the 'authoritative' with the 'non-authoritative' functions, the latter comprising those where 'instead of issuing a command and enforcing it by penalties' the government offered advice, promulgated information, or established such institutions as schools, hospitals, a post office, a national bank, or a government manufactory, without giving them a monopoly within their respective spheres.[4]

Mill was by no means a typical classical economist. In his later years he became an ardent supporter of peasant proprietor-

[1] *Principles*, ed. J. M. Robson (University of Toronto Press, 1965), vol. I, p. xcii. (From the Preface to all editions.)

[2] Hutchison refers to 'Ricardo's almost monistic conception of the objectives of economic policies, and of a simple pseudo-technical kind of means–end relation between policies and their objectives, a pattern which has had great influence ever since. . . . Maximum output was the overriding economic objective' which was, in itself, an expression of the principle of utility. Cf. *'Positive' Economics and Policy Objectives*, pp. 134–5. (Sentence order reversed.)

[3] *Principles*, vol. II, p. 944. The essential question is, of course, whether Mill's readers really took notice of these qualifications. On this point see Scott Gordon, *infra*, pp. 180–205, and the instructive Ph.D. thesis by N. B. de Marchi, *John Stuart Mill and the Development of English Economic Thought: A Study in the Progress of Ricardian Orthodoxy* (Australian National University, 1970).

[4] *Principles*, vol. II, pp. 944, 800, 937.

ship and co-operation, and displayed marked socialist sympathies.[1] In contrast with the laws of production, which partook
of the nature of 'physical truths', he maintained that the laws
of distribution were dependent on the 'laws and customs of
society', thereby indicating that a deliberate redistribution of
wealth was a feasible objective of policy. Moreover, he levelled
a devastating attack on the idea of competition, declaring:

> I confess I am not charmed with the ideal of life held out
> by those who think that the normal state of human beings
> is that of struggling to get on; that the trampling, crushing,
> elbowing, and treading on each other's heels, which form
> the existing type of social life, are the most desirable lot of
> human kind, or anything but the disagreeable symptoms of
> one of the phases of industrial progress.[2]

Here we see Mill's tendency to give priority to moral and
political considerations, over merely economic ones. He
strongly favoured equality, and was much less interested in
economic growth than Ricardo. Indeed, he believed that the
'stationary state' – i.e., the prospective cessation of economic
growth, which his classical precursors had contemplated with
'unaffected aversion' – might well represent an improvement
over the present state of affairs, for

[1] A recent careful student of Mill's social and political thought describes him
as a 'qualified socialist', adding that he was also a 'qualified democrat, and even
a qualified libertarian'. Cf. John M. Robson, *The Improvement of Mankind* (Toronto
and London, 1968), p. 271; also Abram L. Harris, *Economics and Social Reform*
(New York, 1958), chap. II. Many of Mill's qualifications stemmed from his
sense of the historical relativity of social and economic institutions, an outlook
derived from such sources as Coleridge, the Saint-Simonians, and Comte. In this
respect he differed markedly from his Ricardian and Benthamite predecessors.

[2] *Principles*, vol. II, p. 754. Even so, he conceded that 'only through the
principle of competition has political economy any pretension to the character
of a science'. Ibid., vol. I, p. 239. In other words, competition was a necessary
postulate of economic theory. Yet when this assertion is taken in conjunction
with his favourable remarks on co-operation (which to many of his contemporaries was antithetical to competition), one can appreciate how Mill could have
been interpreted quite differently by different readers according to their initial
preconceptions.

For his views on the laws of production and distribution see vol. I, pp. 199–
200; also Hutchison, op. cit., pp. 136–40.

there would be as much scope as ever for all kinds of mental culture, and moral and social progress; as much room for improving the Art of Living, and much more likelihood of its being improved, when minds ceased to be engrossed by the art of getting on.[1]

THE FRAMEWORK OF ECONOMIC POLICY

Mill's intellectual history is far too subtle and complex to be summarized briefly. Indeed, he has been regarded both as the spiritual godfather of the old-fashioned liberals, who favoured a limited and negative conception of the state, and as a precursor of the democratic socialists, who believed that extensions of state activity were necessary for the sake of freedom. His work demonstrates that the defence of laissez-faire, or some equivalent slogan, can be found in conjunction with support for a substantial variety of interventionist measures; and it is necessary to inquire whether this is merely evidence of inconsistency, or whether these two aspects can be reconciled.

The classical ideal of economic policy has conventionally been defined as the maximization of economic freedom within a 'framework' of law and order; but recent research has shown that this 'market-plus-framework' interpretation is oversimplified.[2] In principle, the role of the framework is clear enough: it represents the institutional context within which individuals are to be left free to pursue their own self-interest without either inhibiting the freedom of others or producing socially harmful results. In practice, however, it is no easy matter to distinguish between the framework and the activities taking place within it, for the 'framework' and the 'market' interact upon each other in a manner that changes over time.[3]

---

[1] *Principles*, vol. II, p. 756.   [2] Cf. Samuels, op. cit., chap. I.

[3] Professor Checkland has distinguished between the 'outer' and 'inner' frames. The former 'has three roles: as guarantor of the laws of property and the system of distribution; secondly as an ameliorator of the position of those not capable of meeting the full duties of individualism (education, protection of women and children); and thirdly to act where the market has defaulted (sanitation, roads, etc.). The inner frame prescribes the operation of the market itself, but largely in a negative way of prohibition and the minimizing of coercive

The framework is neither autonomous nor purely of negative significance. Hence, whatever its historical origins, the market mechanism in a capitalist economy is an artefact, not a 'natural' phenomenon. 'The invisible hand which guides men to promote ends which were no part of their intention, is not the hand of some god or some natural agency independent of human effort; it is the hand of the law-giver, the hand which withdraws from the sphere of the pursuit of self-interest those possibilities which do not harmonize with the public good.'[1]

The classical economists did not distinguish clearly between the 'framework' and the activities taking place within it; nor did they draw any hard and fast line between the economic and non-economic spheres, despite the authoritative opinion of Elie Halévy.[2] As already suggested, individual members of the school displayed very different degrees of interest in 'ordnungspolitik' as against 'prozesspolitik', and Bentham himself remarked, 'I do not see that there can exist a code of laws concerning political economy distinct and separate from other codes. The collection of laws upon this subject would only be

---

positions.' See 'The Prescriptions of the Classical Economists', *Economica*, N.S. vol. XX (February 1953), pp. 69–70. Checkland's interpretation represents an intermediate stage between the views of Robbins and Samuels.

[1] Robbins, op. cit., p. 56. Also Nathan Rosenberg, 'Some Institutional Aspects of the Wealth of Nations', *Journal of Political Economy*, vol. LXVIII (December 1960), p. 559, who states: 'Far from assuming a 'spontaneous' identity of interests . . . Smith was obsessed with the urge to go beyond the ordinary market-structure definition of competition and evaluate the effectiveness of different institutional forms in *enforcing* this identity.'

[2] Adam Smith, for example, argued that in addition to its responsibility for defence and justice, the state had 'the duty of erecting and maintaining certain public works and certain public institutions, which it can never be for the interest of any individual, or small number of individuals to erect and maintain; because the profit could never repay the expense to any individual or small number of individuals, though it may frequently do much more than repay it to a great society', *Wealth of Nations*, vol. II, p. 185. Needless to say, this can be seen as the thin edge of a very large wedge.

In *The Growth of Philosophic Radicalism* (Boston, 1955), pp. 489–90, Halévy argued that there was a basic contradiction in Benthamite doctrine between the supposedly 'natural' identity of individual interests in economic affairs and the 'artificial' identity of interests in the science of law. Cf. Robbins, op. cit., pp. 190–2.

a mass of imperfect shreds, drawn without distinction from the whole body of laws.'[1] Admittedly, they recognized that men were better able to perceive their true interest in the market-place, where gains and losses were easier to calculate, than in social affairs, where the consequences of alternative courses of action were less readily discernible. Yet even here there was a difference of degree rather than kind, for they had great faith in the value of education as a means of persuading men to recognize and act upon their true interest. And in matters like poor law and factory legislation, they fully appreciated the intimate interdependence of economic and social considerations.

None of this, however, brings us nearer to solving the problem of the relationship between the general principle of non-intervention and the exceptions to it. Lord Robbins has argued that the classical economists' attitude to government action was determined by expediency, but his account has tended to obscure their fundamental individualistic philosophical bias.[2] Faced with the need to decide the merits of any specific policy proposal, the economists' first impulse was to oppose state intervention as a threat to individual freedom. Yet on further reflection, and after due consideration of the evidence, individual members of the school were often prepared to revise their initial opinion on the grounds that the special circumstances of the case warranted an exception to the general rule. Such exceptions do not, in the nature of the case, fall readily into a neat pattern. For any individual economist they were determined by a variety of factors – his temperament,

[1] Quoted by Robbins, op. cit., p. 192, from Bentham, *View of a Complete Code of Laws*.

[2] Robbins, op. cit., esp. Lecture II. For some perceptive criticisms see Checkland, op. cit., esp. pp. 66–7. Also Frank Knight, 'Theory of Economic Policy and the History of Doctrine', *Ethics*, vol. LXIII (July 1953), who argues that the classical economists never developed a clear or defensible programme of action or a 'theory' of economic policy. 'The central issue of economic policy' he states, 'is the distribution of power between individuals, families, and other groups or organizations and between these and the "community", ultimately the sovereign state. . . . Individualistic utilitarianism does not seem to be much better than dogmatic religion as a "theory" of policy in a free society.' See pp. 281, 284.

his socio-political prejudices, his previous personal commitments on the subject, his evaluation of the weight of argument and evidence pro and con, and his interpretation of past experience and future prospects – occasionally including an estimate of the cost and administrative feasibility of the proposal. Given these variables, one can readily understand why men who shared a common general, theoretical and philosophical position might disagree sharply on particular policy issues.[1] Given the magnitude and significance of contemporary social and economic changes, it is no wonder that individual members of the school sometimes substantially modified and even reversed their earlier opinions on policy questions. Indeed, they would have been culpable had they failed to do so. For to quote McCulloch, who is often regarded as the most narrow and doctrinaire member of the school, to appeal to the principle of laissez-faire 'on all occasions savours more of the policy of a parrot than of a statesman or philosopher'.[2]

THE PROPAGATION OF ECONOMIC IDEAS AND THE PROCESS OF POLICY-MAKING

If, as we have just argued, the classical economists' policy recommendations were on the whole cautious and flexible, how can we account for the widespread misconception that they were dogmatic exponents of laissez-faire? There are, broadly speaking, three reasons for this state of affairs: two minor and one major.

In the first place, it is undeniable that some of their

---

[1] Thus while Smith somewhat illogically defended the usury laws (which set a legal maximum on the rate of interest), Bentham opposed them as a restriction on economic freedom; while Malthus defended the 1815 Corn Law for the sake of a balanced economy, Ricardo opposed it as a serious impediment to economic growth; while Senior was one of the architects of the 1834 Poor Law, McCulloch defended the traditional system of local control against the new principle of centralized administration; and while J. S. Mill supported limited liability on the grounds of non-intervention, McCulloch opposed it in the interests of individualism. Of course, other examples could be cited.

[2] Quoted by Robbins, op. cit., p. 43.

statements invited misrepresentation. This was especially true of Ricardo, who, in the process of imagining 'strong cases' designed to show the operation of general theoretical principles, provided support for the socialist contention that the classical economists propounded an 'iron law of wages'.[1] Secondly, it must be remembered that their work was directly concerned with highly controversial policy questions, so that some misquotation of their views was inevitable, both by their more enthusiastic supporters and by their less scrupulous opponents. But the main reason is that their ideas were quickly taken up by a variety of followers and popularizers who effectively disseminated a watered-down version of classical theory and policy from which most of the warnings and qualifications had been eliminated.

Three major figures stand out among the many popularizers of classical economics: Jane Marcet, whose *Conversations in Political Economy* (1816) was designed to assist the education of well-to-do young ladies; Harriet Martineau, whose astonishingly successful *Illustrations of Political Economy* (1832–4) helped to create that 'vulgar and already outmoded image of the "dismal science" which passed for economic thought among the general public up to the 1870s';[2] and James Wilson, editor of *The Economist*, whose weekly journal played an influential role in the dissemination of the laissez-faire ideology in the 1840s. Obviously political economy did not establish its reputation without a struggle: indeed, its successful propagation as a new orthodoxy has been seen as the outcome of a

[1] According to the 'iron law', wages can rise above subsistence level only temporarily owing to the pressure of population. For a discussion of the classical view of wages see Coats, *infra*, pp. 167–75.

The so-called Ricardian Socialists may be regarded as part of the 'fringe ends' of the classical school, their views being based directly on the classical theory of value. Indeed, as one commentator has remarked, 'for the historian of thought, the real puzzle is why the classics did *not* draw these radical conclusions'. Cf. Gunnar Myrdal, *The Political Element in the Development of Economic Theory* (London, 1953), p. 79; also Schumpeter, op. cit., p. 479.

[2] Mark Blaug, *Ricardian Economics, A Historical Study* (New Haven, 1958), pp. 138–9. For further discussion of Harriet Martineau and other popularizers see Scott Gordon, *infra*, pp. 193 ff. Also his article, 'The London *Economist* and the High Tide of Laissez-Faire', *Journal of Political Economy*, vol. LXIII (December 1955), pp. 461–88.

brilliant campaign conducted by Ricardo's two faithful disciples, James Mill and J. R. McCulloch.[1] A significant number of other persons and agencies also played a part, only a few of which can be mentioned here. The numerous treatises, pamphlets, and articles published by the classical economists became widely known both directly and indirectly through such varied channels as the *Encyclopaedia Britannica*, the fashionable periodicals – especially the *Edinburgh*, *Quarterly*, *Blackwood's* and *Westminster* reviews[2] – and the newspapers. The Political Economy Club, founded in London in 1821, became an influential centre of discussion; and another, far more influential, chamber was the House of Commons. Adam Smith's doctrines were already familiar in Parliament before Ricardo entered the Commons in 1819; indeed, Smith's opinions had been quoted correctly, if partially, on both sides of the great corn law debates of 1814–15.[3] But Ricardo's contributions to the opinion-forming process were far more important not only directly, through his impact on the current issues which immediately concerned him, but also indirectly, by shaping the contemporary 'image' of the political economist. In retrospect, Ricardo may be seen as the epitome of the scientific intellectual, and at the time he was widely acknowledged both among the *cognoscendi* and the laity as the leading contemporary economic authority largely because of the skill, lucidity, and detachment with which he analysed technical problems of currency, banking, trade, and the foreign

[1] Cf. S. G. Checkland, 'The Propagation of Ricardian Economics in England', *Economica*, N.S. vol. XVI (February 1949), pp. 40–52.

[2] Frank W. Fetter, 'Economic Controversy in the British Reviews, 1802–1850', *Economica*, N.S. vol. XXXII (November 1965), pp. 424–37. For the dissemination of economic ideas among the working classes see R. K. Webb, *The British Working Class Reader, 1790–1848* (London, 1955), chaps. 3–7, and on the subject of political economy in the schools see the works by R. Gilmour, J. M. Goldstrom, and A. Tyrrell cited in the bibliography.

[3] A summary of the debates is provided in William Smart, *Economic Annals of the Nineteenth Century, 1801–1820* (London, 1910), chaps. XX, XXII, XXIV. As Jacob Viner remarked of Smith's *magnum opus*: 'Traces of every conceivable sort of doctrine can be found in that most catholic book, and an economist must have peculiar theories indeed who cannot quote from the *Wealth of Nations* to suit his special purposes.' Cf. *The Long View and the Short*, op. cit., p. 221.

Ricardo sat in the House of Commons from 1819 to 1823, Torrens from 1826 to 1827, and 1831 to 1835, and J. S. Mill from 1865 to 1868.

exchanges.[1] It was from Ricardo that subsequent popularizers drew most of the raw material for their propaganda, and it was through James Mill and McCulloch, following Ricardo's lead, that subsequent policy-makers came to appreciate, if slowly and imperfectly, that the economic expert could be expected to make a significant and independent contribution to the solution of current economic and social problems.

The dissemination of economic ideas by intellectuals, journalists, popularizers, and propagandists is but one of several aspects of the subtle and complex process by which economic ideas influence public policy. The general significance of this element necessarily depends on the prevailing administrative, constitutional, and political arrangements. If, for example, the decision-making power is concentrated in the hands of a single ruler or government official, an adviser who is currently in favour, be he amateur or expert, may conceivably determine the choice of policy. In a democracy, on the other hand, the pressure of public opinion may exert a decisive influence on the government's actions, and in these circumstances the historian must examine the role of the mass media, as well as the part played by expert advisers. Early nineteenth-century England lay somewhere midway between these two hypothetical extremes. The mass of the people exerted no direct, and probably little indirect influence on policy; but although Parliament was neither democratically elected nor truly representative, it nevertheless reflected a sufficiently broad and powerful spectrum of opinion to warrant careful consideration by any student of economic and social policy.

No systematic effort has yet been made to study the role of economic ideas in Parliament during the first half of the nineteenth century, but the policy-making process has recently been the subject of active research and controversy, especially in connection with the so-called nineteenth-century 'administrative revolution' and Oliver McDonagh's general thesis

---

[1] For amplification of this point see A. W. Coats, 'The Role of Authority in the Development of British Economics', *The Journal of Law and Economics*, vol. VII (October 1964), pp. 88–95.

concerning the 'pattern of government growth'.[1] The influence
of Bentham and the Benthamites on economic and social
policy has been at the centre of the debate, and although the
issues are still confused,[2] the whole subject is directly relevant
to this volume because of the close relationship between
Benthamism and classical economics. As William Aydelotte
has remarked, on a number of specific issues 'it was the
Benthamites who proved to have the correct answer or, at
least, the answer that was finally adopted'; but his attempt to
test statistically the voting practices of conservatives and radicals in Parliament simply reveals 'the multi-dimensional
character of political attitudes and the spuriousness of a simple
polarity of right and left [which] are now widely appreciated
by those who have made detailed studies of politics in the
twentieth century'.[3] Hence it supports neither the radical
interpretation (which emphasizes the importance of Benthamite influence) nor the tory interpretation (which minimizes it).

The current re-appraisal of the Victorian administrative
revolution has not yet produced any significant new generalizations concerning the influence of ideas on economic and social
policy, nor even any consensus of opinion on the role of
Benthamism. Nevertheless it has shed much valuable new light
on the administrative machinery which forms the essential link

---

[1] See his article, 'The Nineteenth-Century Revolution in Government: A Re-
appraisal', *The Historical Journal*, vol. I (1958), pp. 52–67; also his *A Pattern of
Government Growth, 1800–60: The Passenger Acts and their Enforcement* (London,
1961).

[2] 'There are those who, interpreting Bentham as a laissez-faireist, have ascribed
to him the largest influence in determining the laissez-faire character of mid-
Victorian society. Others, interpreting him as a collectivist, have ascribed to
him the largest influence in introducing collectivism into mid-Victorian society.
Still others have interpreted him as a laissez-faireist who could not, for that
reason, have had any influence on the growing collectivism of the century. And
still others have interpreted him as a collectivist whose particular ideology had
little influence on the emerging institutions, agencies, administrative techniques,
and structures.' Gertrude Himmelfarb, 'Bentham Scholarship and the Bentham
"Problem"', *Journal of Modern History*, vol. XLI (June 1969), pp. 189–206.

[3] William O. Aydelotte, 'The Conservative and Radical Interpretations of
Early Victorian Social Legislation', *Victorian Studies*, vol. XI (December 1967),
pp. 229, 236. This article contains references to earlier phases of the discussion,
some of which are included in the bibliography, *infra*, pp. 211–12. See also
Scott Gordon, *infra*, pp. 180 ff.

between the intellectual's policy recommendations and the legislative process.[1] And it serves as a vivid reminder that the study of economic thought and policy is not a field in which we can expect to trace simple causal connections. This is true even of the most recent times, when we have an abundance of documents and many surviving witnesses[2] whose testimony and written reminiscences can be consulted. In the more distant past, however, the evidence is generally inadequate or misleading, and as we may not fully comprehend the policy-making process (especially if it is dependent on the personal whims of the policy-maker) the obstacles are much more formidable.

Apart from its intrinsic difficulty, research in economic thought and policy has hitherto been seriously inhibited by the professional jealousies of scholarly specialists. Historians of economics, on the one hand, have concentrated unduly on the development of economic theory and the ideas of the great economists, and have consequently failed to study the propagation of economic ideas and the role of the propagandists and popularizers who are often more directly concerned with current policy than the intellectuals. The economic historians, on the other hand, have too often dismissed ideas as either irrelevant or simply a short-term response to crisis situations, neglecting the obvious fact that in any problem-situation there is usually a choice of solutions, a choice that cannot be dictated by circumstances alone.

In studying economic ideas and policy we must strike a

[1] An example is David Roberts's study of the early government inspectors and commissioners in his *Victorian Origins of the British Welfare State* (New Haven, 1960), chaps. 5–8.

[2] Sir Alec Cairncross emphasized this in a lively unpublished paper on 'Writing the History of Recent Economic Policy' delivered at the 1970 Conference of the Economic History Society. Among other warnings he mentioned the temptation to exaggerate the influence of policy, the danger of neglecting the non-economic factors involved, and the fact that policy is not necessarily made by those who write the documents. Commenting on the irrational elements in policy-making, he remarked that 'the atmosphere of a large Government department is frequently almost indistinguishable from that of the loony-bin. I use the term in no pejorative sense; it is simply one of the facts of official life.' One may speculate whether the more modest bureaucratic processes of the early nineteenth century were any more rational. (I am most grateful for Sir Alec's permission to quote from this paper.)

balance between extremes, neither exaggerating the importance of logic and wise forethought nor denying that men are influenced by ideas, even if these merely reflect the accepted 'conventional wisdom' rather than the most up-to-date scientific thinking. The relevant ideas need not be either original or profound, and more often than not they will be coloured by prejudice and vested interest. Yet vested interests, as such, do not determine policy where there is a conflict of interests. As Charles Wilson has argued, the livelier the lobbying, the more numerous the pressure groups, the more necessary is the power of decision, of choosing between alternatives, a power that resides only in the government. Both the mercantile and classical systems, he maintains,

> derived as much from government authority and the 'encroachment of ideas' as they did from the ambiguous, often mutually destructive pressures exercised by private interests. . . . Decisions were taken on the basis of established conventions which might and often did transcend private interests, sometimes very powerful ones. Especially when the alternative choices were neatly balanced, the deciding factor might well be those economic, social, and strategic desiderata which seemed commonplace to the governors of the time.[1]

THE INFLUENCE OF CLASSICAL ECONOMICS ON POLICY

Given the present state of our knowledge and the difficulties inherent in the study of economic ideas and policy, all simple statements about the 'influence' of classical economics are necessarily suspect. Yet it is obviously impossible to provide a comprehensive survey of the subject in this introduction; indeed, the time is not yet ripe for such an undertaking. In

---

[1] 'Government Policy and Private Interest in Modern Economic History', reprinted in Charles Wilson, *Economic History and the Historian, Collected Essays* (London, 1969), pp. 153, 155. The first sentence recalls J. M. Keynes's oft-quoted declaration that 'the power of vested interests is vastly exaggerated compared with the gradual encroachment of ideas'. Cf. *The General Theory of Employment, Interest and Money* (London, 1936), p. 383.

B

order to isolate and evaluate the classical economists' contribution, we would have to take into account the activities of
all the leading contemporary policy-influencing groups, such
as the Tory and Whig reformers, the evangelicals, Owenites,
and trade unionists. However, even in a brief review of this
kind, one such group – the utilitarians or philosophical radicals
– cannot be ignored, for at least two of the economists (Bentham and James Mill) were prominent utilitarians, while in
general, classical economics and utilitarianism constituted
complementary and mutually reinforcing elements in the
liberal-individualistic stream of thought and action. Hence, in
the following paragraphs the utilitarian contribution will be
considered, but only in so far as it is essential to an understanding of our main theme.

In lieu of a general survey of economic and social policy
during the first half of the nineteenth century, it would be
possible to compile a comprehensive catalogue of the classical
economists' policy recommendations or a list of all the known
instances in which individual economists or their ideas made
some contribution to the policy-making process. But in addition to being exceedingly long and tedious, such compilations
would also be highly miscellaneous, for contributions to policy
range from vague influences on the 'climate of opinion' to
specific instances where an economist was directly involved in
policy as an adviser or a member of an official body. Even in
those rare cases when we are confident that an economist's
advice was the decisive factor in determining policy practice,
the process is usually so subtle and complex that a detailed
examination of the evidence is required to support any firm
conclusion. Hence this final section is necessarily illustrative,
rather than exhaustive. It is designed as a supplement to and a
commentary on the reprinted articles and extracts.

The classical economists had no doubts about their ability
to provide solutions to current economic and social problems;[1]

---

[1] *Supra*, pp. 2n.2, 19–20. Indeed, Schumpeter coined the expression 'the Ricardian Vice' to describe the 'habit of piling a heavy load of practical conclusions
upon a tedious groundwork, which was unequal to it yet seemed in its simplicity
not only attractive but also convincing'. Op. cit., p. 1171.

nor did they lack opportunities to shape the course of events.
Adam Smith, for example, was frequently consulted by
ministers of the Crown in the 1770s and 1780s, and his ideas
exerted a direct influence on at least three Prime Ministers:
Lord North, William Pitt, and Lord Liverpool, and a long
series of Board of Trade ministers and officials.[1] Ricardo, as
Professor Sayers has shown in the essay reprinted below,[2]
exerted a major impact on the wartime and post-war currency
and banking debates, on the resumption of cash payments in
1821, and on the Bank Charter Act of 1844 – the most important single piece of nineteenth-century banking legislation.
Senior's case is even more remarkable, for he was the principal
economic adviser to the leaders of the Whig party in the 1830s.
The passages reproduced below[3] from Professor Bowley's
classic study of Senior's life and thought cover three main
topics: his report for the Commission on the Condition of the
Hand-Loom Weavers; the opinion on trade unions which he
submitted to the Home Secretary, Lord Melbourne; and his
ideas and influence on poor law legislation. This by no means
exhausts the range of his policy activities. Senior's views on
factory acts, public works, and education are referred to in
other selections,[4] and his whole career is of interest, for it
displays the evolution of his ideas on policy questions over
three or more decades, during which time he radically changed
his views on the scope and method of economics as a result of
his experiences. Despite his well-known opposition to trade
unions and factory legislation for adults, Senior was never a
doctrinaire advocate of laissez-faire; on the contrary, he
emphasized 'the right, duty, and possibility of intervention for
the common good, and that the only limit to the duty of
Government is its power, without any principle limiting that
power'. As a solution to the Irish problem, he proposed that
the government should 'direct the investment of capital and

---

[1] See for example, Mitchell, op. cit., pp. 152–65. Lucy Brown, op. cit., *passim*.
[2] *Infra*, pp. 33–56.   [3] *Infra*, pp. 57–84.
[4] *Infra*, pp. 111, 119, 91–2, 130–6. See also the biography by S. Leon Levy,
*Nassau W. Senior, 1790–1864, Critical Essayist, Classical Economist and Adviser of
Governments* (Newton Abbot, 1970), esp. chapters VIII–XII and the appendixes,
which contain extracts from several of Senior's policy documents.

undertake productive enterprises', and in the late 1840s he favoured strong legislation to prevent some of the worst evils of bad housing.[1] Senior's collaboration with Chadwick in framing and securing the passage of the 1834 Poor Law Amendment Act symbolizes the association of Benthamism and classical economics in the field of economic and social policy. According to Professor Bowley, Senior was the 'chief analytical force' on the Commission; he wrote the bulk of its Report; he was its leading defender before the Cabinet; and the appointments to the Poor Law Commission were made largely on his recommendation.[2] All this may now seem a somewhat dubious honour, for both the Report and the Act have been severely criticized.[3] Nevertheless, as an example of a classical economist's role in policy making the case is undoubtedly striking, even if regrettable.

No attempt will be made here to consider the careers of other classical economists. The case of Bentham, for example, is especially complicated and still highly controversial.[4] The

[1] The quotations are from Bowley, op. cit., pp. 276 and 248. The following passage from his *Lectures* vividly portrays Senior's awareness of the difficulties of legislating against social evils: '[The government] cannot of course enact that every family shall have five well-built, well-ventilated rooms, any more than it can enact that every family shall live on roast beef, but it can prohibit the erection of houses without drainage, or in courts, or back to back. It can require the streets to be paved, it can regulate their width and the thickness of the walls. In short, it can provide prospectively against the creation of new seats of disease and vice. To deal with those which already exist is more difficult. No one denies the right in the State to interfere to prevent a man from injuring others. It exercises this right when it forbids him to build a row of undrained cottages. But the right of the State to prevent a man from injuring himself supposes that the legislator knows better how to manage the affairs of an individual than the man himself does. In the present case this supposition is true.' See ibid., pp. 266–7.

[2] Ibid., pp. 286–8. Also S. E. Finer, *The Life and Times of Sir Edwin Chadwick* (London, 1952).

[3] See, especially, Mark Blaug, 'The Myth of the Old Poor Law and the Making of the New', *Journal of Economic History*, vol. XXIII (June 1963), pp. 151–84; and idem, 'The Poor Law Report Re-examined', *Journal of Economic History*, vol. XXIV (June 1964), pp. 229–45.

[4] For contrasting views of Bentham's influence on policy see, for example, David Roberts, 'Jeremy Bentham and the Victorian Administrative State', *Victorian Studies*, vol. II (March 1959), pp. 193–210, and Mary Peter Mack, 'Jeremy Bentham', *International Encyclopedia of the Social Sciences*, vol. II, pp. 55–8. See also the references in the bibliography, *infra*, pp. 211–12.

remaining selections reprinted below deal with issues rather than with individuals. The first of these is public works, a subject usually thought to be beyond the scope of classical policy prescriptions. It is certainly true that the classical economists preferred private to state enterprise, but as Professor Black has shown,[1] they were prepared to recommend state intervention to create what would nowadays be termed the 'infrastructure' necessary for economic development. Such public works formed part of the essential institutional 'framework' of a private enterprise economy, and this example not only illustrates the difficulty of precisely defining the framework, but also dispels the notion that the classical economists believed in a natural harmony of interests in economic affairs. Like the immediately preceding selection, it is an extract from a larger work, and it is unquestionably the most comprehensive and successful study of the relationship between economic ideas and policy in the period under review.

Professor Blaug's reappraisal of the classical economists' attitudes to factory legislation serves as a reminder that on most issues their views were more complex and divided than the textbooks suggest.[2] As will be seen, he has no high opinion of their contribution to the public debate. Here, as elsewhere, they ignored considerations of administrative feasibility, their theoretical analysis 'barely rose above the commonplace', and Blaug concludes that the net effect of their intervention was negligible. Dr West's article provides a further example of the differences of opinion within the classical school.[3] Although all its members supported some form of state aid to education, Senior and J. S. Mill had much less confidence in the efficacy of consumer's choice in educational matters than Adam Smith, and they therefore recommended an extension of state control over the school system. Recent interest in the economics of education has inspired a number of studies of the views of earlier generations (several of which are listed in the bibliography), and the early nineteenth-century economists attached

---

[1] *Infra*, pp. 89–103. See also B. A. Corry, *Money, Saving and Investment in English Economics 1800–1850* (London, 1962), esp. chap. IV.

[2] *Infra*, pp. 104–122.   [3] *Infra*, pp. 123–43.

great importance to education. They believed it would not only raise the productivity of labour, by increasing the worker's efficiency and adaptability, and by inculcating habits of attention, obedience, and self-denial; but also that it would significantly enhance the prospects for social reform. Their attack on paternalism stemmed partly from their faith in the educability of man; and their whole approach to economic and social policy was coloured by their persistent habit of underestimating the difficulties of persuading the labourers to adopt bourgeois habits and standards.[1]

It would be inappropriate to conclude this introduction without some reference to free trade, the most familiar of all the classical policy recommendations. Here, as elsewhere, we can perceive the dangers of oversimplifying the relationship between economic ideas and policy, for while most textbook writers take it for granted that the Repeal of the Corn Laws in 1846 represented a victory for classical doctrine, it can be shown that the prevailing economic orthodoxy was a positive embarrassment to Richard Cobden and his fellow-members of the so-called Manchester School. In a sense, Cobden's mid nineteenth-century geo-political ideal of free trade and international peace was merely Adam Smith's conception of commercial society writ large, for Cobden believed that the mutuality of economic interests in a free trade world would effectively restrain the belligerent tendencies of national governments; but there was a great difference between genuine economic analysis and propaganda. In contrast with the uninhibited advocacy of immediate repeal by the Manchester men, the classical economists expressed only cautious and qualified approval of free trade, while Malthus (who was in this respect an exception) even defended the hated 1815 Corn Law. Adam Smith never regarded complete commercial freedom as attainable in practice, and to the Cobdenites' chagrin he and his followers advocated the retention of moderate duties on imports to offset the tax differentials between domestic and imported commodities. Ricardo, the most influential early nineteenth-century economist, recommended a gradual reduc-

[1] See my essay, *infra*, pp. 144–79.

tion of duties on corn imports over a ten-year period, whereas if he and his followers had been doctrinaire defenders of economic freedom they would surely have demanded immediate repeal.[1] As it was, 'the economists were either opposed or indifferent to the campaign' launched by the Anti-Corn Law League, and 'there was no close correspondence between the ideas of the Manchester School and those of classical economists.'[2] Professor Blaug has put the matter even more forcefully.

> The campaign which finally secured the Repeal of the Corn Laws in 1846 based itself, more often than not, on arguments directly contrary to the spirit and letter of Ricardo's works. . . . It is an ironic commentary on the history of Ricardian economics that the fundamental theorem of profits depending on wages and wages upon the price of wheat proved to be the Achilles heel of the anti-corn law agitation, and that John Stuart Mill should have been unable to put much stock in the benefits of repeal, the most basic of all the conclusions of Ricardo's system.[3]

Of course, like all propagandists, the Cobdenites maintained that all parties would benefit from repeal, whereas Ricardo's 'fundamental theorem' implied that if corn prices fell after repeal then money wages would fall *parri passu*, so that the wage earners would be no better off in real terms.[4]

However, this does not mean that the classical economists' ideas played no part whatever in the success of the free trade movement. On the contrary, at every stage in the process there

---

[1] Unlike some past and present-day advocates of free enterprise, Ricardo did not believe that economic freedom could be achieved without cost – and in this case he held that the immediate abolition of restrictions on corn imports would impose excessive burdens on the farming community. Cf. P. Sraffa and M. Dobb (eds.), *Works and Correspondence of David Ricardo* (Cambridge, 1951–5), vol. 4, pp. 243–4, 263–4. On the wider issue of principle, see Hutchison, *'Positive' Economics and Policy Objectives*, pp. 127–8.

[2] William D. Grampp, *The Manchester School of Economics* (London, 1960), pp. 35, 107.

[3] Mark Blaug, *Ricardian Economics* (New Haven, 1958), p. 209. Elsewhere he remarks, 'the hero of the League was Adam Smith, not Ricardo', p. 207.

[4] As Blaug shows, ibid., p. 7, Cobden was well aware of this problem, but chose to ignore it when it suited him.

were leading policy-makers who acknowledged their indebtedness to Smith and his followers. This was true of Shelburne and Pitt in the 1780s; Liverpool, Huskisson and Robinson in the 1820s; Parnell, Poulett Thompson, Francis Baring, and a group of important officials at the Board of Trade in the 1830s; and a substantial number of M.P.s in the 1840s.[1] Here, as in other cases, the precise nature and significance of the classical economists' influence is difficult to specify, and it is virtually impossible to summarize briefly. Economic ideas were never the sole or overriding determinant of policy – indeed, throughout the free trade campaign fiscal needs were always important. Moreover, by the 1840s the belief in the desirability of economic freedom was accepted so widely, and for such a variety of reasons, that it would be ridiculous to attribute it solely to a handful of economists.[2] Yet it would be equally absurd to go to the other extreme and deny any importance to the classical analysis of the market mechanism, which was the most powerful intellectual weapon in the free trade armoury. Not all men are convinced by reasoned argument; but some are, and their convictions played an essential, if not decisive role in the success of the free trade campaign.

The Repeal of the Corn Laws was not the culmination of the free trade movement, which continued into the early 1850s with Gladstone's budgets, reaching a dramatic climax in the Cobden-Chevalier Anglo-French Treaty of Commerce in 1860. By this time popular political economy was a vital constituent of the accepted conventional wisdom,[3] while on a higher

---

[1] Among many relevant studies the following are especially useful: C. R. Fay, *Great Britain from Adam Smith to the Present Day* (London, 1950), chaps. 2–4; Brock, *Lord Liverpool and Liberal Toryism*, op. cit., chaps. 2, 6; Brown, *The Board of Trade, and the Free Trade Movement*, op. cit., part I; Grampp, *The Manchester School*, op. cit., chaps. 4, 5; and Norman McCord, *The Anti-Corn Law League 1838–1846* (London, 1958), chap. 8.

[2] The ramifications of the idea are admirably conveyed in the following passage from the *Edinburgh Review* 1843 cited by Viner, 'Intellectual History of Laissez-Faire', op. cit., p. 55: 'Be assured that freedom of trade, freedom of thought, freedom of speech, and freedom of action, are but modifications of one great fundamental truth, and that all must be maintained or all risked; they stand or fall together.'

[3] But as Scott Gordon shows, *infra*, p. 203, free trade was not the same thing as laissez-faire.

intellectual plane, J. S. Mill's *Principles* exerted a remarkable influence on middle and upper class opinion.

The publication of Mill's first edition in 1848 provides a suitable terminal date for this introduction. During the remaining quarter century of his life, Mill's social and political ideas underwent significant changes, but the main body of his economic analysis was preserved intact throughout successive editions of his *magnum opus*. And there were other classical economists who developed and defended the central doctrines of the school.[1] For many members of the public, the continued economic prosperity under free trade was sufficient proof of the validity of the ruling economic orthodoxy, and political economy enjoyed an unusual measure of public esteem. In the mid 1870s, however, this undeserved reputation was shattered by a number of severe intellectual attacks and by the prevailing depression, for which the economists were unjustly blamed.[2]

It would take at least another volume to trace the classical influence on mid and late Victorian economic and social policy, hence only a few summary remarks will be offered here. Matters are especially complex in the social field, for although there was no general retreat from the interventionist schemes of the 1830s and 1840s, the pace of mid Victorian social legislation slackened until the major advances of the 1870s in education, land reform, and trade union law. In the field of economic policy, however, there was more continuity, and the main trends were entirely in harmony with the classical economists' proposals. Free trade was preserved more or less intact until the early 1930s, despite the vigorous assaults of the fair traders in the 1880s and the tariff reformers in the early 1900s.[3] In government finance, Gladstonian principles ruled

[1] McCulloch, Senior, and Torrens all died in 1864. John Eliot Cairnes (1823–75), who is sometimes described as the last of the classical economists, remained active until shortly before his death. Cf. Blaug, *Ricardian Economics*, chap. 11.

[2] For an account of this period, see T. W. Hutchison, *A Review of Economic Doctrines, 1870–1929* (Oxford, 1953), chap I.

[3] See, for example, Benjamin H. Brown, *The Tariff Reform Movement in Great Britain 1881–1895* (New York, 1943), and A. W. Coats, 'Political Economy and the Tariff Reform Campaign of 1903', *Journal of Law and Economics*, vol. II (April 1968), pp. 181–229.

almost unchallenged, with the emphasis on strict financial economy, balanced budgets, and low taxation. Indeed, this formed the basis of the 'Treasury view' which J. M. Keynes attacked so strenuously in the early 1930s.[1] Again, the conception of a self-regulating currency and sound banking embodied in the Bank Charter Act of 1844 laid the foundations for the late nineteenth-century faith in the gold standard system so that, as Professor Sayers noted,[2] there is a direct line of descent from Ricardo to the return to gold in 1925.

This list is merely illustrative; and it should really include negative as well as positive features. Thus the prevailing economic orthodoxy made certain measures not only unnecessary but also virtually unthinkable, such as exchange controls, restrictions on capital export, large-scale taxation designed to redistribute wealth, and full employment policy. Of course, classical political economy was not always directly or solely responsible for this; but it was by no means a negligible force. Hence there is some justification for Lord Robbins's claim that a grasp of this body of ideas is essential to an understanding of 'the evolution and the meaning of Western liberal civilization'.[3]

[1] For the Treasury view see Winch, op. cit., pp. 109–13. On Gladstonian finance see, for example, Henry Roseveare, *The Treasury, The Evolution of a British Institution* (London, 1969), pp. 139–50, 192–7.

[2] Cf. *infra*, p. 56.   [3] Robbins, op. cit., p. 4.

1 *Ricardo's Views on Monetary Questions*[1]

R. S. SAYERS

[This article was published in T. S. Ashton and R. S. Sayers (eds.), *Papers in English Monetary History*, Oxford, 1953.]

I

The appearance of Dr Sraffa's definitive edition of Ricardo's Works, now in course of publication for the Royal Economic Society, may perhaps be allowed as the occasion for a review of Ricardo's contribution to monetary economics. This paper offers no sensational reversal of established views: the writings of Viner, Clapham, and others of recent years on the controversies in which Ricardo took part and the events arousing those controversies would have undergone no substantial revision had their authors had access to the papers now published more fully – and more conveniently – than before. The purpose of this paper is simply to review as a whole the structure and the development of Ricardo's thought on monetary questions.

David Ricardo's father was a Dutch Jew who made a fortune as a member of the London Stock Exchange. The son, proudly an Englishman,[2] followed him into the business, and though cut off from the family, he had by the time he was twenty-five made so much money that he was able for the rest of his life

---

[1] The substance of this paper was given as a lecture in the University of Oslo on 31 March 1952, and was first printed in the *Quarterly Journal of Economics* (Harvard), February 1953. The author wishes to acknowledge his debt to Dr P. Sraffa, whose loan of proof copies of some of the later volumes made preparation of the review possible at that date. All the references to Ricardo's papers are given by volume and page in the new Sraffa edition – as, for example, in the following footnote, where 'v. 483' means page 483 in volume v of the Sraffa edition.

[2] v. 483 (1823).

to give much of his time to the pursuit of learning and public discussion. He died at the age of fifty-one, having been a Member of Parliament for the last four years. His taste for economics began with Adam Smith's *Wealth of Nations*, then about as old a book as, say, Keynes's *Treatise on Money* is today (but there had been no *General Theory* to supersede the *Wealth of Nations*). His financial business led to a special interest in monetary questions, the subject of his first publication. This was in 1809, Ricardo being then thirty-seven. The writings, speeches, and letters we have now to consider are confined to the brief space of fourteen years, 1809–23 – years covering Napoleon's zenith, England's long climb to victory, and the grim years of post-war readjustment. The publications with which we are most concerned are the four pamphlets, *The High Price of Bullion* (1809), the *Reply to Bosanquet* (1811), *Proposals for an Economical and Secure Currency* (1816), and the *Plan of a National Bank* published shortly after his death. There are important passages in the 1822 pamphlet *On Protection to Agriculture*, in notes commenting on the Report and Evidence published by the Bullion Committee of 1810, in the Evidence he gave before later Committees, in his speeches in the House of Commons, and in the correspondence which fills four volumes in the Sraffa edition.

II

The occasion of Ricardo's first appearance in print was the second stage of the Bullionist controversy, when in 1808 and 1809 the marked depreciation of the pound provoked a second spate of pamphlets and the Bullion Committee's Report. The central issue of the debate was, what caused the depreciation of the pound? It was to this central issue that Ricardo addressed himself, but he – and other Bullionist writers – had first to establish two preliminaries – the meaning of 'depreciation', and the measure of it. Though like everyone else Ricardo was ultimately interested in the commodity value of money, depreciation in terms of goods and services was not the object of his inquiries. He meant by depreciation a fall in value in terms of the standard metal. In the last years of his life, when public attention seems to have been more directly focused on the commodity value of money, Ricardo's insistence on this definition of depreciation may have made for some confusion of issues,[1] but those who read Ricardo had no excuse for any misunderstanding: he was absolutely clear and logical in his use of the concept of depreciation. More and more in the last years he acknowledged the fact of variations in the commodity value of gold and indeed insisted on the importance of these variations, but his first interest in depreciation was a 'City' interest, in the rise in the price of gold, and this was what he always meant by depreciation. The high price of bullion was the sign and measure of depreciation.

In justifying it as a *sign*, he had to explain why he took gold rather than silver as the standard metal. The coinage laws were complicated and the actual state of the coinage further obscured the position, so that intelligent and knowledgeable men could suggest that silver was the standard. Ricardo took his stand from the outset on the position taken a little earlier by Lord Liverpool, that for nearly a century gold had been 'the principal measure of value'.[2] In support of this position Ricardo showed full understanding of the working of bimetallic systems, and he brought the relevant facts to bear. His strength in detailed analysis of fact and relation of facts to established principles is even more in evidence in the next stage of his argument, when he seeks the *measure* of depreciation. Bosanquet, in criticizing the Bullion Report, took the line that he was a practical man basing himself on the real facts of the case. Ricardo mercilessly turns on him with a brain that was in itself the Intelligence Department of a highly successful stockbroker's office: he examines prices of gold and silver, the relation of bar gold to coin, of bills to spot cash, the interest charge related to delays in minting, and so forth, and poor Bosanquet is left cutting a very sorry figure. Apart from the illustration it provides of this particular strength of Ricardo, I find most interest in one point that at first struck me as rather odd. When measuring depreciation, Ricardo in his earlier writings looked only for a

---

[1] At least Blake thought so. See the *Notes on Blake* (1823), vol. iv, p. 330.
[2] See especially *High Price of Bullion* (1810), vol. iii, p. 66. Also vol. iii, p. 176.

rise in the price of gold, a fall in the foreign exchange value of the pound, beyond the current gold export point.[1] This implied another calculation: what, under the extraordinary circumstances of the war, were the costs of shipping gold from London to Continental centres? The answer was eventually thought to be of the order of 4 or 5 per cent, and depreciation, in Ricardo's sense, therefore occurred only when the exchanges were more than this margin away from the Mint par. Now it has always seemed to me sensible to talk of any decline in the currency's gold value as depreciation against gold, and the gold-export point is then the point at which the depreciation becomes great enough to justify shipping gold. This was indeed Ricardo's own usage later. The clue to his earlier attitude is in his general approach to the problem. Over and over again he insisted that he was interested in the difference between actual events (prices of commodities, price of gold, etc.) and what would have occurred had cash payments been maintained. The misbehaviour of the currency was in his view the result of the restriction on cash payments, and the measure of depreciation was therefore considered simply as the degree by which the gold value of the currency had fallen beyond the limits that would have been set by free convertibility.

III

And so I come to the central issue. The fact of depreciation being established, where was the cause to be found? Ricardo's answer was a quite simple Quantity Theory answer that there had been an undue increase in the supply of money: 'Our circulating medium is almost wholly composed of paper, and it behoves us to guard against the depreciation of the paper currency with at least as much vigilance as against that of the coins. This we have neglected to do.'[2] The facts about the note-issues were known only in very small part, and there was little scope here for that skilful analysis of detailed fact in which

---

[1] See, for example, *High Price*, vol. iii, p. 80. In later years he measured depreciation by reference not to the export point but to the Mint par – see, for example, v. 392 (1819), and 204 (1822).

[2] *High Price* (1810), vol. iii, pp. 74–5.

Ricardo so obviously revelled. But this did not worry him. His faith in the Quantity Theory was so strong that in his early writings he came perilously near to arguing in a circle: the pound is depreciated, therefore too much money has been issued, therefore the redundancy of the currency is the cause of the depreciation.[1]

Now Ricardo was often careful to explain that the demand for money could vary so that it was dangerous to expect the price level to move exactly in step with the quantity of money; and it is therefore strange that he should have held firmly to the view that the depreciation was caused solely by the increase in the supply of money. That he, whose influence both on monetary thought and on policy was destined to be so powerful, should have taken this simple Quantity Theory view was a major disaster, and we must seek to understand how it came about. I have just mentioned the paucity of statistical data which Ricardo would most willingly have manipulated in his quest for the truth. Lacking such evidence he was thrown back on other methods, and my guess is that two circumstances were the sources of his diagnosis.

First, there was the earlier history of the controversy. In the early stage, around 1800–2, the degree of depreciation was in any case very small and the interpretation of events was singularly difficult. There was little then to choose between the various views put forward, and either party may have been right. Into this obscurity there suddenly shone a beam of light from Ireland. In 1802–4, the Irish currency depreciated sharply in terms of English currency, and it was not at all difficult to show that this Irish depreciation was due to excessive creation of money in Ireland. This event and its easy diagnosis would naturally be prominent in the mind of an intelligent amateur – as Ricardo was at that stage – and he was all too ready to jump to the conclusion that exactly the same thing was now, in 1809–10, happening to the English currency.[2]

[1] See, for example, ibid., 81.

[2] Professor Frank W. Fetter has prompted me to emphasize that the absence of direct evidence that Ricardo read the Irish report before he wrote *The High Price of Bullion* is so complete as to render highly conjectural the suggestion that

The second leg upon which Ricardo's interpretation stood was the result of more conscious reasoning and it has obvious connections with other Ricardian doctrines. It emerges when he is facing an alternative answer given to that central question, what caused the depreciation of the pound? The Anti-Bullionists generally argued that the depreciation was due to an adverse balance of international payments, due particularly to special government payments overseas and to heavy corn imports after bad harvests. But, said Ricardo, why is the void in the balance not filled at once, without any significant depreciation, by expanding exports of commodities? Why is gold any different from commodities in this respect?[1] He assumes, you see, that the slightest fall in our export prices – the fall implied by the movement to gold export point – will sufficiently stimulate the export of commodities, just as it stimulates the export of gold. Instead of this happening, the development of exports to fill the gap was being prevented by the rise in home prices consequent upon the increase in the supply of money. Ricardo would thus have been very much at home among those of our contemporaries who stress the difficulty of transferring resources to the export trades while the inflationary pressure continues; he would have been surprised at the difficulties encountered in his own day by Lancashire manufacturers and merchants in their search for fresh outlets when their export trade was barred by Napoleonic advances. It is important to remember this fundamental position of Ricardo, usually tacitly assumed but clear enough to forfeit the respect of the pamphleteers from the trading communities of Lancashire and the Midlands.

Responsibility for the excess issues was laid by Ricardo at

---

he was directly influenced by it. The works (of Locke, Stuart, Smith, Liverpool, and Thornton) we know him to have read immediately before writing (see Sraffa's note, iii. 7, and many passages, especially iii. 81, in *The High Price*) were all written before the Irish episode. Ricardo may, however, have been influenced by pamphlets or conversations about the Irish episode before he decided to put his views systematically before the public, and for the latter purpose reinforced himself by studying and quoting the standard authors.

[1] This argument is most explicit in the 1811 Appendix to *The High Price* (iii. 103) and in the *Reply to Bosanquet* (iii. 207). In 1819 he was still arguing that a 'highly manufacturing' country such as this could always easily acquire any quantity of bullion it wanted. (*Commons Evidence*, vol. v, pp. 408–9.)

the door of the Bank of England. He argued that the issues of the country banks were automatically governed by the Bank of England, justifying this by analogy with the established theory of the distribution of the precious metals.[1] The amount of his notes a country banker could push into circulation depended on the local price level; this was dependent on the London price level, and this in turn was governed by the amount of money created in London by the Bank of England. The conclusion exonerating the country banks from all blame for the excess issues was held even by less extreme Bullionists[2] in the earlier phases of the controversy. Like other parts of Ricardo's doctrine, there was an assumption here of instantaneous adjustment to a long-run equilibrium. In later days, especially as some of the facts became known, opinion swung round rather against the country bankers,[3] and Ricardo did occasionally concede that, in this as in other respects, there might be some friction in the transition to the long-run effect which alone his intellectual blinkers generally allowed him to see.[4]

What happened was thus, in Ricardo's view, determined by the Bank of England. What precisely was happening to the size of the Bank of England's note-issue, and to the volume of its discounts, was known or deduced only from occasional figures published in response to official inquiries. Ricardo believed, on the basis of such figures as were available to him, that the Bank issues had risen unduly,[5] though he acknowledged that firm

---

[1] Most clearly stated in *Reply to Bosanquet* (1811), chap. VII (iii. 230). Cf. *High Price of Bullion*, vol. iii, p. 87. For a later statement (still almost unqualified) see v. 375.

[2] e.g. H. Thornton, *Paper Credit* (1802), p. 216.

[3] This complex question has been most acutely discussed by E. Wood, in his *English Theories of Central Banking Control, 1819–58*. His broad conclusion is that the size of their London balances weighed heavily among the country bankers' considerations of liquidity, so that the London supply of money did fairly directly and quickly affect the supply of money in the provinces; but this is not quite the Ricardian approach.

[4] I have taken the phrase 'intellectual blinkers', as applied to Ricardo, from Professor L. C. Robbins. For an example of Ricardo's late qualification of his extreme view on this topic, see v. 375 (1819).

[5] iii. 86. Ricardo rarely said this outright: more frequently he was content to say that since the Directors were under no restriction and had every incentive to expand the issue, it *must* have been expanded.

conclusions depended not only upon the actual figures but also upon assumptions as to the changing habits of the people in the use of money substitutes.[1] But it was not so much by reference to the event as by demonstration that the operative principles of the Bank were bound to lead to over-issue, that Ricardo relied for his explanation of the origin of the inflation. The 'company of merchants' – he never tired of this description of the Bank's character[2] – had before 1797 been restrained by the fear of losing their cash reserve, and had therefore restricted their discounts when the gold was running down. The Restriction of Cash Payments removed this restraint and the Bank Directors, by their own admission before the Bullion Committee, now took no heed of the foreign exchange position but simply met 'the needs of trade' – and at a fixed rate of discount – as well as meeting the needs of the government. Indeed, having regard to the stated principles of Bank operations, 'it is a matter of surprise that our circulation has been confined within such moderate bounds'.[3]

The remedy was to reimpose the restraint that had prevented excess issues before 1797 – to compel, that is to say, the Bank of England to cash notes in the standard metal upon demand at a fixed price. Until that was done, the company of merchants could not be expected to restrain sufficiently their profitable business of lending to traders. This was the quite simple remedy for what Ricardo regarded as a quite simple wrong. As he would have no truck with arguments about government needs or the adverse balance of trade,[4] he had, at any rate in the earlier years, no apprehensions about the alleged evils of Resumption.[5] He did, nevertheless, give a good deal of thought to the long-term settlement to be sought. In particular, he considered and at least once changed his mind on the question of choice of standard, and he advocated the bullion system

[1] *High Price of Bullion* (1809), vol. iii, p. 86, and *Commons Evidence* (1819), vol. v, pp. 389–90.

[2] Ricardo was *not* himself a merchant!

[3] The broad line of attack is repeated in many passages, perhaps most clearly in chap. VII of the *Reply to Bosanquet* (iii. 215) from which the quotation is taken.

[4] See, for example, *Notes on Trotter* (late 1810), vol. iii, pp. 392–3.

[5] e.g. *Reply to Bosanquet*, vol. iii, pp. 244–5.

known as his Ingot Plan, rejected by his own generation but adopted a century later.

IV

Incidentally to his establishment of the fact of depreciation, Ricardo explained how with bimetallic laws a country adopts as the effective standard whichever of the two metals happens to be over-valued and that the English coinage arrangements of the eighteenth century had, given the relative values in the outside world, made gold the effective standard.[1] Ricardo did not like the hazards of these eighteenth-century arrangements,[2] but he had no doubt that the precious metals were better than any conceivable alternative.[3] The more open question was, silver or gold? On this Ricardo changed his mind at least once. In the early writings no preference emerged – the important thing then was to get back to a metallic standard, though it would not be unfair to surmise that Ricardo was then content that it should be gold, since he never troubled, when arguing that gold had in fact been the standard, to say that he wished it otherwise. The instability of the precious metals in the late war years forced him to think it over. The considerable effect of the fortunes of war on the values of the precious metals 'should never', he wrote to Trower[4] six months after Waterloo, 'be neglected in any future discussion on this subject'. Gold, because it was so useful for army and other payments in foreign lands, was subject to extraordinary variations in demand, from which the more bulky silver was comparatively free. The bulk of silver – the very quality that underlay its greater stability – was, of course, a disadvantage for circulation, but if the Ingot Plan were adopted, paper would provide the most usual medium of circulation, and the objection would lose most of its force.[5] So in 1815–16 he was publicly advocating a silver

---

[1] *High Price of Bullion*, vol. iii, p. 66. *Reply*, vol. iii, p. 176.

[2] *Principles*, vol. i, pp. 368–9.

[3] Letter to Trower (2 March 1821), vol. viii, p. 350. Cf. *On Protection* (sec. V), vol. iv., p. 223; *Evidence*, vol. v, p. 388.

[4] 25 December 1815 (vi. 344).

[5] Letter to Malthus, 17 October 1815 (vi. 301); *Econ. and Secure Currency*, vol. iv, p. 63.

standard. After the first post-war years had shown how right he had been in his prediction that 'when peace comes we shall not want for advocates for a continuance of the Restriction Bill',[1] he felt it necessary to concentrate his fire mainly on the overriding desirability of Resumption, and came to think of the choice of metal as a question 'of little importance'. But he still thought about it, and once more changed his mind on the ground that improvements in silver mining would make silver a falling standard.[2]

v

While his interest in the question of the standard faded, Ricardo put great energy into the advocacy of his 'Ingot Plan'. This became, at a very early stage, an integral part of Ricardo's proposals for Resumption of cash payments; it was at the same time intended as a permanent reform of the monetary system, and it was destined to become a practical legacy to the twentieth century. The plan first appeared in the 1811 Appendix to the *High Price of Bullion*,[3] and was introduced as a reply to the objection to resumption that the Bank would have to accumulate a stock of gold wherewith to substitute the circulating small notes by gold coin. Though it was thus proposed as a measure to meet a practical difficulty, it is perfectly clear that from the outset Ricardo perceived that the essential condition of a gold standard is not in gold coinage but convertibility into gold for international transactions. On this first occasion of mentioning it, he said that it might be tried 'for three or four years . . . and if found advantageous, might be continued as a permanent measure'.

At the end of the war Ricardo again put forward the Plan, not this time at the tail end of an appendix but as the central proposal of the pamphlet *Proposals for an Economical and Secure Currency*.[4] Then, early in 1819, the question of Resumption was

---

[1] *Notes on Trotter* (1810), vol. iii, p. 400.

[2] *Evidence*, vol. v, pp. 390-1 and 427. Ricardo also favoured gold because it was the traditional standard: 'I do not like a change without there is a very manifest advantage in it.' Letter to McCulloch, 3 January 1819, viii. 3.

[3] iii. 123-7.

[4] There were two editions in 1816 and a third (a mere reprint) when public interest was renewed in 1819. For the Ingot Plan see iv. 66-7.

the subject of inquiry by Committees of both Houses of Parliament, and Ricardo's Plan – on which he himself gave evidence[1] – was immediately in the forefront of discussion both inside and outside the Committees. Both Committees were won over[2] not to a permanent measure but to temporary adoption of the Plan to ease the transition to a full gold standard. Ricardo was sorry that it was a merely temporary measure, but thought that its success would win over even the Bank Directors so that England might have permanently the paper circulation he so much preferred.[3] Meanwhile, he was practical enough to judge that Parliament had taken a sensible course, for there was opposition in two important quarters: the Bank of England and the common people. The Bank Directors were narrow enough to object on the ground that their charter protected them from the obligation to pay in bullion,[4] and it was in deference to this objection that special bars were prepared and stamped at the Mint;[5] they were also worried about the forgeries of small notes, the many executions for which were exacerbating popular feeling.[6] Also, though preference expressed at the Bank's counters at first favoured notes,[7] there was some popular hankering after gold coin, and this, fanned by Cobbett's ravings into a belief that *any* paper money was unstable, helped to ensure the suppression of the Plan two years later.

All that Ricardo said, from 1811 onwards, about the problems of Resumption was based on the assumption that an intelligent government would adopt his Ingot Plan, at least as a transitional measure. He therefore brushed aside difficulties that would arise through an attempt to accumulate a new supply of gold in the Bank of England, and addressed himself wholly to the question of the adjustment of the supply of

[1] He was not a member of the Commons Committee; he actually entered the House a few days after it had been appointed.

[2] See Mallet's Diary, quoted v. 365–6.

[3] See Letters to McCulloch, 8 May and 22 June 1819, and to Sinclair, 11 May 1820 (viii. 26–8, 39, and 186).

[4] viii. 27.   [5] They were called 'Ricardoes'. (For details, see v. 368–70.)

[6] v. 201. For discussion of this question, see A. W. Acworth, *Financial Reconstruction in England, 1815–22* (London, 1925), pp. 95–9.

[7] Cf. Acworth, op. cit., p. 94.

money and the price level to the price of gold that would be enforced by the decision to resume cash payments. Given his view that prices were adjusted pretty quickly – though not instantaneously[1] – to changes in the volume of the note-issue of the Bank of England, a contraction of this issue, more or less proportional to the extent to which the price of gold was to be reduced, would appear to have been the logical conclusion from Ricardo's general position. But he was never quite as unworldly as this, and always insisted upon the necessity of a gradual contraction.[2] As early as 1811, he was suggesting[3] that the Bank of England might try the experiment of reducing by stages their note-issues: this, he supposed, would prove his general point by causing proportionate approaches of the price of gold towards the Mint par. Similarly, as early as 1811 he had written to Perceval (Prime Minister and Chancellor of the Exchequer) proposing that further depreciation be prevented by Bank of England sales of gold at the ruling price (£4. 15s. 0d.) followed by gradual reduction of this selling price as successive contractions of the note-issue brought the general level of prices down.[4] All such proposals were rejected until 1819 when the influence of Ricardo was at its zenith and his expositions before the Parliamentary Committees were masterly and, in the event, convincing.

Now it is notable that in these expositions in 1819 he was careful to say that he would not have advocated a very early return to par if the gap to be closed were anything like as wide as it had been in some of the earlier years. The extent of depreciation was now only about 4 per cent, and from Ricardo's general argument it followed that a contraction of the note-issue by 4 per cent or thereabouts would be sufficient to bring the exchanges and the price of bullion back to par.[5] The

[1] 'They do not immediately conform, but I do not think it very long before they do.' (Lords' *Evidence*, 1819, v. 452.)

[2] See, for example, v. 2, 34, and 40 (1819).

[3] Letter to Perceval, 27 July 1811 (vi. 43–5).

[4] Letter of 27 July 1811. Perceval rejected the proposal by letter of 2 August (vi. 43–5). Cf. Letter to Tierney, vi. 67–70.

[5] Sometimes (e.g. speech of 24 May 1819, v. 10) Ricardo said 3 per cent; at others (e.g. speech of 8 February 1821, v. 73) he said 4 per cent; on 4 March 1819 Commons' *Evidence*, v. 385) he had said 5 or 6 per cent.

Bank's part would be to contract its issues (by contracting its lending to government and traders together[1]) and to *sell*, not buy, gold.[2] He thought an interval of a year adequate for comfortable completion of the operation, though he would concede a maximum of two years to allow for the unreasonable timidity certain to be evident in some quarters.[3] He expressly adhered to the opinion, implied in the challenge thrown out nine years earlier,[4] that the Bank should try the experiment of reducing their issues and see what effect that had in 'the short period of three months'.[5] He did now acknowledge that the process of Resumption might cause 'some little difficulty'[6] – a qualification that had not appeared in the corresponding passages of 1811[7] – but he was still absolutely confident in the event, and he maintained this confidence in the face of challenges based on the discordances between movements in the note-issue and the price level since the end of the war.[8] Even given the narrowness of the gap to be bridged, resumption should be gradual, and Ricardo was willing to allow the Bank Directors discretion in the precise timing of resumption.[9]

VI

In the event the fall in prices within the next three years was much more than 5 per cent. By the end of 1821 Ricardo admitted it to be 10 per cent and in 1822 it was generally reckoned as much more than this.[10] The discomforts of this fall of prices were widely laid at Ricardo's door: 'Every ill which befalls the country is', he complained,[11] 'by some ascribed to Peel's bill, and

---

[1] *High Price of Bullion*, vol. iii, p. 81.

[2] Speech of 24 May 1819 (v. 13).

[3] *Evidence*, 1819, vol. v, pp. 440 and 451.

[4] Letter to *Morning Chronicle*, vol. iii, p. 152. *Reply to Bosanquet*, vol. iii, p. 195.

[5] *Evidence*, 1819, vol. v, p. 371.

[6] *Evidence* (before the Commons' Committee), 1819, vol. v, p. 396; cf. 416, 440, and 10.

[7] *Reply to Bosanquet*, vol. iii, pp. 245–6.

[8] See for example, Lords' *Evidence*, vol. v, pp. 417–20.

[9] 'A Discretion to accelerate, but not to retard, the successive reduction of prices at which they would give Bullion in Exchange for their Notes.' v. 440.

[10] Clapham, *Econ. Hist. Modern Britain*, i. 602.

[11] Letter to Trower, 11 December 1821, xi. 122.

Peel's bill is invariably ascribed to me.' He repudiated responsibility in terms that have come down to us in two private letters,[1] in the draft of a Letter to a Newspaper,[2] all dating about Christmas 1821, and in published form in the pamphlet *On Protection to Agriculture*[3] written three months later. Nothing in his letters during the remaining year and a half of his life affords any evidence of any modification of his view. But there is a story that Ricardo 'recanted'.[4] The story as given by William Ward is this:

> Now Mr Ricardo lived to change this opinion, and shortly before he died expressed that he had done so; the late Sir W. Heygate[5] was with him, and he said 'Ay, Heygate, you and the few others who opposed us on the cash payments have proved right. I said that the difference at most would be only five per cent, and you said that at the least it would be twenty-five per cent.'

Sir James Graham gave the story some support in his *Corn and Currency*:[6] 'Mr Ricardo', he alleged, 'varied in the application of his own test; for in 1819 he contended that 3 per cent[7] was the full amount of the depreciation; whereas, before his lamented death in 1823, he admitted his original error, and confessed that the bill of 1819 had raised the value of the currency at least 10 per cent.' Graham's reference is to Ricardo's speech in the Commons on 12 June 1822,[8] but the speech does not bear the interpretation of any recantation, and its meaning is repeated in speeches of February and June 1823.[9] I find it easier to suppose that Ward and possibly Heygate followed Graham in misinterpreting this passage than that Ricardo changed his

[1] To Trower, ix. 122 and McCulloch, 2 January 1822, ix. 140–1.

[2] v. 515–21.   [3] iv. 223–8.

[4] Viner's discussion and references (*Studies in the Theory of International Trade*, pp. 176–7) enabled me to track this down.

[5] Heygate was Lord Mayor of London, 1822–3, and M.P. for Sudbury. He was not on the 1819 Committee; but twice in the Commons crossed swords with Ricardo on the Resumption. (See v. 17 and 203.)

[6] 3rd ed., 1827, p. 39.

[7] This figure was taken from Ricardo's Commons speech on 24 May, 1819. (See v. 10, esp. footnote 2.)

[8] v. 209.   [9] v. 255 and 312.

mind in the last few weeks of his life without leaving any
record in the letters of those weeks.[1]

In fact it was in the last of the speeches just referred to that
Ricardo stated most clearly his consistency with his own analysis of the position in 1819:

> The difference in 1819, between paper and gold, was 5 per
> cent, and the paper being brought, by the bill of 1819, up to
> the gold standard, he had considered that, as the value of the
> currency was only altered 5 per cent, there could be no
> greater variation than 5 per cent, in the result as to prices.
> But this calculation had always been subject to a supposition,
> that no change was to take place in the value of gold. Mr
> Peel's bill, as originally constituted, led the way to no such
> chance. . . . It was a bill by which, if they had followed it
> strictly, the Bank would have been enabled to carry on the
> currency . . . in paper, without using an ounce more of gold
> than was then in their possession . . . no doubt gold had
> altered in value; and why? Why, because the Bank, from the
> moment of the passing of the bill in 1819, set their faces
> against the due execution of it. . . . By their measures they
> occasioned a demand for gold, which was, in no way, neces-
> sarily consequent upon the bill of 1819. . . .[2]

In short, all the rise of prices beyond 5 per cent was due to the
Bank's scramble for gold, and Ricardo thought his sole error
in 1819 had been in assuming that an intelligent Bank of
England would make reasonable efforts to operate in con-
formity with the spirit of the Act of 1819, which embodied the
Ingot Plan for the very purpose of avoiding a scramble for
gold.

Ricardo estimated the damage done by the Bank's action as
a 5 per cent appreciation in gold against commodities which,
added to the 5 per cent appreciation in paper against gold as

[1] We have for these weeks letters to McCulloch, Mill, Malthus, and Trower,
to any one of whom it would have been natural for Ricardo to mention a
change of opinion on a subject in which he had been supremely interested.

[2] v. 311–12. Cf. 254–5 (26 February 1823); and the Draft Letter to a Newspaper, v. 519–20.

forecast in 1819, made it 'necessary to raise the value of paper 10 per cent instead of 5 per cent'.[1] In the 1822 speeches he was rather less categorical, admitted that 'he had very little ground for forming any correct opinion on this subject', but thought that 5 per cent was about the degree of appreciation he would have expected to result from a demand for £15 or 20 millions' worth of gold.[2] It may be that Ricardo was wrong in this – he himself insisted that it was impossible to isolate for measurement the effect of one among a number of simultaneously operative causes.[3] But there was no confession of error except on the one matter of the assumption about the behaviour of the Bank. If in 1819 Ricardo could have foreseen the course of events following the Resumption Act, his advice would not have been against restoration of the former gold parity (as would follow from the Ward–Heygate–Graham recantation story[4]); it would have been 'Restore the gold parity, adopt my Ingot Plan, but do not leave this incompetent and prejudiced company of merchants in charge of the operation.' It is possible, indeed likely, that such a course would still have led to grave difficulty, because Ricardo had ignored the lack of adjustment in 1819 between the internal price and income structure and the foreign exchange position; but this is a charge that was levelled at Ricardo only in later years.

VII

For Ricardo this bungling of the Resumption by the Bank of England was the last straw, and he devoted some of his last energies to putting into pamphlet form his proposals for superseding this intolerable company of merchants. The attack was never on the ground of dishonesty or the deliberate subordination of the public interest to private ends. On the contrary, Ricardo again and again defended the integrity of the Directors, from the beginning to the end of his controversies

---

[1] v. 312.

[2] v. 209.

[3] e.g. *Evidence*, 1819, vol. v, pp. 417–21.

[4] For Ricardo repeatedly said he would oppose return to parity if that had implied a large measure of price adjustment (see above, p. 44).

about them.[1] Very rarely he was willing to acknowledge other virtues in them: in 1811 he specifically refrained from charging them with incautiousness in their discount business,[2] though if he had known what Clapham revealed to us in the official history,[3] he would have been sharply critical. As lately as 1819 he privately expressed[4] 'full confidence in the wise checks which have been put on by the Directors' in the first phase of the Resumption operation. But these bouquets were exceptional and, quite apart from his general objection that a corporate body should not be entrusted with such power,[5] as the years went by Ricardo found more and more counts on which to indict the Bank. In his first comments on the Bullion Report, he characterized the Bank Court as 'notoriously ignorant of the most obvious principles of political economy',[6] and he particularized by pointing to the evidence given by the Governor and Deputy Governor and even by Jeremiah Harman.[7] From 1819 he broadened the front of his attack, accusing them of ignorant prejudice in their unwillingness to accept his Ingot Plan[8] and complaining that because of their prejudice they were using the forgeries problem as an excuse instead of really trying to produce an unimitable note.[9] Ricardo obviously found their criticism of his own scheme very aggravating, and when the Directors added the crime of turning the path back to the gold standard into a ploughed field, he referred to the Bank in Parliament as 'a timid body' which 'seldom saw its own interest'.[10]

[1] e.g. Letter to *Morning Chronicle*, 24 September 1810 (iii. 152). Speeches in the Commons, 1819 and 1822 (v. 14 and 18, 143). Cf. the suppressed part of letter to Tierney, 11 December 1811 (vi. 70).

[2] *Reply to Bosanquet*, vol. iii, p. 215.

[3] *The Bank of England*, vol. ii.

[4] Letter to Trower, 25 September (viii. 79).

[5] Letter to McCulloch, 4 December 1816 (vii. 103).

[6] iii. 133. Cf. v. 18 (1819) and v. 143 (1822).

[7] iii. 358–9, 369, and 377.

[8] e.g. viii. 21 and ix. 141.

[9] See viii. 350 (1821) and iv. 225–6 (1822). The recent researches of Mr A. D. Mackenzie have revealed that, even if they did use it as an excuse, the Directors were at least making considerable efforts to improve the technique of bank-note production.

[10] Speech of 8 February 1821, v. 76–7. Cf. remarks in Letters, ix. 15, 140–1, 176, and 202.

His attitude towards the Bank was also affected in the later years by the controversies over the Bank's profits. The inflation of its discounts, coupled with its comparative freedom from reserve obligations, meant that the Bank had been enabled to increase its profits very substantially,[1] though Ricardo was surprised that the increase had not been greater, and indeed thought this additional proof that the Directors did not know how to manage their business.[2] There was a clear case, he thought, for revision of the bargain between the Bank and the Exchequer;[3] it was 'lamentable to view a great and opulent body like the Bank of England, exhibiting a wish to augment their hoards by undue gains wrested from the hands of an over-burthened people'.[4] Ricardo also joined Grenfell and others in urging that the Directors were breaking their own bye-laws in refusing to make bigger distributions to stockholders, and in concealing the actual profit figures.[5] He did not pursue this particular matter very far,[6] but the attitude of the Directors in it was no doubt just one more circumstance confirming him in the view that this set of ignorant bunglers should be deprived of the privileges and responsibilities which were anyway inconsistent with the spirit of the time.

When he introduced his Ingot Plan in the 1811 Appendix to the *High Price of Bullion*, Ricardo wrote solely of continuance of the right of note-issue in the Bank of England. The idea that the right should be removed from the Bank and vested in a governmental body appears to have come to him from J.-B. Say. Say had been commissioned by the French Government to study economic conditions in England, and he included in his

---

[1] *Economical and Secure Currency* (1816), vol. iv, p. 52.

[2] Letter to McCulloch, 8 May 1819, viii. 27.

[3] vi. 333. Cf. speech of 31 May 1822, by which time he was urging that 'every farthing made by the Bank ought to belong to the public' (v. 193), and Letter to J.-B. Say, 24 December 1814 (vi. 166).

[4] *Economical and Secure Currency* (1816), vol. iv, p. 93. This is an unusual sentence to find in Ricardo whose writings are generally dispassionate, and it is not surprising to learn that its actual wording was suggested by Mill (see vii. 5).

[5] See, for example, iv. 110 (1816).

[6] He did not, for example, take up Allardyce's campaign after the latter's death (see iv. 113).

unpublished report a currency plan[1] which, it seems, he sent to Ricardo. In an important letter[2] of 24 December 1814, Ricardo commented on this plan, which provided for a government note-issue. Ricardo thought the history of abuse would make all peoples reluctant to leave this business to governments.

> My only doubt is whether Government will under all temptations rigidly abide by its own rules. In justice the public ought to derive the benefits which result from the substitution of a paper for a more valuable currency, but it has hitherto been given to a company of Bankers or merchants because they were more under the control of authority and could not with impunity use so formidable an engine to the injury of the public.

The seed thus sown in Ricardo's mind germinated slowly but surely. The pamphlet on an *Economical and Secure Currency* in 1816 was concerned mainly with the return to gold, the Ingot Plan, and the disposal of the Bank's profits; but in its very last lines Ricardo, following the train of thought inspired by Say's document, suggested that after the expiration of the Bank's charter in 1833, the right to issue notes might be vested exclusively in 'commissioners responsible to parliament only'.[3]

Annoyance at the Bank's mishandling of the Resumption of Cash Payments, and perhaps also their 'lamentable' attitude over the allocation of profits,[4] led Ricardo to develop the notion seriously in the last year or so of his life. In the summer of 1823, letters to Malthus and Mill[5] told of his writing the pamphlet which appeared posthumously in 1824, *The Plan for the Establishment of a National Bank*. The problem that had troubled him when he wrote to Say nine years earlier, the danger of abuse by governments, was solved by Ricardo in a manner directly anticipating the Liberal Yellow Book of 1928. Commissioners should be appointed over whom 'ministers would have much less influence . . . to make them swerve from their duty, than what they have possessed, and have indeed

---

[1] See Sraffa's note 3, vi. 165.   [2] vi. 164–5.
[3] iv. 114.   [4] See p. 50 above.
[5] 3 and 7 August (ix. 325–6 and 329).

exercised, over the Bank of England'.[1] The profits of issue would automatically be enjoyed, as Ricardo thought they should be, by the State. The Commissioners would regulate their issues on the principle that later became known as the Currency Principle and was embodied in the arrangements for the Issue Department of the Bank of England.[2]

Having developed – in some detail – a plan for currency issue by National Commissioners (we should nowadays say a National Board), Ricardo looked back over his shoulder to see what might happen to the restricted Bank of England. What he saw caused him no worry at all. 'It would still have profitable means of employing its own funds'[3] in the second of its previous lines of business – the banking line. But this was not all: 'Suppose I am wrong, and that the company were dissolved, what inconvenience would commerce sustain from it?' And he answers his question by explaining that the country could get along perfectly well without the Bank: the funds deposited with it would not be lost to the community, but would simply go to other operators in the market. He quoted[4] Richardson's evidence to show that the Bank's discount business was not an overwhelming part, and argued that Richardson and other operators could perfectly well replace the Bank in this side of its business. It is significant both of Ricardo's general position and of his view of the Bank Directors that neither in published work nor in private letters did he make any reference whatever to the special responsibility of the Bank as a prop to the market in times of trouble – as, we should say, a lender of last resort. He did, of course, always acknowledge the risk of internal drain in times of panic, but took the line that no system could provide protection against such calamities.[5]

[1] Letter to Mill, ix. 329. The matter is developed fully in the pamphlet at iv. 282–3.

[2] The pamphlet opens with the distinction between the currency function and the banking function of the Bank of England, a distinction that was destined to become regrettably prominent in the controversies of subsequent decades. See iv. 276 and 293.

[3] iv. 278.   [4] iv. 280.

[5] e.g. Lords' *Evidence*, vol. v, p. 456.

VIII

Though the habit of ascribing to Ricardo great influence on the Bullion Report has now disappeared – thanks to the researches of Professor F. W. Fetter[1] – the passages I have just reviewed afford basis for a claim that Ricardo was the father of the system adopted by the Bank of England after its internal revolution at the beginning of the 'forties and, after Peel's conversion, embodied in the famous Bank Charter Act of 1844. His direct influence on events was thus at least as great after his death as it had been when in 1819 he carried the country back to gold at the old parity. After 1819 he lived long enough to complain that the operation had been bungled. Would he equally have complained, in mid-century, that the application of the Currency Principle had been bungled? I doubt whether he could have done. Though Ricardo continually acknowledged the variability of the demand for money to support a given price structure,[2] he made no provision in his system for meeting such variations. Moreover, he did not at any stage foresee the important role that was to be played in the nineteenth century by banking manipulation of the rate of interest. Consistently with his attitude on other issues, he retarded the rate of interest as determined by the forces that we should regard as long-run forces. An early statement of his position on this question is to be found in his Second Letter on the Bullion Report,[3] where he argued against Sinclair's claim that an increase in the supply of money lowered the rate of interest: 'the rate of interest for money is totally independent of the nominal amount of the circulating medium. It is regulated solely by the competition of capital, not consisting of money.' Even before this, however, Ricardo did, in his longer explanation given in *The High Price of Bullion*,[4] concede that the rate of interest would be momentarily

---

[1] 'The Bullion Report Re-examined', in the *Quarterly Journal of Economics*, August 1942, p. 655 et seq. Reprinted above.

[2] e.g. Lords' *Evidence* (1819), vol. v, pp. 420–1.

[3] iii. 143–4 (September 1810). Cf. iii. 25–6 (September 1809) and i. 363–4. Ricardo derived his view from Adam Smith (*Wealth of Nations*, bk. ii, ch. IV) and Hume (Essay 'Of Interest', in *Political Discourses*).

[4] iii. 88–94.

affected: additional notes offered on loan by the Bank 'would for a time affect the rate of interest . . . they would be sent into every market, and would everywhere raise the prices of commodities, till they were absorbed in the general circulation. It is only during the interval of the issues of the Bank, and their effect on prices . . . interest would, during the interval, be under its natural level. . . .' These acknowledgements of short-period disturbances became more regular, though hardly more prominent, in later expositions.[1]

To say that Ricardo ignored everything but the long-run forces would therefore be a grave injustice, but it is the fact that his real interest was confined to these forces, to the exclusion of short-period disturbances. This emphasis not only prevented him from realizing the potentialities of banking policy, but also lent to much of his exposition an air of unreality that weakened its political effect, and I would go so far as to say that it prevented him from perceiving certain major inconsistencies in his general position. He assumed that the effect of increased money in forcing prices upwards was almost instantaneous,[2] and it was largely on this that he based his belief that a 'gap' in the balance of payments would be almost instantly filled by expansion of exports of commodities.[3] This view was, it seems, based not merely on *a priori* arguments but also on a genuine belief that this was how things happened in English trade. Ricardo appears to have drawn, in his own mind, a sharp distinction between agriculture, in which variations in supply necessarily implied considerable variations in price,[4] and manufacturing industry which could adjust output and exports easily on the appearance of the smallest variations in price.[5] This naïve view of economic structure could be held only by a man whose time was largely spent in the City and on his estate in Gloucestershire, and who never (as far as I know)

[1] e.g. Speech of 1 July 1822 (v. 222): 'The general level of interest would be restored in less than six months.' Cf. iv. 233 (1822).

[2] For example as late as 1819, see v. 452.

[3] See p. 38 above.

[4] So giving rise to the phenomenon of rent, the theory of which he helped to develop, or at least to promulgate.

[5] Cf. v. 408–9.

went into the great industrial areas of the Midlands and the north. I confess I have a sneaking sympathy for the Member of Parliament[1] who asked 'Where has the Honourable Member [Mr Ricardo] been? Has he just descended from some other planet?'

What I find more shattering is the inconsistency between on the one hand this view that long-run effects come quickly and easily, and on the other hand Ricardo's continual complaints of the distributional evils of a variation in the value of money. Ricardo often said that an increase in the supply of money was not genuinely stimulating to industry and trade; it merely encouraged the worst and most disturbing class of speculation.[2] But his main case against inflation was that it caused injustice between debtor and creditor, and between one section of the people and other sections.[3] In 1821 he publicly went much further: 'By altering a distribution of property thus, an alteration would be made in the demand for some commodities; there would be a deficiency of supply to the new taste which came to the market, with the increase of property; and there would be too much for the taste of those whose resources had fallen.'[4] Writing to Mill in 1816 he had not been quite as firm; but it is interesting to find him mentioning the sources of friction: 'the resistance which is offered – the unwillingness that every man feels to sell his goods at a reduced price, induces him to borrow at a high interest and to have recourse to other shifts to postpone the necessity of selling.'[5] In all such passages there seem to be two circumstances hindering Ricardo's path towards the whole truth: the attractions of Say's Law, and his lack of touch with the industry and trade of Britain outside London. On the first he had, as is well known, controversy with Malthus extending over years, but when Ricardo died, the truth still lay in the wide gap that separated the two of them. A few more years might have given him the opportunity to

[1] Brougham (see v. 85).
[2] e.g. Appendix to *High Price of Bullion* (1811), vol. iii, pp. 122–3; iii. 134 (1810).
[3] e.g. iii. 96 and 134 (1810); Letters to McCulloch, 9 June and 4 December 1816 (vii. 37 and 103).
[4] Speech in the House of Commons, 9 April 1821, v. 127–8.
[5] vii. 67.

C

move just that little further that would have made his views on monetary questions very much more helpful.

Even so, the Ricardian legacy, the lasting fruit of a mere fourteen years' attention to these matters, was remarkable. His first essay, *The High Price of Bullion*, reinforced the teachings of the Bullion Report, and it was then only a matter of time before the worst monetary fallacies hitherto prevalent became the happy hunting-ground of cranks rather than the respectable resort of serious thinkers. In a more positive way, the theory of purchasing-power parity, to which his work at least gave impetus, proved an anchor of sanity in the whirlpools of currency confusion a hundred years later. His permanent influence on institutions was substantial: he must share responsibility for the Bank Charter Act of 1844 which gave the English currency system its peculiar form and seriously retarded the development of central banking. On the credit side, he can claim some responsibility for the gold bullion system, in substance the Ricardian Ingot Plan, adopted by Britain in 1925. For the transformation of the Bank of England from a company of merchants to a board of national commissioners Ricardo can, of course, claim no credit, but it would perhaps have been a satisfaction to him. He might still be left with his doubt 'whether Government will under all temptations rigidly abide by its own rules'.

2 Nassau Senior and Classical Economics

MARIAN BOWLEY

[This article is edited from M. Bowley, *Nassau Senior and Classical Economics*, London, Allen & Unwin, 1937, pp. 258–62, 276–81, 288–97, 328–34.][1]

I THE HAND-LOOM WEAVERS REPORT

Senior's other excursion into the field of social policy between 1831 and 1847 was in connection with the Commission on the Distress of the Hand-loom Weavers of which he was a member. It seems probable that Senior was himself responsible for the writing of the Report, and it bears all the marks of his style and methods of arrangement.[2] That he attached importance to the analysis and conclusions of the Report, and to his own work on it, is shown in a letter from him to de Tocqueville:

> I take advantage of the privilege of General Hamilton to send you a copy of a Report on Hand-loom Weavers, which I printed a few days ago, after having given to it the leisure of nearly two years. If you can find time to look through it, you will find that it treats at some length many important questions.[3]

---

[1] The author draws attention to the fact that her book was published in 1937, and some of the views expressed therein may need to be modified in the light of subsequent research.

[2] This is suggested also by an unpublished letter to Whately (Senior MSS.) dated 1 February 1841. 'I send you a little pamphlet which together with the Hand-loom Weavers Report has occupied all my leisure since November. I have inserted in the Hand-loom Weavers Report besides this, two considerable articles on Embezzlement and the Irish Linen Board, [and] an elaborate paper on combinations among workmen. It is a frightful picture and has cost the perusal, painful in every sense, of many folios. I have nothing more on [that] report now than Emigration, which I shall dismiss rather summarily, for the weavers are not good emigrants, and education – on which I shall have Kay's assistance.'

[3] Letter to de Tocqueville, 27 February 1841, *Correspondence and Conversations of Alexis de Tocqueville with N. W. Senior*, 1872, vol. I, pp. 21–2.

After a comprehensive and sympathetic account of the condition of the hand-loom weavers, the Report goes on to the analysis of the causes of those conditions by an application of wage theory. Since wages depend on the supply and demand for labour, it is argued, unduly low wages in any occupation must be due either to an excessive supply of labour, or to a diminution of demand.[1] On the side of supply in hand-loom weaving there were continuous tendencies to excessive supply, due to the agreeableness and freedom of independent working, to the ease of learning to weave and of hiring looms, and to the fact that it was an occupation in which it was possible for every member of a family to contribute to income, since children could be employed on the subsidiary occupations. As a result, according to the Report, weavers in many ways suffered from all the disadvantages of a casual supply of labour, and had a tendency to increase in numbers despite the appallingly low level of earnings.[2]

On the side of demand, the competition of power looms and the instability of trade diminished both the volume and the regularity of the demand for their labour. The bulk of the fluctuations in the demand for weavers fell on the hand-loom weavers, who as a class had been reduced to the reserve of the industry for times of active trade.[3] The problem was summarized in the following way:

> The general result of our inquiries as to the condition of the hand-loom weavers and its causes may be thus summed up. We have shown that though there are many differences in the respective conditions of different branches of hand-loom weavers, yet as a body they are in a state of distress; and that the great cause of this distress is a disproportion between the supply of hand-loom labour and the demand

[1] *Report of the Commission on the Condition of the Hand-loom Weavers*, 1841, pp. 22–3.

[2] The Hand-loom Weavers inquiry led Senior to raise as an additional objection to the allowance system of outdoor poor relief, that it acted as a subsidy to a decaying branch of industry encouraging the formation of pools of underpaid labour subsisting partly on the rates. *Remarks on the Opposition to the Poor Law Amendment Bill by a Guardian*, 1841, pp. 78–83.

[3] *Report on the Hand-loom Weavers*, p. 23.

for it: the demand being in many cases deficient, in some cases decreasing, and in still more irregular, while the supply is in many branches excessive, in almost all has a tendency to increase, and does not appear in any to have a tendency to adapt itself to the irregularities of the demand.

If we are right in believing that the low rate of the wages of the hand-loom weavers arises principally from a disproportion between the supply of their labour and the demand for it, it must follow that no measures can effectually raise their wages except by getting rid of that disproportion, or even improve them except by diminishing it; still, however, while this low rate of wages continues the condition of the weaver would be improved by any cause which should render the demand for his labour more steady, or should diminish the price or improve the quality of the commodities on which his wages are expended.[1]

The problem confronting the Commission was similar in many ways to that of the modern depressed areas – that of a declining industry dependent to some extent on a foreign market in a period of considerable trade fluctuations. It was no more possible to produce a remedy like a rabbit out of a hat then than now, and the Commission was reduced to making general recommendations with the objects of steadying the demand for the labour of the hand-loom weavers, lowering the cost of living, and increasing the mobility of the weavers themselves. In this connection a discussion of the mischievous effects of the Corn Laws in causing sudden and unforeseeable changes in the state of trade came into the Report. Apart from the hampering effects of these Laws on the expansion of trade, the variations in the price of corn and in the quantities imported caused, according to the Report, sudden fluctuations in the home demand for manufactured goods, and dislocated credit and markets by necessitating sudden movements of specie. These variations were bad for all industries, but *a fortiori* for the marginal producers of a depressed industry, since a bad harvest not merely raised the price of food, but increased the supply of

[1] *Report on the Hand-loom Weavers*, p. 48.

labour among those who, like the hand-loom weavers, had the opportunity to work harder to make up their wages, just at the times when the demand for their labour had fallen off. The inevitable results were a fall in money wages and a rise in the cost of living at the same time. The Commission attempted to bring home the distress caused by these disturbances:

> Very few even of our best-paid workmen have the economy and providence which enable the high wages of one period to meet the low wages or inactivity of another. With almost all of them low wages produce immediate distress, and want of employment immediate destitution. We do not believe that anyone who has not mixed with the working classes, we do not believe that we ourselves, can adequately estimate how much mental and bodily suffering, how much anxiety and pain, how much despondency and disease are implied in the vague terms 'a fall of wages' or a 'slack demand for labour'.[1]

Although the Commission was convinced of the harmful effects of the protective system and of the Corn Laws in particular, it pointed out that their removal could not produce any fundamental change in the conditions of the hand-loom weavers, since the principal cause of their distress was the competition of power looms. It made, however, a general recommendation in order to help the weavers by improving the quality of some of the goods they bought, particularly house room. The duty of the government was intervention in this matter:

> Of the modes in which the labourer can expend his income, the legislature ought to encourage those which contribute to the general welfare of his family; and of these the principal is the improvement and adornment of his habitation. Where that is miserable, nothing else that is for the common benefit is likely to be attended to.

[1] *Report on the Hand-loom Weavers*, p. 67. According to the Report the hand-loom weavers attached great importance to the reform of the Corn Laws.

On the following page of the Report the way in which this might be done is explained:

> With all our reverence for the principle of non-interference, we cannot doubt that in this matter it has been pushed too far. We believe that both the ground landlord and the speculating builder ought to be compelled by law, though it should cost them a percentage on their rent and profit, to take measures which shall prevent the towns which they create from being the centre of disease. . . . If like the higher classes the labourers were aware of the danger and refused to encounter it, better habitations would be provided for them. But where tenants are to be found for every hovel and cellar where family after family occupy rooms which are vacant by the disease or death of the previous tenants, the builder has no pecuniary motive to provide better accommodation than his customers require. We repeat, therefore, our belief that this is not one of the matters which can be safely abandoned to the parties immediately concerned.

The Commission was in fact prepared to support the recommendations of the public health enthusiasts as to regulation and examination of plans for new buildings, compulsory drainage, inspection and disinfection of old, and the condemning of those past repair. The Commission made the further suggestion that in order to prevent these restrictions raising the cost of houses to the labourers, the duty on Baltic timber should be abolished.[1]

Of those remedies which might apply specifically to hand-loom weavers by increasing their mobility and willingness to enter other industries, education occupied the chief position, and the Commission had no hesitation in recommending compulsory education provided gratis by the State.[2] Emigration was turned down as unsuited to the physique and inclinations of the weavers themselves.[3] Finally, Senior himself regarded

[1] *Report on the Hand-loom Weavers*, pp. 71–3 et seq.
[2] Ibid., pp. 121–4. See pp. 267–8 of original text for an account of Senior's views on education.
[3] Ibid., pp. 118–20.

legislation to prevent trade unions limiting entry into certain trades, as one of the easiest and most effective remedies.[1]

From the tone of the Report it is obvious that if Senior and his colleagues had known a remedy for the distress of the hand-loom weavers, they would not have turned it down for the sake of the principle of non-interference. But inevitably the only real solution lay in the hands of the weavers themselves – the abandonment of the branches of hand-loom weaving which were economically dead, and the decrease or limitation of the supply of labour in those which were not. Thus the Report concludes:

> But we must add, and we make the statement with great sympathy for the persons on whose situation we are commenting, that there are branches of hand-loom weaving which no conduct on the part of those engaged in them is likely to make adequate sources of comfortable support for a family.[2]

It is evident that the attitude of Senior and John Stuart Mill marked an important breach with the preceding generation. It is one thing to maintain, as a principle, that the duty of government is to keep out except in special cases, however liberally that phrase is interpreted. It is quite another to assert the right, duty, and possibility of intervention for the common good, and that the only limit to the duty of government is its power, without any first principle limiting that power. This is what Senior and effectually J. S. Mill were asserting in 1847.[3] Senior's own evolution and application of this principle of government is sufficient evidence of his divergence from the original Benthamite principle of non-intervention. The same may be said of John Stuart Mill. Nor is it difficult to explain why this has not been realized in the former case, while it has in that of the latter. Most of the writings in which Senior's

[1] *Report on the Hand-loom Weavers*, p. 118.
[2] Ibid., p. 120.
[3] Cf. Leslie Stephen, *English Utilitarians*, vol. III, chaps. 3 and 4. J. S. Mill, *Autobiography*, chap. 7.

evolution is displayed are either embodied in government reports, or are in the form of memoranda written for various members of the inner circle of the Whig party to which he acted as general adviser on social and economic questions, or else are contained in his unpublished lectures. Of the few non-theoretical writings published, the most important, the *Letter* on the Irish Poor Laws, naturally had a circulation limited to people interested in the Irish question; the *Letters on the Factory Act* were certainly open to laissez-faire interpretation in view of the common habit of reading a general condemnation of a wide movement into criticism of a particular part of it; while the only article directly connected with English social problems, viz., 'The English Poor Law', was published anonymously in the *Edinburgh Review*.[1] It was thus not to be expected that any outside the circle in which he moved should know anything about those of his opinions which might modify the popular idea that economists had got left behind.

Sufficient has been said to show that Senior, no less than John Stuart Mill, thought that the function of government was not limited to intervention in special cases outside the general category of police, and that laissez-faire was not necessarily the normal rule. Surely if the two most distinguished members of the second generation of classical economists had reached this position, it is unreasonable to suggest that the teachings of the classical economists have been a dead weight on later generations. Indeed, there is little doubt that much of the actual work of reform has been carried out by people who have been educated and influenced by either classical economics or utilitarian philosophy, or both; it is impossible to deny the debt of such reformers and administrators as Chadwick, Sir James Stephens, the Cornewall Lewises, Lansdowne and Sir Robert Peel, and Lord Howick, to mention only some of Senior's contemporaries, to both Bentham and the classical economists.

[1] This article was reprinted in 1865 in *Historical and Philosophical Essays*, vol. II.

II SENIOR ON TRADE UNIONS

In 1830 Senior was asked by Lord Melbourne to consider the position of the law of trade combinations, and to make recommendations for reform. Lord Melbourne and his colleagues in the Cabinet considered that the existing position of the law gave far too much encouragement to strike organizations. In this Senior agreed with them, and he believed that a drastic strengthening of the law was necessary.

Assisted by another lawyer, Tomlinson, he made inquiries, and finally recommended the most intolerant measures which, if they had been enforced, and provided they had not provoked a revolution, would have effectively hampered the Trade Union Movement. This group of proposals may be summarized as follows:

1. A law making clear the common law prohibitions of all conspiracy and restraint of trade.

2. All solicitations, peaceful or otherwise, to form unions, all threats to blacklegs or to masters were to be forbidden and severely punished. Picketing, however peaceful, was to be prohibited and ruthlessly punished.

3. Employers, or their assistants, were to be authorized to arrest men soliciting or picketing without warrant, and take them before any Justice of the Peace.

4. Masters who encouraged combinations and strikes were also to be severely punished.[1]

If these measures were not found to be adequate, Senior recommended that funds subscribed for the purposes of combinations and deposited in savings banks or elsewhere should be confiscated.

After deliberation, Lord Melbourne and his colleagues decided that these astounding recommendations were politically impossible, and in any case probably undesirable, and the Report was relegated to the files of the Home Office. The Report, however, contained a good deal of other interesting

[1] The original report is not available. This account is taken from the Webbs' *History of Trade Unionism*, chap. 3. The Webbs had access to the original.

material, and numerous recommendations which Senior incorporated in the *Report on the Hand-loom Weavers* in 1841, and published in his *Historical and Philosophical Essays*. Whether in 1841 he still really thought that the recommendations of his original Report were satisfactory it is impossible to say, but it is evident that in 1830–1 he was sufficiently alarmed to make recommendations which in practice would have undone the work of the Philosophical Radicals in achieving the repeal of the Combination Laws in 1824–5.

In 1841 he explained his objections to trade unions as due to the effect that their restrictive policy had on the mobility and freedom of labour:

> As the object of the combinations among workmen is the increase of their wages and the general improvement of their condition, and as they have adhered to them for many years, at the expense of great and widely spread occasional suffering, at a sacrifice of individual liberty, such as no political despotism has ever been able to enforce, and with a disregard of justice and of humanity, which only the strongest motives could instigate, it may be supposed that combinations have been found to produce the benefits for which such enormous evils have been voluntarily incurred. We believe, however, that, with a few exceptions, the tendency of combinations has been precisely the reverse of their object, and that, as hitherto directed, they have led to the positive deterioration of the wages and of the condition of those who have engaged in them, and of the far more numerous body who are excluded from them.[1]

It must be remembered that at the time of Senior's early Report, and even when he wrote again in 1841, that the active unions were practically confined to skilled trades. Naturally, therefore, strikes were called without much regard for the large body of workpeople who would, for the time being, lose their wages quite involuntarily. Although Senior seriously failed to appreciate the significance of the Labour Movement

---

[1] *Historical and Philosophical Essays*, 1865, vol. II, p. 117. Reprinted from p. 31 of the *Report on the Hand-loom Weavers*, 1841.

in its early nineteenth-century phases, its contemporary appearance was in fact not such as to encourage anyone who was a sincere believer in individual liberty, though his original recommendations cannot be justified on any grounds whatever. Even the most ardent opponents of the old Combination Laws, such as Francis Place, hoped that their abolition would bring about the natural death of active trade unionism.

The duty of the State in this matter was, Senior believed, to protect the right of the labourer to dispose of his labour as he liked. The government, he said, would be guilty of 'acts of omission if it does not protect the labourer from injury on the part of those who assume to dictate to him what he shall do and what he shall not do'. It would fail on the other hand by acts of commission if it should oblige labourers to do and not to do things because such actions might damage their own interests or those of their employers, and the wealth of the community. In short, Senior declared that, apart from keeping the peace and protecting individuals from each other, the duty of the government is to leave everyone to follow what they believe to be their own interests.[1]

It is evident that Senior felt the difficulty that most Liberals have always felt with regard to the position of trade unions with respect to individual freedom. Whether or not we agree with his particular opinion of the real influence of trade unions at the time he was writing (and in this connection the Webbs' extremely sympathetic account of the early nineteenth-century Labour Movement gives very considerable support to it[2]), it must be admitted that Senior had laid his finger on one of the most important of the economic and social aspects of trade unionism in emphasizing the lack of solidarity of interests between different sections of the working classes.

Despite his fierce recommendations, it appears that he had not any real desire to return to the pre-1824 state of the Combination Laws, for he stigmatized the old laws as oppressive

---

[1] *Historical and Philosophical Essays*, 1865, vol. II, p. 122. These opinions were reprinted from pp. 98–118 of the *Report on the Hand-loom Weavers*, 1841.

[2] *History of Trade Unionism*, chaps. 2 and 3.

and demoralizing, since, he explained, they confounded 'men's ideas of right and wrong' by laying down that —

> each man's separate attempt to raise his own wages was blameless, but that any concerted effort was a crime; that a mere agreement to make such an effort was a crime, and that an assault or a riot exposed its actors to far severer punishment when used as evidence of a combination to raise wages, than when regarded as merely endangering the persons and property of their fellow-subjects.[1]

He admitted, too, that the administration of the old law had been 'partial and oppressive'.

His suggestions were, he said, tentative, as he felt that he did not know the complete facts. In the first place, he recommended that the common law against conspiracies should be modified, as it still made practically every act of a workman, as a member of a combination, illegal. Secondly, that the law should be strengthened against combinations to force discharges of individual labourers, or to force the use or prohibition of certain sorts of machinery. Thirdly, that the encouragement of strikes and combinations by masters should be severely punished by fines. Fourthly, that picketing should be made a criminal offence. Fifthly, that injury to witnesses or to people who stood out against combinations should be compensated from public funds. Finally, he added in a true philosophical-radical spirit:

> We have to add . . . only an earnest wish that no preamble in the spirit of that of the 6 George IV denouncing combinations as 'injurious to trade and commerce, and especially prejudicial to the interests of all concerned in them' [should be included]. We firmly believe in the truth of this preamble. We believe that the general evils and general dangers of combinations cannot easily be exaggerated. We believe that if the manufacturer is to employ his capital, and the mechanist and chemist his ingenuity only under the dictation of his shortsighted and rapacious workmen, or of his equally

[1] *Historical and Philosophical Essays*, vol. II, pp. 124-5.

ignorant and rapacious rivals; if a few agitators can command and enforce a strike which first paralyses the industry
of the peculiar class of workpeople over whom they tyran-
nize, and then extends itself in an increasing circle ... we
believe, we say, that if this state of things is to continue we
shall not retain the industry, the skill, or the capital, on
which our manufacturing superiority, and, with that superiority, our power, and almost our existence as a nation,
depends. But though we believe in the truth of these
premises, they are not the grounds on which we wish now
to proceed. Our immediate object is to give freedom to the
labourer; and we firmly believe that as soon as he is made
master of his own conduct he will use his liberty in the way
most useful not only to himself, but to the rest of the
community.[1]

Altogether Senior's attitude to trade unions was a peculiar
combination of panic fear of turbulent workpeople, a genuine
belief in the damage and injustice done by them to the excluded
groups such as the unskilled, the hand-loom weavers, etc., and
to industry as a whole, and too great a willingness to think of
the instigators and organizers of unions as unscrupulous
ruffians imposing on the ignorance of their fellows.

III THE POOR LAW PROBLEM

It is necessary to point out that although Senior was not a die-
hard supporter of the policy of laissez-faire, he was on general
grounds to begin with opposed to the principle of the Poor
Laws, and in particular to that of relief to the able-bodied. So
far the historians are correct, but they have not, with the
exception of Mackay, made any attempt to discover the extent
of, and reasons for, this disapproval in the light of either the
Poor Law Report or the Amendment Act itself.[2] It would be

---

[1] *Historical and Philosophical Essays*, vol. II, pp. 171–2.

[2] The Webbs (*English Poor Law History*, Part II, vol. 1, p. 86 n. 1) appear to be
surprised that Senior changed from opposing relief to the able-bodied to sup-
porting it. If they had not been so convinced that all the economists, including
Senior, were dogmatic and prejudiced they would have appreciated the reason
for his original opposition better. (See pp. 74–5 below for Senior's own explanation.)

possible, to some extent, to reconstruct Senior's philosophy of the Poor Law, as we may call it, from these sources together with the Preface to the *Foreign Communications on the Poor Law*. But there is, fortunately, a perfectly clear statement in an article by him in the *Edinburgh Review* of 1841,[1] which, together with the published and unpublished letters and papers of the period of the inquiry itself, give us ample material. The objection that the article of 1841 contains wisdom after the event is not valid, as the earlier papers give adequate though scattered support to the same view. It was at a somewhat later date towards the end of the 1840s that Senior's opinion underwent some modification.[2] There is a real difficulty, however, in using the earlier papers in that some purport to be the expression of the views of the whole Commission, though as Senior was without doubt the most active member of it, it is obvious that he at least agreed with the ideas expressed. As to whether they were original or not, it is unimportant. On a subject which had occupied public attention, and that of economists in particular, for as long as the Poor Laws had, it would be invidious to attempt to decide.

Senior himself was under the influence of the prevailing ideas of individual freedom and self-determination, and it was from this angle that he considered the place of the Poor Laws in the social fabric. His opinions can be summarized as follows from the 1841 article. He saw the progress of society as the gradual evolution of individual freedom. The first major step in the process had been taken with the abolition of serfdom, which gave the individual labourer legal personal freedom. Legal freedom of occupation had, however, only evolved gradually with the decay of the guild and apprenticeship system, while actual freedom had been hampered by the existence of the Poor Laws and the Laws of Settlement which were an integral part of their administration. The effect of the Settlement Laws on the effectual mobility, and therefore freedom, of labour was obvious, but the connection of the actual Poor Laws with it

---

[1] 'English Poor Laws', *Edinburgh Review*, October 1841; reprinted in *Historical and Philosophical Essays*, 1865, vol. II.
[2] Lectures, 1847–52, Course I, lecture 7. See below pp. 76–7.

needed some explanation. Senior's view of personal freedom was that of the recognition of personal responsibility for self-support, and the support of a family, in ordinary contingencies of life, such as old age and sickness, as well as for the other actions for which responsibility was recognized by the civil and criminal law. The fundamental principle of the Poor Laws was inconsistent with this concept, for they were based on the idea that the labouring classes were peculiarly unfitted to look after themselves in a way tolerable with common ideas of humanity or compatible with the safety and welfare of the State. The abolition of the Poor Laws was therefore an essential step in the recognition of the freedom and responsibility of the labouring classes. The Poor Laws were a badge of their fundamental inferiority. It followed that if poor laws were considered necessary they must be framed so as to hinder the process of emancipation as little as possible.

This point of view is illustrated frequently throughout the Commission papers, in which both current practice and proposed remedies were examined from this aspect. Thus in a letter to Lord Althorp about the labour-rate, he says, after examining its numerous disadvantages:

> The great fault of a Labour-rate is that it destroys the distinction between pauperism and independence. The inquiries of the Commissioners have convinced them that it is only by keeping these things separated, and separated by as broad and as distinct a demarkation as possible, and by making relief in all cases less agreeable than wages, that any thing deserving the name of improvement can be hoped for. But under the Labour-rate system, relief and wages are utterly confounded. All the wages partake of relief, and all the relief partakes of wages. The labourer is employed not because he is a good workman, but because he is a parishioner. He receives a certain sum not because that sum is the value of his services, but because it is what the vestry has ordered to be paid. Good conduct, diligence, skill, all become valueless. Can it be supposed that they will be preserved? We deplore the misconception of the poor in thinking that wages are

not a matter of contract but of right; that any diminution of their comforts occasioned by an increase of their numbers without an equal increase of the fund for their subsistence is an evil to be remedied not by themselves, but by the magistrate – not an error, or even a misfortune, but an injustice.[1]

Further on in the same letter he adds:

When what now remains of repugnance to relief or of degradation in accepting it has been destroyed by its being merged in wages, when all the labourers have been converted into a semi-servile populace, without fear but without hope, where can we look for the materials of improvement?

Similarly in an earlier letter in 1832 he expresses his fundamental criticism of the Settlement and Poor Laws:

To suppose that a man can support his family by his wages; that he is to exercise any providence or economy; that anything is to be hoped from voluntary charity; that the poor can manage their own affairs without the interference of the rich; that a man's wages ought to depend on his services, not his wants; seem to be views which those who have long resided in pauperized districts reject as too absurd for refutation. . . .

The present system gives the labourer low wages, but at the same time easy work. It gives him also, strange as it may appear, what he values more, a sort of independence. He need not study to please his master, he need not bestir himself to seek work, he need not put any restraint on his temper, he need not ask relief as a favour, he need not fear that his idleness, or drunkenness, will injure his family; he

[1] Letter to Lord Althorp, March 1833, explaining the views of the Commission on the Labour-rate with reference to a proposed Bill for the better employment of Agricultural Labourers, by facilitating the introduction of a Labour-rate. *Appendix D to the first Report from the Commissioners on the Poor Laws*, p. 2. *Parliamentary Papers*, 1833, vol. XXXII. The Bill was passed in March 1833 as a temporary measure, was twice amended, and finally expired in 1834.

has, in short, all a slave's security for subsistence without his liabilities to punishment.[1]

It is difficult to decide just how far at this period Senior regarded a poor law offering relief to the able-bodied as advantageous in the backward state of development of England. It seems to me probable that, while wishing to leave open the way to future development by breaking down the traditional right to relief, he considered some provision for relief to be desirable, if some safe method of administering it could be devised. In a letter in 1832 on a proposed Agricultural Labourers' Employment Bill which aimed at facilitating the introduction of the labour-rate, on which his opinion had been asked by Lord Melbourne, he inveighed against the provision of additional 'eleemosynary funds' on account of the discouragement they offer to foresight and thrift:

I have gone through the Agricultural Labourers' Employment Bill, and I must say that next to the 43rd Elizabeth, the usury laws, the apprentice laws, and a few other choice specimens, it appears to me as mischievous an attempt at legislation as ever was made.

It aims at providing a new fund for eleemosynary assistance. Now we know that it is the nature of any such fund to create its own demand, to raise up a fresh body of claimants; after which the distress is greater than before the fund was created. It is the old story of the children who made a wall across the valley to keep the cuckoo in. They raised the wall just over the level of the bird's usual flight, and when they found that it just skimmed over the top they thought that if they had laid only another row of stones it would have been kept in. So it is with every definite provision for the poor. Fresh and fresh applicants appear encouraged to depend on such support, and to relax their own industry and

[1] Letter from Senior to the Lord Chancellor, 14 September 1832 (Senior MSS.), written to explain Senior's general opinions. At this date he explained that the Commission were agreed as to the nature and sources of the evil of the Poor Laws, but had not discussed remedies. Almost exactly similar passages occur in Senior's Preface to his *Lectures on Wages*, published 1830.

frugality; fresh funds must be raised, and in turn fall short of the distress. The cuckoo still skims over the wall.

Finally, his last criticism of the Bill is that it admits 'the most dangerous of all principles, the principle that the poor are in fact the owners of the land, and that to the extent of their wants'.[1]

In the later papers frequent passages occur in which he objects to the recognition of a right to relief both on the grounds given above, and because he sees no logical limit to the principle between admitting relief from some people's incomes and confiscation of the whole of rent and profits. There is, for instance, a passage in his History of the Passing of the Poor Law Amendment Act, in an account of the discussion of the labourer's right of appeal against the Guardians, etc., as follows:

> If, therefore, the guardians or vestry expressly commanded the overseer to refuse relief to A B, and A B should consequently perish, it did not appear that any body could be punished. Now though this is the law in the greater part of Europe, and is a much safer system than our own, yet it seemed to me a change which Parliament would not knowingly sanction, and which ought not to be introduced surreptitiously.[2]

He was unable, nevertheless, to resist the temptation to slip in an amendment while the Bill was in the Lords, which enabled all relief to be treated as a loan, of which ne says that it was:

> a most important change in principle, as in fact, by enabling all relief to be treated as a loan, it amounts to a denial of the

---

[1] Letter to Lord Melbourne, 10 March 1832. (Senior MSS.) This Bill appears to be the same as the one about which Lord Althorp made inquiries, see note 1 on p. 71 above.

[2] Senior's History of the Poor Law, pp. 81–2 of the MS. (There are several copies of the manuscript, including one in the Goldsmiths' Company's Library of Economic Literature (University of London) and one deposited in the Library of the London School of Economics. The paging varies in the different copies, and all page references given here are to the latter copy.)

right to gratuitous relief: a right which has existed from the 43rd Eliz. until the present time.[1]

He also expressed his approval of the general anti-Poor Law sentiment of the speech in which Brougham introduced the Bill into the Lords, for though he admitted it to be untimely he remarked:

> Indeed as these views, though perhaps unguardedly expressed, are in a great measure, indeed almost to the whole length, founded on truth, I am not sure that this powerful exposition of them by suggesting to many persons doubts as to the justice and expediency of the whole system, did not induce them to concur more readily in its restriction and modification.[2]

The inference from these passages seems obviously that Senior submitted to relief to the able-bodied merely as a concession to public opinion in England. On the other hand, in a letter to Lord John Russell in 1836, on the Third Report of the Commission of Inquiry into the Condition of the Poor in Ireland, he said that he had changed his mind on this matter, as far as England was concerned, since writing the *Letter to Lord Howick on a legal provision for the Irish Poor* in 1831. He explained that his chief objection in the past had been due to the difficulty of administering relief to the able-bodied:

> In that letter [i.e. to Lord Howick in 1831] I protested against any compulsory provision for the able-bodied or their families. The only change that subsequent experience has produced in my opinion is that I now believe that in England,

[1] Senior's History of the Poor Law, p. 228. It is interesting to notice that in 1848 he had changed his opinion and thought that a right to relief must be admitted where relief was administered by officials. Course I, lecture 7. The statement that a right to gratuitous relief was admitted in 43 Eliz. is not strictly accurate. According to the law, relief to the able-bodied was to be given only in the form of employment and thus was only in return for work. This, of course, Senior knew, but the failure to make the employment effective had in his opinion resulted in gratuitous relief and he generally spoke of it as such.

[2] Ibid., pp. 203–4. Senior had sent Lord Brougham a summary of the Bill preparatory to the latter introducing it in the House of Lords. Brougham's speech consisted of a violent and most untimely denunciation of the principle of poor laws.

or in any country in which the standard of subsistence is high, a provision for the able-bodied in strictly managed workhouses, in which their condition shall be inferior to that of the independent labourer, may be safely and even advantageously made. But as this is not the state of Ireland, as the standard of subsistence in that country is so low that any provision which the State could offer must be superior, as far as physical comfort is concerned, to that obtained by the independent labourer, this change of opinion does not apply to Ireland, and I am forced, therefore, so far as Ireland is concerned, to adhere to that letter.

Though it is impossible to give any exact date to this change of view, it would, I think, be fair to put it at the beginning of the period between writing the letter to the Lord Chancellor in September 1832, and the writing of the Introduction to *Statement of the Provision for the Poor in Parts of America and Europe* in the first few months of 1835. In any case, the letter to Lord John Russell seems to prove fairly conclusively that, considering the stage of development and the traditions of England, Senior did not ever really believe that abolition of all relief to the able-bodied was desirable if its abuse could be prevented.[1] It will appear more clearly in later sections describing the possible remedies that he recognized the necessary slowness of a process of depauperization, only expressing a pious hope that some time the ideal state would be realized in which the necessity for provision would be so small that the Settlement Laws would be altogether abolished.

[1] 'Letter to Lord John Russell, etc.', 14 April 1836, published in *Parliamentary Papers*, vol. LI, 1837.

In the *Statement of the Provision for the Poor in Parts of America and Europe*, 1835, he remarked that in those countries such as Switzerland where a right to relief had been admitted, the system had worked well where the principle of 'less eligibility' had been enforced, pp. 84–8. The Advertisement to the *Statement* is dated 10 June 1835.

It has sometimes been thought that Senior's conversion to the idea of relief to the able-bodied was only forced upon him by circumstances, since he had stated in the *Introductory Lecture*, 1826, and the Preface to the *Lectures on Wages*, 1830, that relief would inevitably produce over-population. This is not correct. All he said was that the abuse of the Poor Law had produced local over-population in some districts, and that emigration would enormously facilitate the carrying through of a reform – an opinion that he still held in 1834.

It must be remembered that neither Senior himself, nor the Commission, ever suggested at any time the desirability of abolishing relief for old age, sickness, sudden emergency, or catastrophe, but on the contrary were anxious to make it more effective.[1] From among the numerous references to this we may perhaps select the following from a letter to Lord Lansdowne in 1834 explaining the main objects of the Commission's Bill. Referring to their recommendation of the workhouse test, Senior wrote:

> In the first place our recommendation applies only to the able-bodied and their families. The aged and impotent, the true poor as they are called in the 18th Eliz., are excluded. It is true, that even for the aged and impotent, the workhouse will in many, perhaps even in most cases, be the least objectionable mode of bestowing compulsory charity, and we trust that by a proper classification of workhouses, and assigning distinct and comparatively comfortable abodes to the impotent, they will be far more effectually relieved than at present. But we have carefully avoided making such a measure obligatory.[2]

Senior's general standpoint, which seems to have remained unchanged between 1832 and 1841, was that under the un-reformed system relief of all types tended to create its own demand by destroying the incentive to energy and providence; that reform must by definition remove this discouragement by making the position of the independent able-bodied labourer more eligible than that of the able-bodied pauper; that it must also differentiate as far as possible between those who attempted to provide for old age, sickness, etc., and those who did not.[3]

---

[1] Cf. the *Letter to Lord Howick on a legal provision for the Irish Poor*, 1831.

[2] Letter to Lord Lansdowne, 2 March 1834, explaining the main objects of the Commission's Bill. (Senior MSS.)

[3] It is interesting to notice in this connection that, while the Bill was in the House of Lords, Senior and Sturges Bourne suggested that overseers should be enabled, under certain regulations, to make contributions from the rates towards the establishment of benefit and saving societies, and help with the subscriptions of members. Cf. Senior's History of the passing of the Poor Law Amendment Act.

It is obviously consistent with this eminently reasonable attitude that machinery should exist to deal with any distress that eventually arose. To this end the Poor Law must distinguish between poverty and pauperism; between a low standard of living and inability and/or unwillingness to reach even that low standard. If this vital distinction was lost sight of, the Poor Law would always be a machine for increasing pauperism, and would finally ruin the hope of an ultimately higher standard of living by the destruction of the means of achieving it – the efficiency of labour.[1]

Substantially Senior held this opinion when he went to lecture at Oxford for the second time in 1847, but he had modified his emphasis, showing more appreciation of the difficulties of providence on a very small income. He pointed out that the government can mitigate the hardships of poverty by providing that no one shall perish by destitution, and regarded this as desirable, something worth while achieving for itself, not merely as a provision necessitated by the imperfect development of the country. On the intrinsic dangers of such provision and its liability to abuse his opinion was unchanged, but it is clear that he had been impressed by the success of the reformed Poor Law both in depauperizing the agricultural labourer and in proving the possibility of administrative efficiency.[2] The soundness of the general principles of the 1834 Act had shown that it was possible to make provision of this sort without increasing the need which it was supposed to relieve.

* * *

[1] This opinion was restated in the pamphlet published during the controversy as to the continuance of the centralized administration in 1841. (*Remarks on the Opposition to the Poor Law Amendment Bill by a Guardian.*) In this pamphlet he maintains that the allowance system has been put down; the industry, etc., of the labourer have again become of value to him; the comfort of the aged and infirm secured; the education of pauper children commenced; and early marriages decreased; also that wages had risen, employment had become steadier, and corruption been repressed (p. 54). This optimistic account, not by any means altogether unjustified, was written, it must be remembered, before the problems of the general mixed workhouse had come to the fore.

[2] Course I, lecture 7. Senior's letter on the Irish Poor Law is sufficient evidence that he distinguished not only between destitution and poverty but also between the different causes of destitution.

It remains only to attempt to estimate Senior's influence on the amendment of the Poor Laws. It is clear that the realization of so many of the Commission's original recommendations in the actual Act was due to Senior's untiring persistence, and in this sense his own statement that for good or evil the main responsibility for the inception of the system of 1834 rested on him is undoubtedly correct.[1] But it is impossible to disentangle the respective parts played by him and Chadwick in making the particular suggestions. Senior was certainly responsible for most of the suggestions for the reform of the Settlement Laws, though Chadwick agreed with him. It seems probable that they decided independently on the merits of the workhouse test. On the administrative side Chadwick is known to have been the dominating influence, but Senior appears to have decided on the necessity of some sort of centralization independently. In any case it is evident that they had much in common in their views, and we know that Senior's attention was drawn to Chadwick by some of his papers on administration. That he finally got him into the main Commission of Inquiry and recommended with great warmth his appointment as one of the Central Administrative Commissioners shows that he relied considerably on his judgement.[2]

Whether Senior or Chadwick was originally responsible for any particular suggestion is really, however, unimportant, for practically every suggestion included in the Report had been recommended at some time or other by people not connected with the Commission of Inquiry. But it is clear that the introduction of the workhouse system and the sweeping simplification of the Settlement Laws were the two objects that

[1] *Correspondence and Conversations of Alexis de Tocqueville with N. W. Senior,* 1872. Letter from Senior to de Tocqueville, 18 March 1835, pp. 12–13.

[2] In a letter to Lord Melbourne on Appointments, 30 June 1834 (Senior MSS.)., he wrote of Chadwick as 'the only individual among the Candidates, perhaps I might say in the country, who could enter into the office of Commissioner with complete prearranged plans of action. He was the principal framer of the remedial measures in the Report and the sole author of one of the most important and difficult portions, the union of parishes', and as having 'communicated more information than any other of our Assistant Commissioners, indeed, almost as much as the rest of them put together', when he had been an Assistant Commissioner.

Senior had most at heart; in both cases he met with only partial success. By the time the Bill was passed, the former had been left entirely dependent on the Commissioners, and its enforcement would depend on their personal views. This, of course, was what happened; the first Administrative Commissioners, appointed largely on Senior's recommendation, introduced the workhouse test into the majority of pauperized rural areas, but as the memory of the old abuses faded, the restrictions on outdoor relief to the able-bodied slackened, and another burst of liberality appeared in the 1850s.[1] As to settlement, Senior was really more successful; he managed to dispose of at least a number of heads and leave it simplified to marriage, parentage, apprenticeship with some limitations, a qualified form of residence, and a qualified form of settlement by estate.

This success, partial though it was, at least sufficed to get rid of the worst pauperization of the agricultural labourer, an achievement largely due to Senior's insistence that this was the essence of the problem. His further hope of gradually eradicating all pauperism has only partially been realized, and by modern methods of insurance rather than by the workhouse system; but even to the most enthusiastic supporters of the principle of 'less eligibility' realization of this ultimate aim was always something an Utopian aspiration. The failure of the workhouse scheme to take the form recommended in the Report of 1834 was a much greater disappointment, and in 1862 Senior regarded the cherished workhouse system from which he had hoped so much with something like horror. He had never anticipated the evolution of the general mixed workhouse with every sort and grade of pauper jumbled up together, nor the complete failure of the Poor Law Commissioners to make adequate provision for the education of pauper children. Thus in his evidence before the Select Committee on Poor Relief in 1862, in answer to a question about the intentions of the original Commission as to classification, he said:

> Yes, we recommended that in every union there should be a separate school. We said that the children who went to the

[1] For an account of the administration of Poor Relief after 1834 see Mackay, *History of the English Poor Law*, and Webbs, op. cit.

workhouse were hardened if they were already vicious, and became contaminated if they were innocent, and we recommended that in every union there should be a building for the children, and one for the able-bodied males, and another for the able-bodied females, and another for the old; we supposed the use of four buildings in every union.

and added in reply to a supplementary question:

We never contemplated having the children under the same roof as the adults.[1]

On education he was equally critical of the administration and vigorous in his defence of education for pauper children. In reply to the suggestion that it was unfair to the independent labourer to educate pauper children at the expense of the rates, he said:

I feel that if a guardian refused to allow a child to be educated because some money could be saved to the parish by so refusing, it would be an act of wickedness and cruelty.

and again:

I think that parents who send their children to work instead of allowing them to be educated, are guilty of cruelty and wickedness to their children, and I do not think the guardians ought to require any parent to be guilty of such conduct.

He went on to maintain that children had a right to education, in replying to a question as to whether a parent had the right to claim education for his children at the public expense:

Certainly at the public expense, if he cannot do it at his own. I take it that the duty to educate children is as much a duty as the duty to feed them.

Finally, he emphasized his old theory that ignorance and pauperism have a great deal to do with each other:

[1] Third Report of the Select Committee on Poor Relief, 1862, *Parliamentary Papers*, 1862, vol. X, Senior's evidence, questions 6905 and 6906.

I believe that there is nothing which creates paupers so much as ignorance, and that to require a child to work, perhaps that he may earn sixpence a day by scaring birds, instead of going to school would be not only very wrong, but very short-sighted.[1]

It is perfectly clear that this was not mere wisdom after the event. The Report of 1834 had recommended the education of pauper children; the Report on the Hand-loom Weavers had recommended free education without specific limitation to any particular class; he had pointed it out as one of the most useful fields for government intervention in his lectures in 1847.[2] No one, however, is disposed to deny the educational enthusiasm of the Utilitarians or of the classical economists, and it is unnecessary to enlarge upon it, but it has been less generally realized that the workhouse system visualized in the *Poor Law Report* of 1834 and that evolved by the Administrative Commissioners were two very different things.

In its Report in 1834,[3] the Commission of Inquiry recommended a strict classification of the inhabitants of workhouses just in order that different types of destitution should be treated differently: that the aged and infirm should be looked after in reasonable quiet and comfort; the children educated, and kept away from the depressing influence of the adults, so that they at least might start with a fair chance of independence; the sick of all sorts given proper medical attention in infirmaries; the able-bodied separated from the rest and the two sexes from each other, in order to make possible a more rigorous treatment.

[1] Third Report of the Select Committee on Poor Relief, 1862, *Parliamentary Papers*, 1862, vol. X, Senior's evidence, questions 6686, 6687, 6690, 6694. The Committee suggested that, in his enthusiasm for education, Senior had underrated both the achievements of the Poor Law authorities in educating indoor pauper children, and the objections and difficulties to their undertaking the education of outdoor paupers' children.

[2] *Poor Law Report*, 1834, pp. 253, 255–8, 301 (1894 reprint). *Report on the Hand-loom Weavers*, see p. 61 above. Lectures, 1847–52, Course I, lecture 6. In the pamphlet *Remarks on the Opposition to the Poor Law Amendment Bill by a Guardian* (p. 54; cf. p. 77, note 1 above) Senior cited as one of the achievements of the Act of 1834 that the education of pauper children had been started.

[3] *Poor Law Report*, 1834, pp. 252–9.

Senior summarized the recommendations in a letter on the Forest of Dean[1]:

> I should recommend four Workhouses to be built: one for able-bodied men, one for able-bodied women, one for the old and sick, and one for the children. The two for the able-bodied should be at a distance from one another, and need be very small; for if tolerably managed (that is, cleanliness and regularity enforced, stimulants prohibited, and work required) they would scarcely ever have half-a-dozen inmates. That for children would of course contain a school. That for the aged and sick would be an Almshouse and Hospital.

It is strange to find the word 'almshouse' used in connection with any part of the workhouse system, but it undoubtedly conveyed the idea of the Commission of Inquiry with regard to the aged.[2]

Why, with all these good intentions, did the plans for distinctive treatment of the main categories of poverty miscarry so completely between 1834 and 1839 that the first three or four decades of reforming effort in the twentieth century have been devoted to destroying the workhouse system that resulted?[3] In the first place, no doubt, part of the trouble was due to the failure of the Commission of Inquiry of 1834 to think out all the administrative difficulties involved in their plan. Not only did the urgency and complexity of the problem prevent the laying down by law of the details of the new system, but the unpopularity of the proposed reforms forced the Commission to acquiesce in leaving out specific references to the organization and administration of the workhouses from the final Bill. It is fairly evident, however, that considerable responsibility for the miscarriage of the original plans rests with Sir G. Nicholls, perhaps the most energetic and the least subtle of the Administrative Commission.[4]

---

[1] Letter to Robert Gordon, Esq., India Board, 4 April 1834, on the Relation of the Forest of Dean to the new Poor Law. (Senior MSS.)

[2] See pp. 76 above.

[3] See Webbs, op. cit., pp. 122–48.

[4] Nicholls appears to have been mainly responsible for the introduction of mixed workhouses both in England and Ireland. Cf. Webbs, op. cit., pp. 122–33; and Nicholls's own *History of the English Poor Law*, vol. II, chaps 16–18.

Despite these admitted failures of the Amendment, there is much to be said in favour of Senior's attempts to deal with the problem of destitution. His attitude may, I think, be fairly summarized as follows: He believed that over-population in the crude sense did not exist in England, that every able-bodied adult could earn enough to live on if unhindered in his attempts. The various forms of allowances not only dragged wages down so as to make this impossible, but assisted the survival of irregular and decaying trades by a concealed form of subsidy. The result was a serious obstacle to the most productive distribution of labour. Apart from philosophical considerations these arguments were and still are the main justification of the principle of 'less eligibility'. Unemployment as a recurrent phenomena Senior was not prepared to deal with except on this principle, for, while he admitted the difficulty of providence on a small income, to make no distinction between those who did and those who did not save was, he believed, unjustifiable. Apart from this problem of unemployment, however, he favoured the provision of relief in what may be called cases of personal misfortune.[1] The criticism that the workhouse test failed to distinguish between unemployment due to personal and impersonal causes is legitimate, and is the most serious that can be made against the Amendment. But it must be remembered that though everyone has been aware of this for a long time, the remedies, such as they are, have only been found after prolonged and stormy experience.

To us, in the complacency of the twentieth century, it appears that, in common with others of his generation, Senior under-estimated the difficulties of saving on a small income and over-estimated the flexibility of the economic system. That neither he, nor his contemporaries, were blind to the human difficulties of adaptability is, however, certain; and his greatest failure, the analysis of and provision of relief for urban destitution due to unemployment, lay in just that field in which modern failure is so painfully evident. Senior, too, it should be remembered, recognized several classes of destitution due to infirmity, childhood, and old age, and was clear that each of

[1] Cf. Senior's *Letter to Lord Howick on a legal provision for the Irish Poor.*

these should be treated differently, in infirmaries, schools, and almshouses. Even for these classes he avoided recommending rigidly uniform treatment, and the Commission carefully refrained from recommending the application of the workhouse test to them.[1] At least the fundamental principle that a poor law is not and cannot be a general cure for poverty was enunciated once and for all in the Report of 1834.

Thus although the classification and the administrative machine recommended by the Commission are out of date today, and were open to criticism even in their own day, it is difficult to see any really significant difference between its outlook and the outlook of the modern reformers of the Poor Law on these problems.

[1] See p. 76 above.

3 The Classical View of Ireland's Economy

R. D. COLLISON BLACK

[This article is edited from R. D. Collison Black, *Economic Thought and the Irish Question, 1817–1870*, Cambridge University Press, 1960, pp. 86–8, 159–68, 201–2.]

At least up to the time of John Stuart Mill, the classical economists were agreed that no change in the system of landed property was necessary to the improvement of Ireland; economic development could best be achieved through the retention of that system, and the adjustment of Irish agriculture to the capitalist type of mixed farming.

This conviction followed logically from the economists' method of viewing economic development in terms of the comparative rates of increase of population and capital.[1] In 1817, it seemed clear to such writers as Malthus and Ricardo that the extremely low standards of the majority of the Irish people were the result of a continuing tendency for population growth to outstrip capital increase. Employment opportunities were thus few, and money wages in them extremely low, but the people were able to support themselves, because of the comparative ease with which land could be obtained, through sub-division, and a sufficient quantity of potatoes raised from it.[2]

[1] By capital was normally meant circulating capital – 'funds destined for the support of labour' – but the term was often used in a looser sense. See the present author's article 'The Classical Economists and the Irish Problem', *Oxford Economic Papers*, vol. V, no. 1 (March 1953), especially p. 28.

[2] See Malthus to Ricardo, 17 August 1817: '. . . the predominant evil of Ireland, namely a population greatly in excess above the demand for labour, though in general not much in excess above the means of subsistence on account of the rapidity with which potatoes have increased under a system of cultivating them on very small properties rather with a view to support than sale' (*Works and Correspondence of David Ricardo*, ed. Sraffa, vol. III, p. 175).

The system gave no incentive to produce more than this, and thus the great majority of the people were idle and indolent.

If they were to be raised out of this condition and given higher material standards, then the growth of population must be checked, and the increase of capital promoted.[1] That it was desirable thus to raise material standards most political economists of the time did not doubt, although Ricardo pointed out that it was not the only course that might be chosen. 'Happiness is the object to be desired,' he reminded Malthus, 'and we cannot be quite sure that provided he is equally well fed, a man may not be happier in the enjoyment of the luxury of idleness than in the enjoyment of the luxuries of a neat cottage, and good clothes. And after all we do not know if these would fall to his share. His labour might only increase the enjoyments of his employer.'[2]

However, once granted the premiss that improvement of material standards was to be sought, it clearly followed that capital growth must be made to outstrip population growth, and the classical economists reasoned that the most effective single step that could be taken to achieve this was the abolition of the cottier system, and the introduction of the English type of agriculture in its place. Such a change would in fact operate to check population and stimulate investment simultaneously.

Malthus, and all who shared his beliefs, constantly stressed that population would be stimulated where it appeared easy

[1] Most economists tended to regard increase of capital as a long-term remedy, and reduction of population as the main source of short-term improvement. Ricardo, however, classed Ireland among those 'poor countries where there are abundant means of production in store' in which accumulation of capital would be the 'only safe and efficacious means' of reducing the pressure of population against subsistence. So long as the people remained ignorant and indolent, reduction of their numbers would cause an equal fall in food production, and thus be of no benefit – *Principles, Works and Correspondence*, ed. Sraffa, vol. I, pp. 99–100.

[2] Ricardo to Malthus, 4 September 1817, *Works and Correspondence*, ed. Sraffa, vol. VII, p. 185. See Ricardo's note (no. 225) to p. 382 of Malthus's *Principles* in his *Works*, ed. Sraffa, vol. II, pp. 336–8: 'It has been well said by M. Say that it is not the province of the political economist to advise: he is to tell you how you may become rich, but he is not to advise you to prefer riches to indolence, or indolence to riches.'

for the labourer to obtain food and shelter for a family.[1] No-
where did it appear easier than in Ireland, so long as sub-
division of land was permitted. By the consolidation of holdings and the conversion of the cottier into a wage-labourer,
buying his food and renting his cottage, a deterrent might be
imposed on improvident marriages, and population be checked.
At the same time, the loss of potato ground would make the
labourer dependent on the employer for his subsistence, and
give him a new incentive to work. This was Ricardo's argument: to Malthus's contention 'That the necessity of employing
only a small portion of time in producing food does not
always occasion the employment of a greater portion of time
in procuring conveniences and luxuries' he replied: 'Certainly
not, if the choice be in the power of the labourers, in which
case their wages must be high, or rather they must be well paid
for their work. As certainly yes, if labour be low, and the
choice be in the power of the capitalists.'[2] Left to themselves,
the Irish labourers might prefer potatoes and idleness: employed by capitalists, either in agriculture or industry, they
could be made to produce 'conveniences and luxuries' and
might develop a taste for their products, which would come
to be a part of their accepted standard of life, as with the
English labourer. In other words, if industry replaced idleness
a very considerable increase in the wages-fund would be
possible, but the abolition of the cottier potato-truck system
would be the condition precedent for this.

With the land minutely sub-divided neither an increase of
productive efficiency, nor an influx of fresh capital to aid it,
could be hoped for.[3] Hence the population and capital aspects
of the problem were inter-related: to improve agriculture and
give scope for investment in it, it was necessary to clear the

[1] 'Such is the tendency to form early connections, that with the encouragement
of a sufficient number of tenements, I have very little doubt that the population
might be so pushed and such a quantity of labour in time thrown into the market,
as to render the condition of the independent labourer absolutely hopeless. . . .' –
Malthus, *A Letter to Samuel Whitbread, Esq., M.P., on his Proposed Bill for the
Amendment of the Poor Laws* (London, 1807).

[2] Ricardo, *Works and Correspondence*, vol. II, pp. 349–50.

[3] This is clearly indicated by statements such as those of Torrens, quoted in
ch. II, p. 19 of original text.

D

land of the improvident cottiers who encumbered it and consolidate it into more efficient farm units: to employ the displaced population and raise their real income, it was necessary to encourage investment.

So, as the classical economists saw the problem, the replacement of the cottier system by a capitalistic agriculture was the key to the economic regeneration of Ireland; but though this was necessary to the solution of the problem, it was not sufficient. The adjustment must be accompanied by a series of other measures designed to promote capital growth and control population. The remainder of this book will be devoted to the examination of the proposals which stemmed from this conception of the problem, and the manner of their transition into policy.

Analysed in classical terms, the situation in Ireland appeared as one mainly of chronic under-employment, which must compel steps to increase the demand for labour, and reduce the supply of it. Yet however vigorously and judiciously such a programme might be pursued, it could only succeed after a period of some years. In the meantime 'the boundless multiplication of human beings satisfied with the lowest condition of existence'[1] created a serious problem. Not all could succeed in the competition for land, so that to the crowds of under-employed cottiers in rural areas were beginning to be added crowds of unemployed labourers in the towns and villages, and a poor potato crop, which was a frequent occurrence, brought the majority of the working population to the brink of destitution.[2] These conditions might be eradicated by measures for economic development, but until they were, the question of immediate relief for those without means of support was too large to be ignored. Moreover, it was recognized by economists and administrators alike that cottiers could not always be

---

[1] From *Report of the Select Committee on the State of Disease, and the Condition of the Labouring Poor in Ireland* (1819 [409]), vol. VIII, p. 97.

[2] Though the condition of the majority of the Irish labourers was certainly one of under-employment, there seems to be ample evidence that many 'landless men' were unemployed in the modern sense. See evidence of A. Nimmo before the Select Committee on the Condition of the Labouring Poor in Ireland (1819 [409]), vol. VIII, p. 101.

transmuted into wage-labourers without delay; there was bound to be a difficult 'period of transition' during which the population displaced by clearances would require assistance.[1]

PUBLIC WORKS

The subject of public works receives comparatively little direct discussion in the writings of the major classical economists. The fullest treatment is that of Adam Smith, who listed among the duties of the sovereign 'that of erecting and maintaining those public institutions and those public works, which, though they may be in the highest degree advantageous to a great society, are, however, of such a nature that the profit could never repay the expense to any individual or small number of individuals, and which it therefore cannot be expected that any individual or small number of individuals should erect or maintain'.[2]

Among such public works Smith listed those 'which facilitate the commerce of any country, such as good roads, bridges, navigable canals, harbours, etc.', but argued that for the most part they might be 'so managed as to afford a particular revenue sufficient for defraying their own expense, without bringing any burden upon the general revenue of the society'.[3] Where public works could not be so managed, Smith maintained that they should wherever possible be managed by local authorities and financed out of local taxes, in preference to their being made a responsibility of the central government.

Most of Smith's followers appear to have acquiesced in these views: there is no direct discussion of public works in Ricardo's *Principles* or Mill's *Elements*, but passages in McCulloch's *Principles* appear to reflect Smith's ideas fairly closely.[4] McCulloch took a somewhat wider view than Smith, for he considered it 'the duty of government . . . to assist, by making

---

[1] See Lewis, *Local Disturbances in Ireland* (London, 1836), pp. 313–21; *Report of Geo. Nicholls, Esq., on Poor Laws, Ireland* (1837 [69]), vol. LI.

[2] Smith, *Wealth of Nations*, bk. V, chap. V, pt. III.

[3] Idem.

[4] McCulloch, *Principles of Political Economy*, pp. 279–84.

grants, in enabling roads to be carried through districts, and bridges to be constructed, where the necessary funds could not otherwise be raised'. 'As a general rule, however,' he added, 'government ought to be exceedingly shy about advancing funds for the prosecution of undertakings that have failed in the hands of private individuals, or that will not be engaged in by them', and gave the example of Irish canals as a case in point.

From such statements as these, it has customarily been inferred that the English classical school was uniformly opposed to anything more than the barest minimum of public enterprise, and insistent on that being managed according to the strictest criteria of economy. This is a view of their attitude which was shared by contemporaries. Even J.-B. Say, usually closely identified with the doctrine of laissez-faire, felt that the English attitude to public works was sometimes unduly rigid:

> Il me semble qu'en Angleterre on est trop porté à croire qu'un édifice public, un pont, un canal, un bassin de navigation qui ne rapportent pas l'intérêt des avances et les frais d'entretien qu'ils coutent ne méritent pas d'être construits; d'où résulte une sorte de préjugé contre les établissements que les associations particulières ne veulent pas entreprendre, et qui ont besoin d'avoir recours à l'appui et aux fonds du gouvernement, c'est à dire, de la nation.[1]

That a general presumption against the State undertaking any enterprise which could be tackled by private initiative exists in the writings of the English classical economists is beyond all question – but their whole philosophy on the subject of public works cannot be deduced from this. The presumption against public enterprise in classical economics was always associated with a recognition that a certain minimum of State activity was inevitable and essential. It is usually taken for granted that these activities were confined to defence, police, and administration of justice – what modern writers refer to as 'keeping the ring'. Yet it is clear that most of the classical authors believed that the State would not merely have to keep

[1] J.-B. Say, *Cours complet d'économie politique pratique*, 7th ed. (Brussels, 1844), p. 453.

the ring, but also build it; the passages already cited from Smith and McCulloch are typical enough in this respect. If they also show something of that narrow insistence on the criterion of profitability in public works, of which Say complained, that would seem to be because, though general in form, they were primarily made with the British economy in mind. In such a society, where the volume of trade and commerce was already large, the basic facilities of communication and exchange were largely inherited from the past, and it would be legitimate to apply fairly strict tests of profitability to any improvements or extensions of them. With a considerable volume of capital seeking investment outlets, it would also be right for the government to be 'exceedingly shy' of undertaking works where private agencies were available.

It was the tendency to take this background for granted which led the classical economists, explicitly or implicitly, to minimize the role of government, and especially the central government, in undertaking construction and other enterprises. On the other hand, when their attention was specifically directed to societies in which the essential public works were lacking, they were quite prepared to place it among the essential duties of the State to undertake them. Thus when that staunch interpreter of classical orthodoxy, Miss Harriet Martineau, visited the United States and turned her attention to the question of the right of Congress to use public funds for internal improvements, she afterwards wrote that 'to an impartial observer it appears ... that some degree of such power in the hands of the general government is desirable and necessary'.[1] Professor Carter Goodrich has shown how, in the American discussions of the period, advocacy of Federal action on internal improvements was frequently combined with acceptance of laissez-faire, the improvements being thought of as necessary to create the basic structure within which private enterprise could function unhindered.[2]

Similarly, when Senior came to deal specifically with the case

[1] H. Martineau, *Society in America*, 2nd ed. (London, 1837), vol. II, p. 215.
[2] C. Goodrich, 'National Planning of Internal Improvements', *Political Science Quarterly*, vol. LXIII, no. 1 (March 1948), see especially pp. 42–3.

of Ireland in his *Letter to Lord Howick* of 1831, he advocated a vigorous programme of economic development which included advances by the government for the building of roads, canals, railways, and harbours, as well as drainage and reclamation of waste lands – a programme very much akin to that which Whately later endorsed as Chairman of the Irish Poor Inquiry Commissioners in 1836, and one which seems to echo the suggestions made by Rooke for improving the market outlets for Irish agriculture in 1824.[1]

The necessity of qualifying the definition of the proper sphere of public action according to circumstances was specifically recognized and stated by John Stuart Mill:

> In the particular circumstances of a given age or nation, there is scarcely anything, really important to the general interest, which it may not be desirable or even necessary, that the government should take upon itself, not because private individuals cannot effectually perform it, but because they will not. At some times and places there will be no roads, docks, harbours, canals, works of irrigation . . . unless the government establishes them. . . . In many parts of the world, the people can do nothing for themselves which requires large means and combined action; all such things are left undone, unless done by the state.[2]

The expression of such views by Mill is not surprising, but it may be suggested, in the light of the evidence given here, that most of his predecessors in the classical tradition would not have dissented from them. That there must be a certain basis of public works to facilitate economic activity they all accepted; where possible the cost of these works ought to be borne by those who would most directly benefit from them, and where they could be undertaken by private agencies (as, for example, in the case of railways) then the government should certainly exercise no more than a regulatory function in connection with them. But these conditions might not

---

[1] Senior, *A Letter to Lord Howick*, pp. 45–6; Rooke, *Principles of National Wealth*, p. 137.

[2] Mill, *Principles*, bk. V, chap. XI, § 16.

everywhere be fulfilled, and where they were not, then the State must assume the duty of constructing and maintaining the requisite works.

Normally the orthodox economists thought of public works as contributing to the institutional framework within which private economic activity could be successfully carried on. A considerable programme of such works might be necessary to bring a country up to the point where private enterprise could function to the fullest advantage in it, but in their view it should certainly not be necessary to introduce public works into a developed private system in order to maintain the volume of employment in it. In such a case, all government expenditure would be liable to the same criticism – that of diverting funds from private to public use, since if the funds were left in private hands they might be used to employ productive labour, whereas the government would normally employ them unproductively. In fact, transfer of funds from private to public use meant conversion of capital into revenue, and was to that extent undesirable.

The assumption underlying all this – that the fund destined for the maintenance of labour might be indefinitely increased without creating an impossibility of finding employment for it[1] – was not, however, accepted by all the economists of the period. To those who feared the possibility of general overproduction, public works naturally appeared in a more favourable light. Malthus, for example, felt that the tendency of public expenditure to convert capital into revenue might be 'to a certain extent, exactly what is wanted' and contended that 'in our endeavours to assist the working classes (in a period of depression), it is desirable to employ them in those kinds of labour, the results of which do not come for sale into the market, such as roads and public works'.[2]

Views of this kind were not uncommon in the period of distress which followed the Napoleonic wars, when underconsumption theories were enjoying a considerable vogue. The majority of these theories, including Malthus's, relate

---

[1] See Mill, *Principles*, bk. I, chap. V, § 3.
[2] Malthus, *Principles*, p. 51.

primarily to the conditions of industrial society and reflect a fear that the continued investment of capital in industry must produce a flood of manufactured products for which no market can be found. Some of their authors were nevertheless prepared to apply the theories to less-developed agricultural economies where 'redundant population' presented a problem.

A remarkable example of this is to be found in the now forgotten economic writings of Major-General Sir William Sleeman, an officer in the service of the East India Company from 1809 to 1854.[1] Sleeman mingled under-consumptionist ideas clearly derived from Malthus and Sismondi with observations based upon his Indian experience. The behaviour of Indian princes who devoted their wealth to the construction of irrigation canals and aqueducts, seeking only 'the gratitude of society and the approbation of the Deity' appeared to Sleeman much more worthy of approval than the activities of Western merchants and manufacturers based on calculations of profit and the desire for accumulation of capital.[2] Like Malthus, Sleeman was impressed with the necessity of maintaining a body of unproductive consumers in society, and argued that in countries like India the great landed proprietors and the government might confer a double benefit on the mass of the people by giving them employment in the construction of public works which would ultimately improve the productive capacity of the economy. The other country which Sleeman thought especially suited to benefit from a scheme of extended public works was Ireland. 'Perhaps the legislature could hardly confer a greater blessing upon Ireland, than the formation of a few such great works, out of means levied from Absentees, in a tax upon their incomes; and the revenues arising from these might be given to small communities, or deserving Irish families, on condition of their keeping them in a state of efficiency.'[3]

Thus Irish landlords were to be compelled by taxation to do

---

[1] Sleeman's two economic works were: *On Taxes, or Public Revenue, the Ultimate Incidence of their Payment, their Disbursement, and the Seats of their Consumption,* by An Officer in the Military and Civil Service of the honourable East India Company (London, 1829); *Analysis and Review of the Peculiar Doctrines of the Ricardo or New School of Political Economy* (Serampore, 1837).

[2] [Sleeman], *On Taxes,* pp. 182, 200–3.   [3] Ibid., p. 212.

what Indian princes did for 'the approbation of the Deity', and afford employment to their people.

Although at one stage, Sleeman does say 'I should be glad to see a public debt contracted in every district of India, provided I could feel assured that the amount of the loan would be spent in the formation of works useful to the people, and that the interest of the debt should be permanently enjoyed by people residing in these districts',[1] he is generally suspicious of the growth of public debt, and tends to adhere to Adam Smith's principles for the financing of public works from tolls and local taxes.

The proposition that where unemployment exists the government should attempt to eliminate it by undertaking public works, financed not by taxes but by loans, is to be found quite clearly and generally stated in the work of another very little-known contemporary of Malthus, W. R. A. Pettman, a captain in the Royal Navy. In an *Essay on Political Economy*, published in 1828,[2] Pettman declared that

> the burden of debt is much less to be feared than the burden of idleness; but a debt that produces incomes, and an expenditure that finds employment for millions of the population who, but for such expenditure, would not be able to sell their labour, is not a burden, but a capital. . . . The community at large are benefited by the public money being expended in building palaces, improving harbours, cutting canals . . . in short, on any public works that find employment for the labouring classes, and thereby create in them an ability to purchase and consume the commodities produced by each other.[3]

Among the 'Propositions and Suggestions' which Pettman based on this line of argument was one for the government to borrow money and employ it in the reclamation of waste lands in Ireland.[4]

Hence a review of writings on public works in the first half

[1] Sleeman, *On Taxes*, p. 223.

[2] W. R. A. Pettman, *An Essay on Political Economy, Parts I and II* (London, 1828).

[3] Ibid., pt. II, pp. 74 and 105.   [4] Ibid., p. 119.

of the nineteenth century reveals the co-existence of two attitudes towards public works policy, which were sharply distinct though not, in this respect, contradictory. On the one hand, orthodox writers envisaged public works as part of the necessary infrastructure of a free-exchange economy, to be built up, if need be, in order to give full scope to the natural forces of economic development. On the other hand, those who were sufficiently unorthodox to see employment as an end which must be deliberately sought, conceived of public works as a valuable means of achieving it, with the possibility of their aiding economic development thrown in as an additional advantage.

Ireland at the time was a backward agricultural region with a serious population problem, and to such a region, clearly, both these arguments for public works could be readily applied. They are to be found constantly recurring in various guises in the numerous works, English and Irish, which put forward solutions for the Irish problem year after year through the whole period covered here. 'Public works' was indeed one of the clichés of this endless debate, and, like all clichés, many writers were none too clear as to the reasons why they were using it. The most obvious reason was that so many Irish were palpably half-idle and half-starved and public employment could give them work and food. Those who advocated the expenditure of public money on these grounds usually argued that it would be counterbalanced by a consequential reduction in the outlay needed for military and political establishments in Ireland.[1] In fact, the reasons offered for giving employment were often as much political as economic; officially as well as unofficially, the hope was frequently entertained that by giving work the people might be prevented not only from joining Whiteboy raiding parties at night, but also from attending Repeal gatherings by day. 'I have got O'Connell in the net. He cannot get out', wrote Anglesey to Holland in 1831, with rather hasty optimism. 'Now, then, send me money to employ the People, without a moment's loss of time. Then, pass quickly a few popular bills ... and finally, pay the Priests, and I

[1] See, for example, *Reflections on the State of Ireland in the Nineteenth Century* (London, 1822), p. 109.

promise you shall never hear more of O'Connell, or of any such fellow.'[1] The prophecy was not fulfilled, whether or not because the advice was not heeded, and twelve years later, when the Tories had succeeded the Whigs, Lord Devon passed on to Peel a letter from one of his land agents, who wrote: 'I wish the Government would *promptly* put in circulation a large sum of money to neutralize the labourers. All the discontented small shopkeepers, etc., would derive advantage from the extensive employment. . . .'[2]

Those who looked beyond the immediate tranquillizing effects of wages and employment usually envisaged public works as a means of creating new facilities for private enterprise, by which permanent employment could be provided after the public works were completed. This argument was very concisely summarized in 1831 by C. W. Williams, whose interest in Irish public works stemmed from his being a director of the Dublin Steam Packet Company, and much interested in the growth of inland navigation: '1. The population want employment. 2. That can only be supplied by the pursuits of agriculture, trade or commerce. 3. These cannot be promoted without intercourse and interchange.' These, in turn, depended on such public works as roads and canals in which, Williams contended, Ireland was sadly deficient.[3]

A few years later, the same argument was frequently put forward in reference to railways. The building of railways would not only afford much direct employment, but when completed the lines would improve access to markets so greatly as to open many new opportunities for employment in agriculture and industry.[4]

Arguments of this type, contemplating increasing the public works equipment of the Irish economy to a point which would allow the rapid development of private enterprise, were quite

[1] Anglesey to Holland, 29 January 1831 (Anglesey Papers, T. 1068/7).
[2] Alfred Furlong to Devon, 18 June 1843 (Peel Papers, B.M. Add. MSS. 40530).
[3] C. W. Williams, *Observations on an Important Feature in the State of Ireland, and the Want of Employment of its Population* (Westminster, 1831), p. 7.
[4] See *Second Report from the Railway Commissioners, Ireland* (1837–8 [145]), vol. XXXV, p. 91.

in accord with classical orthodoxy. They also evaded one of the most common criticisms of public employment at the time – that the expenditure could not be continued indefinitely, and that when it came to an end, the labourers would be no better off than before, possibly even worse.[1]

Some other schemes of public works proposed for Ireland rather over-stepped the limits which most classical economists would have prescribed for State activity, since they aimed not merely at creating the appropriate foundation for economic development, but at undertaking that development deliberately – in part at least. The proposals for arterial drainage and the reclamation of waste lands put forward by Poulett Scrope, Thornton, and John Stuart Mill[2] might be regarded as coming into this category, since they aimed at a fundamental change in the conditions of occupation and cultivation of land.

Proposals of this kind were always met by the objection that they could be undertaken by private enterprise – and that the fact that they were not was proof that they would be an un-profitable speculation.[3] If government, then, were to under-take the works, it would be diverting funds from more to less profitable uses, and so retarding rather than advancing eco-nomic growth. Advocates of large-scale works met these criticisms by saying that the projects they wished to see under-taken were of a long-term character, affording a genuine return, but too slowly to interest private speculators; moreover, they were projects too large for the private investor in a country like Ireland, where capital was scarce.[4]

[1] 'So long as money is expended in carrying on public works, a scanty means of subsistence may be afforded the poor labourer engaged, but at the expiration of the outlay you will not find the wretched man or his miserable family improved in the least degree in their prospects; but, on the contrary, he would be found inhabiting his former hovel, with his physical strength much impaired by hard toil merely for a scanty support' – A. C. Buchanan, *Outline of a Practical Plan for the Relief of the Poor of Ireland* (Brighton, 1837), pp. 9 and 10. See also Bryan *Practical View of Ireland*, p. 220; W. T. Thornton, *Over-population and its Remedy* (London, 1846), p. 418.

[2] See chap. II, p. 30 of original text.

[3] See Bryan, p. 220; E. Wakefield, *An Account of Ireland, Statistical and Political* (1812), vol. I, p. 85.

[4] See 'Hints for the Cultivation of the Peat-bogs in Ireland', *The Pamphleteer*, vol. IX (1817), p. 84.

It was also possible to use the argument, stated generally by Mill, that where private agencies did not exist or were inadequate, the tasks which in better circumstances would fall to them must be undertaken by the public authorities. More rigid economists could counter this with a point which had considerable force in reference to Ireland, before the Famine at least – it could be said that if the government took on these tasks it would sap the initiative of potential private employers, and encourage them perennially to look to the government to do what properly they ought to do themselves. In Ireland the main potential employers were the landowners, and there can be little doubt that many of them were all too ready to seek the expenditure of public money which would benefit their estates or put their tenants in funds to pay increased rents; this was a tendency which Ricardo found as prevalent and as exasperating in 1823 as did Charles Wood in 1846.[1]

There was in fact something of a tradition in Ireland in the early nineteenth century that public works and jobbery went hand in hand, and that every man of any influence did his best to get whatever pickings he could from public expenditure.[2] In the light of this, it is not surprising that ambitious schemes of government enterprise were usually received with more enthusiasm in Dublin Castle than in Whitehall or Westminster. Thus when Anglesey was Lord-Lieutenant in 1828 his frequent and impassioned pleas for 'money to employ the people' met with but a cool reception from Peel, then Home Secretary.

While I admit the melancholy fact that there is a great want of employment for the poor in Ireland, and admit also, that an increase in the demand for labour would be of the utmost advantage to society in that Country, I must at the

---

[1] Ricardo to Trower, 24 July 1823: 'It is a favourite plan with many, for Government to lend capital to Ireland, in order that the people may be employed. Against such a scheme I have the most decided objections, which I never fail to urge. If the greater part of the Irish members could have their way, we should not only grant a vast number of charitable loans, but we should encourage all sorts of manufactures by bounties and premiums' – *Works and Correspondence*, vol. IX, p. 313; Wood to Bessborough, 9 September 1846, quoted in chap. IV, p. 115 of original text.

[2] E. Wakefield, vol. II, p. 803; Inglis, *Ireland in 1834*, vol. I, p. 237.

same time express a doubt whether ultimate advantage would arise from the creation of such a demand by the continued application of large sums of public money [wrote Peel]. In voting the public money in aid of local improvements, it must be borne in mind that, with the best intentions on the part of Government, it is not easy to prevent occasional abuse in the expenditure. . . . It must also be borne in mind that too great a facility on the part of Government in applying the public money in furtherance of such objects has a tendency to discourage local exertions, and to afford an excuse for the indifference and neglect of those, who ought to apply some part of their influence and their wealth in promoting the improvement of their Country.[1]

Very similar views can be found expressed in the speeches and writings of Whig statesmen, such as Russell,[2] while, almost forty years later, Gladstone was if anything more rigid in his attitude: speaking in 1865, he showed no inclination to relax his classic principles of public finance in the case of Ireland:

There is, I think, a tendency to claim that public expenditure in Ireland shall not be limited to the amount required for the purposes in view, or fixed to the spot which is deemed most for the general convenience and efficiency of the public service, but that it shall be applied for the benefit of a particular locality and in a fixed degree. Against that principle and every modification of it I entirely protest . . . what is the public expenditure? What is a tax? It is money taken by the Government out of the pockets of the people. What right have the Government to take that money? Simply the necessity which exists to satisfy the public wants. And if

---

[1] Peel to Anglesey, 26 July 1828 (Anglesey Papers, T. 1068/1).

[2] See Russell's memorandum 'State of Ireland – July 1847' (P.R.O. 30/22/6): 'In my opinion no aid similar in character to that of the public works, or the rations, should be administered by the Public Treasury. If England were to countenance, which she would not, such continued expenditure, we should run the risk of making large portions of the people permanent paupers. . . .'

Also Wood to Bessborough, 25 September 1846: 'We are well disposed to help those who will help themselves, but we shall get into a scrape if we do nothing but make advances of money with a distant prospect of repayment' (P.R.O. 30/22/5).

they proceed to satisfy the public wants, are they not bound to do so in the best, most efficient, and at the same time most economic manner in their power?[1]

Much as the various ministers of the period may have wanted to limit public expenditure in Ireland, the endemic distress of the country frequently forced them to depart from the principles which they enunciated. At the beginning of the nineteenth century, many parts of Ireland lacked such fundamental works as roads and bridges, and the administrative mechanism which existed for their construction and maintenance was rudimentary and inefficient. Reform in these respects was clearly necessary and inevitable, for political as well as economic reasons. Apart from this, periodic famines compelled the undertaking of relief works and at various times more ambitious schemes seemed to provide a means of conciliating Ireland. Hence while in principle every government was always opposed to the extension of public expenditure, in practice the State became involved in a series of public works programmes in Ireland, some undertaken *ad hoc*, others of a continuing nature.

The policy pursued with regard to public works in Ireland over the half-century here examined could certainly not be described as inaction, but it would be equally difficult to characterize it as planning. W. O. Henderson has been somewhat over-generous in writing that 'the improvement of the Shannon navigation and the varied activities of the Public Works Commissioners [in Ireland] showed that English statesmen were no hidebound doctrinaires. Since a policy of laissez-faire was inappropriate when applied to Ireland a policy of capital investment was adopted.'[2]

That successive governments did invest a large amount of capital in Ireland is manifest, but a consistent policy of investment did not really exist. If any general principle can be said to have motivated the various ministers who authorized public

[1] *Hansard*, 3rd ser. vol. CLXXVII, col. 679 (24 February 1865).
[2] W. O. Henderson, Review of Court's 'Concise Economic History of Britain from 1750 to Recent Times', *Kyklos*, vol. VIII (1955), p. 441.

works for Ireland, it was the idea, here contended to have been respectably founded in classical theory, that if a basic equipment of public works were provided it would enable the economy to function of its own accord, lifting it into the stage where laissez-faire would become appropriate. But what the proper extent of the basic equipment would have to be was never clearly thought out. Would roads, bridges, and harbours be enough, combined with loans for approved purposes, leaving it to the initiative of private parties to take these up? Or was it necessary to go further and positively undertake some large-scale schemes of development? While many, like Scrope, who had specifically studied Irish affairs, advocated the latter, the main body of classical doctrine sanctioned no more than the former. Ministers vacillated, and ultimately quailed at the prospect of proposing the heavy expenditures which special schemes must necessarily have involved.

This is not to deny that much was achieved by the patchwork of *ad hoc* measures which did reach the Statute Book: the Land Improvement Acts alone were a valuable aid to Irish economic improvement. Yet what was done certainly failed to produce the situation which the classical economists would have regarded as the desirable outcome – where further special public expenditure would be rendered unnecessary by the 'natural' forces of economic development taking over. The main reason for this is not hard to discover; it was perceived, though only partially, by Harriet Martineau when she wrote:

> The impression which every day's observation strengthens in the traveller's mind is, that till the agriculture of Ireland is improved, little benefit can arise from the large grants which have been, and still are, made for public works. If public works which are designed to open up markets for produce should stimulate the people to the improvement of production, it will be a capital thing; but, till some evidence of this appears, there is something melancholy in the spectacle of a great apparatus which does not seem to be the result of any natural demand.[1]

[1] H. Martineau, *Letters from Ireland* (London, 1852), p. 17.

Miss Martineau here came close to the heart of the matter: public works could be of little value unless they improved the basic industry of the country. Without security of tenure, however, opening markets gave the people no incentive to improve their agriculture. The absence of land reform, then, largely nullified the potential benefits from public works.

4 The Classical Economists and the Factory Acts – A re-examination

MARK BLAUG

[This article was first published in the *Quarterly Journal of Economics*, vol. 72, May 1958.]

I

British historians of the Industrial Revolution are unanimously of the opinion that early factory reform was achieved in the face of strong hostility from the economic experts of the day. It does not matter whom we consult: Toynbee, Trevelyan, the Hammonds, Cunningham, Clapham; the classical economists are always depicted as unalterably opposed to the Factory Acts.[1] But if we turn to the historians of economic thought a very different interpretation emerges. Marshall, for instance, asserts that the classical economists 'supported the factory acts, in spite of the strenuous opposition of some politicians and employers who claimed to speak in their name'; he cites McCulloch and Tooke as examples in point.[2] In his *History of Economic Analysis*, Schumpeter flatly declares that 'Most "classic" economists supported factory legislation, McCulloch especially.'[3] K. O. Walker, in an article which examines the question in some detail, concludes that 'the direct influence of the political economists on labour legislation was negligible' and that 'any influence that was exerted tended to favour, rather than oppose, the passage of the Factory Acts'.[4] Lionel

---

[1] For a recent example see R. G. Cowherd, *The Humanitarians and the Ten Hour Movement in England* (Boston, Mass., Kress Library of Business and Economics, 1956), pp. 5–6, 9–10.

[2] *Principles*, pp. 47, 763n. See also Marshall's *Industry and Trade*, pp. 763–5.

[3] (New York, 1954), p. 402.

[4] K. O. Walker, 'The Classical Economists and the Factory Acts', *Journal of Economic History*, I (November 1941), p. 170. See also L. R. Sorenson, 'Some

Robbins's study of *The Theory of Economic Policy in English Classical Political Economy* deals briefly with this issue; he suggests that the classical authors generally favoured regulation of child labour while disapproving of legislation for adults.[1]

How can we account for such widely divergent interpretations of what is, after all, a matter of record? One answer is that the evidence which has so far been considered is highly selective.[2] Moreover, little attention has been paid to the successive phases of the factory reform controversy: generalizations have been advanced on the basis of writings published at different times and under distinctly different circumstances.

The fact of the matter is that the attitude of the classical writers was conditioned at each stage of the debate, by the degree of regulation that had already been achieved. Many a factory Bill, whose introduction had been bitterly opposed, met with approval once it became law. Although the classical economists supported the *principle* of granting protection to children, they were aware that the unavoidable consequence was a shorter working day for adult operatives; rather than to countenance that they preferred to dispense with the benefits of regulated child labour. Thus, we are faced on the one hand with differences of opinion among the classical economists as to the desirability of further restrictions on the employment of children, and on the other hand with a general tendency towards rear-guard action designed to prevent the effective regulation of adult labour.

For this reason the question whether the classical economists did or did not favour the Factory Acts cannot be answered. This much, however, is a matter of pure academic interest. The real significance of the discussion lies in the opportunity which it affords to study the quality of classical policy-pronouncements. Were their opinions based upon economic considera-

---

Classical Economists, Laissez-Faire, and the Factory Acts', ibid., XII (Summer, 1952), which reaches similar conclusions. Sorenson documents the assertion made above about the opinions of economic historians.

[1] (London, 1952), pp. 101–3.
[2] This is particularly true of Walker's analysis which deals only with the literature up to 1833.

tions, such as the effects of shorter hours on employment and real wages, or solely upon fundamental value judgements embodied in the tenets of laissez-faire? In the concluding section of this paper I shall attempt to evaluate the merits of the classical economists' position in the light of their own analytical apparatus and the relevant factual knowledge available to them.[1]

II

The history of factory legislation in England begins with Peel's Bill of 1819. An earlier Act of 1802, regulating the labour of parish apprentices, was an extension of the Poor Laws, not a Factory Act; no new power of the State was at issue. Peel's Bill, however, did raise the question of State interference in private industry; it reduced the working day of children under sixteen to twelve hours and prohibited altogether the employment of children under nine years of age. The Act applied only to the cotton factories and inadequate inspection provisions made it largely inoperative. Nevertheless, there was opposition to the Bill, particularly from the House of Lords, in the form of an appeal to 'that great principle of Political Economy, that labour ought to be left free'. The proponents of Peel's Bill, on the other hand, defended the measure on the grounds that children were not 'free agents'.[2] Economists took little interest in the debate; Malthus alone gave public support to the measure.[3]

Additional restrictions on child labour in the cotton factories in 1825 and 1831 improved but little upon the Act of 1819. But with the publication of Oastler's letters on 'Yorkshire Slavery' and the appearance of Sadler's Committee Report (1833), the movement for factory reform began to assume a

---

[1] The presentation of the argument has gained in clarity through the criticisms of Mr M. Leiserson.

[2] W. Smart, *Economic Annals of the Nineteenth Century* (London, 1910), vol. I, pp. 688, 702–3; Walker, op. cit., p. 175.

[3] T. R. Malthus, *Essay on Population*, 5th ed. (London, 1817), p. 282. Only some dozen tracts appeared on Peel's Bill in contrast to the flood of pamphlets that accompanied the legislation of the 1830s and 1840s. See J. B. Williams, *A Guide to the Printed Materials for English Social and Economic History, 1750–1850* (New York, 1926), vol. II, pp. 192–4.

more radical tone. Lord Ashley's motion of a Ten Hours Bill, applicable to all persons under the age of sixteen, led to the appointment of a Royal Commission to collect further evidence. The Commissioners – Thomas Tooke, Edwin Chadwick, and Southwood Smith – proposed several amendments to Ashley's Bill to prevent interference with the free employment of adults.[1] The final version, known as Althorp's Act, limited the working day of persons between thirteen and eighteen to twelve hours a day and of those between nine and thirteen to nine hours a day.[2]

After the passage of Althorp's Act it was necessary to employ children in part-time relays since the work of the adult spinners and weavers depended, for technical reasons, upon the labour of their young assistants. The factory inspectors devised a variety of schemes for co-ordinating the work day of different categories of labour but none of the plans proved completely successful. The relay system soon became one of the major devices for evading legislative control. The leaders of the Ten Hours party were quick to point out that it was impossible to separate the adult from the child for purposes of legislative control; in short, they did not attempt to disguise their ulterior aim of limiting the hours of adult labour by means of placing restrictions upon the hours of children. Classical political economy, however, sanctioned a limit on the employment of children below 'the age of consent' so long as this could be achieved without encroaching upon the working hours of adults. Consequently, economists arraigned themselves against the Ten Hours movement as its ultimate purpose became increasingly evident.[3]

[1] See M. W. Thomas, *The Early Factory Legislation* (London, 1948), pp. 55–6.

[2] In addition, night work was abolished for those under eighteen, and the scope of regulation was extended to all textile factories, with the exception of lace and silk mills. Furthermore, employment for children was made conditional upon attendance at school for two hours a day and machinery of inspection was provided to supervise the enforcement of the Act.

[3] As one of the advocates of shorter hours put it bitterly:

'They could not refuse to protect children, but they are "political economists", and though, as men, they could no longer screw up their minds and hearts so far as to sacrifice any more limbs and lives of infants, the science would not suffer them to invade the "freedom of industry" by involving the adults in that

The years between the Acts of 1833 and 1844 mark the first phase of the debate; at this point there was still great variety in the attitudes of individual economists. It was only in the 1840s that something like a uniform position began to emerge. Nevertheless, all the leading arguments in the controversy make their appearance at this stage of the discussion.

The first to commit himself, even before the passage of Althorp's Act, was John Stuart Mill. Writing in a popular weekly in 1832, he expressed a desire to see 'a law established *interdicting* altogether the employment of children under fourteen, and *females of any age*, in manufactories'.[1] He anticipated objections to such a law drawn from the 'non-interference philosophy' and admitted that he, too, was a partisan of this principle 'up to a certain point'. He drew attention, however, to a significant exception:

> The case in which it would be to the advantage of everybody, if everybody were to act in a certain manner, but in which it is not in the interest of any individual to adopt the rule for the guidance of his own conduct, unless he has some assurance that others will do so too. There are a thousand such cases; and when they arise, who is to afford the security that is wanted, except the legislature?

The case of child and female labour is a typical example, he went on to say; here private and public benefit must diverge unless a universal compact can be secured. This argument could have been applied with the same force to the labour of adult males but Mill failed to carry it through.[2]

Robert Torrens supported Ashley's Ten Hours Bill when it

---

protection which they were obliged to give the child. It is this absurd attempt to separate the adult from the child in its labour, that has rendered every Act that has ever been passed to give protection to children almost void.' C. Wing, *Evils of the Factory System Exposed* (London, 1836), p. 17, quoted by Thomas, op. cit., p. 89.

[1] 'Employment of Children in Manufactories', *The Examiner*, 29 January 1832, p. 67. The article appeared anonymously; for evidence of Mill's authorship, see *Bibliography of the Published Writings of J. S. Mill*, ed. N. MacMinn, *et al.* (Evanston, Illinois, 1945).

[2] In his *Principles* (1848), however, Mill pursued the argument to its logical conclusion. See *infra*.

came up for debate in Parliament, but with an important qualification. Since the Corn Laws had raised the cost of food and thus depressed real wages, the working class was entitled to shorter hours without a reduction in money wages. Still, the tariff on agricultural produce should be lowered so as to 'create a margin on which your short time might safely stand'.[1] In a work published shortly before the passage of Althorp's Act, he declared:

> The evidence presented by the Royal Commission of 1832 makes it imperative on Parliament to interpose, to shorten the hours of labour, and to save the infant labourer from the cruel oppression of excessive toil. But while humanity cries aloud for such intervention, and while it must be promptly and freely granted, the truth should at the same time be declared, that a Bill for regulating the hours of labour, though framed by a consummate wisdom, cannot reach the root of the disease.[2]

The 'root of the disease', of course, is the Corn Laws.

George Poulett Scrope took a similar view in his *Principles of Political Economy*: the Factory Bill is 'a measure which in a healthy state of society would be a needless interference, though in the existing circumstances of the country, it seems to us highly desirable'.[3] *The Westminster Review* (under the proprietorship of Colonel Perronet Thompson, an ardent Benthamite and free trader) varied the argument: it condemned Althorp's Act as a 'restrictive blunder' and depicted the Ten Hours Movement as 'the stalking-horse to cover and protect – the Corn Laws and West Indian Slavery'.[4] Within a decade this became the standard reply of the Anti-Corn Law League to the factory reform movement.[5] The Corn Laws were

---

[1] *Hansard's Parliamentary Debates*, 3rd series, vol. XV, pp. 414–15. See also Sorenson, op. cit., pp. 253–4.

[2] *Letters on Commercial Policy* (London, 1833), p. 73.

[3] (London, 1833), p. 51; also pp. 241, 358.

[4] *Westminster Review*, April 1833, pp. 380–1. See also G. L. Nesbitt, *Benthamite Reviewing* (New York, 1934), pp. 147–8.

[5] See A. E. Bland, *et al.*, *English Economic History: Select Documents* (London, 1919), pp. 611–12; J. Morley, *The Life of Richard Cobden* (London, 1910), pp. 166–70.

made the scapegoat of distress in the factory districts, and cheap bread was hailed as the nostrum to remedy all ills.

While the Factory Act of 1833 was still under discussion, Lord Ashley solicited McCulloch's views on the question. McCulloch had spoken approvingly of factory legislation in 1827, adding the warning, however, that 'no further interference ought, in any account, to be either attempted or tolerated'.[1] Now he wrote to Ashley: 'I would not interfere between adults and masters; but it is absurd to contend that children have the power to judge for themselves on such matters.'[2] McCulloch's modern reputation as a friend of factory reform is largely based upon this private communication, penned under the stimulus of the shocking disclosures of Sadler's Committee Report. It is to be noted, however, that the argument goes no further than the admission that children are not 'free agents', a notion that was rapidly becoming a commonplace.

Indeed, in the pages of the *Edinburgh Review* McCulloch continued to deprecate the case for legislative control. In 1835 he devoted a major article to Ure's *Philosophy of Manufactures*, a crass apology for the factory system.[3] 'That abuses have existed in some factories is certain,' McCulloch admitted, 'but these have been rare instances; and, speaking generally, factory workpeople, including non-adults, are as healthy and contented as any class of the community obliged to earn their bread in the sweat of their brow.' He saw no reason to object to the exclusion of children under thirteen years of age from factory employment provided that they were properly looked after at home. But in view of parental attitudes among the lower classes, it was likely, he argued, that children turned out of factories would become delinquent paupers. The factory system, he observed, did imbue children with disciplined habits and allowed them to extend material assistance to their

---

[1] *Edinburgh Review*, June 1827, p. 35.

[2] Quoted by Robbins, op. cit., pp. 101–2. See also G. Ramsay, *An Essay on the Distribution of Wealth* (Edinburgh, 1836), pp. 102–3, for the same argument.

[3] On the basis of personal experience, Ure testified that child labour in factories 'seemed to resemble a sport': children, working twelve hours a day, spent nine hours in idle contemplation and 'sometimes dedicated these intervals to the perusal of books'.

parents. Nevertheless, 'the Legislature did right in prohibiting altogether the employment of children in mills under nine years of age.' Lest these words give comfort to factory reformers, McCulloch hastened to add that the limitation of hours was 'a matter of great nicety and difficulty'; on the whole, he concluded, the less the textile trade is 'tampered with' the better.[1] Senior's *Letters on the Factory Act* (1837) is too well known to require discussion. Its importance lies in the fact that it carried the debate out of the realm of such general considerations as the proper 'age of consent', the character of parental supervision, or the priority of free trade over factory legislation. Senior accepted Althorp's Act as it stood but argued that, given the cost structure of the typical textile mill, further reductions in hours would wipe out the margin of profit.[2] Senior's thesis proved to be a serviceable argument against the extension of regulation and in the next round of discussions which took place in 1844, several members of Parliament succumbed to its logic.[3] Senior's fellow economists, however, did not take it very seriously: *Letters on the Factory Acts* is hardly mentioned, much less analysed, in the economic literature of the day. The records of the Political Economy Club clearly suggest that Senior's argument was not accepted by his colleagues: they objected to his unrealistic estimate of capital investment upon which his conclusions were grounded.[4] But one of Senior's basic assumptions, that output would fall proportionately with the reduction of hours, was not challenged and became an essential feature of the classical analysis of factory legislation.

[1] *Edinburgh Review*, July 1835, pp. 464–7.
[2] Contrary to popular belief, fostered by Marx's attack, Senior did not advance a general theory that profits are produced in the 'last hour'. Even on his own assumptions, Senior's calculations actually show no more than that a shortening of the working day by one hour would cause profits to fall from 10 to 8 per cent, given a constant output per man-hour. See K. Wicksell, *Lectures on Political Economy* (New York, 1934), vol. I, pp. 194–5.
[3] See A. E. Bland, *et al.*, op. cit., pp. 605–6.
[4] See Walker, op. cit., pp. 171–2.

III

A new Factory Act was passed in 1844 which lowered the working hours of children to six and one-half hours and that of 'young persons' (boys below eighteen and girls below twenty-one) to twelve hours. This Act proved to be a stepping-stone to the Ten Hours Bill of 1847 which finally secured a fifty-eight hours' week for 'young persons' and for women of all ages. The passage of both measures was accompanied by an intense discussion that marked the high point of three decades of debate. Economic arguments became more concrete and were now clearly divorced from the precept of non-interference. However, there were no dramatic conversions to the Ten Hours camp.[1] At the Political Economy Club in 1844, Edwin Chadwick put up this question for debate: 'Is legislative interference between the Master and the Adult labourer, to regulate the hours of work, expedient?' The diary of one of the participants reveals that Charles Buller, the radical philosopher, was the only member to vote in favour of such interference.[2] Chadwick, Senior, Torrens, and Tooke answered the question in the negative. McCulloch admitted much of Buller's reasoning but thought the matter could not be settled in general terms. The views of John Stuart Mill at this point are not clear; but in an article on 'The Claims of Labour' for the *Edinburgh Review* (1845) he referred to the Ten Hours Bill as falling into the category of 'quack schemes of reform'.

The prevailing economic argument against the Ten Hours Bill is set forth in Torrens's *Letter to Lord Ashley* (1844), a curiously neglected work.[3] Torrens begins his discussion with a strong condemnation of the principle of 'leaving things to

[1] There is some evidence that Dr Thomas Chalmers, a leading Scottish divine and author of several economic treatises, was finally won over by the Ten Hours campaign in 1847. If so, Chalmers was a singular exception. See C. Driver, *Tory Radical. The Life of Richard Oastler* (New York, 1946), pp. 476–9.

[2] *Proceedings of the Political Economy Club, 1821–1920* (London, 1921), vol. VI, pp. 287–8.

[3] Sorenson, op. cit., contends that Torrens was definitely sympathetic to factory legislation. The evidence for this comes from Torrens's Parliamentary speeches in the 1830s while *Letter to Lord Ashley*, the most important of Torrens's writings on the Factory Acts, is not considered.

their course'. The concept of 'free agents', however, is not mentioned at all. His analysis is largely concerned with 'the delusion' of the operatives that 'upon the passing of a Ten Hour Bill, they would receive the wages of twelve hours for the work of ten'. Torrens lays it down as an incontrovertible fact that 'the rate of profit in this country is already approaching the minimum at which no margin remains for an advance of wages'; 'capital to an enormous amount already emigrates from our shores'.

Torrens's conclusion is that the Ten Hours Bill would check production and diminish wages: 'Enact your Ten Hours Bill and one of two events must inevitably ensue: – the manufactures of England will be transferred to foreign lands, or else the operatives must submit to a reduction of wages to the extent of 25 per cent.'[1]

There is no mention in Torrens's pamphlet of the possible productivity effects of a shorter working day. Yet this had long been a favourite argument of the factory reformers. Robert Owen had testified in 1818 before Peel's Committee that a reduction from fourteen to twelve hours a day in his factory at New Lanark had actually resulted in an increase of output.[2] Speaking in the House of Commons in 1844, Lord Ashley recalled Owen's testimony by way of an attack on Senior's 'last hour' theory. Reviewing the successive Factory Acts since 1819, he pointed out: 'you had no diminution of produce, no fall in wages, no rise in prices, no closing of markets, no irresistible rivalry from foreign competition, although you reduced your hours of working from 16, 14, 13, to 12 hours a day.'[3] The implication is that productivity per man-hour had risen with each reduction in the length of the working day.

Ashley's argument is loose, of course: dynamic factors un-

---

[1] *A Letter to Lord Ashley* (London, 1844), pp. 64–5, 71–3. Torrens's argument was reproduced in the popular journals: see the article on 'Protection of Labour', *The Economist*, 6 April 1844. Typically, however, *The Economist* based its case on laissez-faire (see Scott Gordon, 'The London *Economist* and the High Tide of Laissez-Faire', *Journal of Political Economy*, LXIII (December 1955), pp. 478, 483).

[2] See B. L. Hutchins and A. Harrison, *A History of Factory Legislation* (London, 1911), pp. 19–23.

[3] *The Ten Hours Factory Bill. The Speech of Lord Ashley, M.P. in the House of Commons on Friday, 10 May 1844* (London, 1844), pp. 15–16.

related to shorter hours might account for the facts. The same argument, however, more carefully stated, appears in a popular treatise of the 'forties, William Thornton's *Over-Population and Its Remedy*. Thornton reviewed the whole question in the light of the imminent repeal of protection. If 'the daily labour of British operatives were shortened', he thought it 'very possible that their wages would fall'. But once the Corn Laws were abolished, lower food prices might leave real wages constant, or even raise them, despite the fall in money wages owing to a Ten Hours Bill. Moreover,

> It is not quite certain that a diminution of produce would result from shortening the duration of labour. Persons who are not obliged to work so long may work harder than before, and may get through the same quantity of work in a short time as formerly occupied them for a longer period. . . . If so, the limitation of labour to ten hours daily would not in any circumstances reduce wages, and at all events the reduction might be either prevented or neutralized by the establishment of free trade in food.[1]

Unhappily, Thornton's analysis made no impression on his contemporaries. McCulloch, for example, continued to discuss the regulation of hours along traditional lines. 'We should be inclined to think', he wrote in 1846, 'that the existing regulations respecting factory labour in this country are about as reasonable and judicious as they can be made.' Then he went on to praise Torrens's *Letter to Ashley* as 'the best tract in opposition to the ten-hours project'.[2] In the fourth edition of his *Principles* (1849), he added a few pages on the Factory Acts, lauding the Act of 1844 as consistent with 'claims of humanity' and 'the interest of manufacturers' but roundly condemning the Bill of 1847 because it tended to restrict the hours of adults. At this point he turned to a new argument. The conditions of the working class, he declared, rest ultimately upon the size of the wages fund relative to population; the real issue,

---

[1] (London, 1846), p. 399.
[2] *The Literature of Political Economy* (London, 1846); London Reprints No. 5 (1938), pp. 294–6.

therefore, is not whether eight, ten, or twelve hours constitutes the 'proper' length of a working day.

> If . . . the longer be introduced by the customs of the country, in preference to a shorter period, it is a proof that there is, if not an excess, at all events an extremely copious supply of labour; and that the labourers are, in consequence, obliged to submit to the drudgery of lengthened service . . . it is difficult to perceive how the hours of work . . . should be lessened by a legislative enactment without at the same time, and by the same act, reducing wages.[1]

John Stuart Mill touched briefly on the economic objections against the Factory Acts in his *Principles* (1848). Whether a reduction of hours without a cut in wages would inevitably displace labour was, he said, 'in every particular instance a question of fact, not of principle'. For the most part his analysis of factory legislation dealt with the propriety of government intervention along the lines laid down in his earlier article of 1832.[2] If a nine-hour day were proved to be in the interest of the working class, Mill reasoned, state action would be required 'not to overrule the judgment of individuals respecting their own interest, but to give effect to that judgment'. He concluded: 'I am not expressing any opinion in favour of such an enactment . . . but it serves to exemplify the manner in which classes of persons may need the assistance of law, to give effect to their deliberate collective opinion of their own interest.' He condemned the Acts of 1844 and 1847, however, on the grounds that they excluded working-women from factories, although women were 'free agents' as much as men.[3]

[1] *Principles of Political Economy*, 4th ed. (London, 1849), pp. 427–30. See also McCulloch's *Treatise on the Circumstances Which Determine the Rate of Wages* (London, 1851), pp. 93–7, and *Treatises and Essays* (Edinburgh, 1859), pp. 453–4.

[2] Mill's argument here is nothing but an early example of Pigou's famous distinction between private and social costs, as W. J. Baumol pointed out: *Welfare Economics and The Theory of the State* (Cambridge, Mass., 1952), pp. 15–16, 150–2.

[3] J. S. Mill, *Principles of Political-Economy*, Ashley edition, pp. 964–5, 959. Senior took the same view on female labour: *Industrial Efficiency and Social Economy*, ed. S. L. Levy (London, 1929), vol. II, pp. 307–8.

IV

The Ten Hours Bill of 1847 had failed to abolish the system of employing children in part-time shifts; consequently, it was possible to keep adult male operatives at the bench for fifteen hours a day without violating the letter of the Act of 1847. Renewed agitation at last secured the 'normal working day' for women and children in 1853: hours of legal employment and meal times were specified in greater detail so that it became difficult to employ relays. The scope of the Ten Hours Bill was extended in the 1860s, although industries other than textile were not covered until the Consolidating Act of 1878. The minimum age of child labour was now raised to ten, the employment of women was further restricted, and sanitary inspection and safety-regulations were improved. None of this legislation, except the details of sanitation, was applicable to adult males but their weekly hours, of course, were almost everywhere scaled down to sixty or less.

Meanwhile, fragmentary statistical data on the effect of the Act of 1847 had been gathered by the factory inspectors. The initial consequences were partly obscured by a severe trade depression. Wages in textiles fell, but much less than the 16 per cent reduction in hours or the 10 per cent reduction in piece rates. After the revival of prosperity in the 1850s, Horner and Tooke declared that the Ten Hours Bill had not depressed either earnings or output owing to an increase in the intensity of labour.[1]

There is no indication that economists shared the belief that shorter hours had paid for themselves through a rise in output per man. New editions of Mill's *Principles* in the 'fifties and 'sixties reveal no alterations with respect to the topic under discussion. Cairnes's writings contain no explicit discussion of the Factory Acts. Fawcett, however, delivered a lecture on the question in 1872 in the midst of a new campaign for a nine-hour day. At the outset he expounded the familiar theme of the free agent:

[1] See G. H. Wood, 'Factory Legislation, considered with reference to the Wages, etc., of the Operatives Protected thereby', *Journal of the Royal Statistical Society*, Vol. LXV (June 1902), p. 297.

It certainly appears to me that it is quite as desirable to pass a law limiting the number of hours which a child is permitted to work, as it would be undesirable to impose similar restrictions upon men and women. If grown-up persons overwork they do it of their own free will.

Moreover, he had no patience with Mill's 'hypothetical argument' in favour of state intervention. This is 'the old story', Fawcett complained, which requires us to believe in the collective wisdom and infallible judgement of the legislature. He proceeded to examine the notion that a diminution of hours could increase the efficiency of labour and thus leave output unaffected. He admitted that there was some factual evidence which might be adduced on behalf of this argument. Still, he insisted that generally entrepreneurs could be trusted to maximize profits and, thereby, to achieve an optimum length of the work day from the viewpoint of maximizing output per man-hour.[1]

The success of the Nine Hours Movement, Fawcett warned, would open the way to a campaign in favour of eight hours, and so forth. Already, England 'can scarcely hold her own in some trades in which she once had an almost undisputed supremacy'. When the Nine Hours Law came up for debate in Parliament, Fawcett spoke against it on the grounds that 'this House has no right to interfere with the labour of adults' or to place the employment of women on a different footing from the employment of men.[2]

Although Jevons is not a classical economist, his treatment of the Factory Acts contains some instructive differences as well as similarities to the classical analysis. Jevons denied, first of all, that the question can be decided once and for all on 'some supposed principle of liberty'. The same principle, if it existed, would apply to adult women whose hours were already regulated. Moreover, a mass of 'paternal legislation', such as the Truck Acts, the Coal Mines Act, and a series of Bills relating to merchant shipping and the fencing of machinery, had long

[1] H. Fawcett, *Essays and Lectures on Social and Political Subjects* (London, 1872), pp. 36, 113–15, 120.
[2] H. Fawcett, *Speeches on Current Political Questions* (London, 1873), pp. 122 ff.

ago been sanctioned for the protection of adult men. On the face of it, he saw no reason to prohibit State action in the matter 'if it could be clearly shown that the existing customs are injurious to health and there is no other probable remedy'.[1]

At the same time, Jevons's analysis is quite innocent of the type of consideration introduced by Thornton.[2] Jevons believed it to be 'an economic fallacy' to suppose that shorter hours could give rise to any counterbalancing advantage other than the workmen's enjoyment of more leisure.[3] Then, ignoring Mill's contention that private interests were fundamentally interdependent, he concluded:

> When we observe, too, that trades unions are already constantly wrangling with employers for a reduction of hours, while individual workmen are generally ready to work overtime for a moderate inducement, we shall be led to think that there is no ground whatever for legal limitation of adult male labour in the present day.

v

The classical analysis of the Factory Acts consisted of two quite separate strands of thought. On the one hand, factory legislation was criticized in terms of the doctrine of 'freedom of contract' between enlightened economic agents. On the other hand, it was held that something like a Ten Hours Bill would spell the ruin of British industry if unaccompanied by a drastic fall in money wages. We will examine each argument in turn.

In so far as the problem was treated as a matter of enlightened individualism, the attitude of the classical economists was unambiguous: where self-interest was plainly unenlightened, as in the case of children, they recommended intervention by the State, differing only about the proper age of consent and the scope of parents' right of supervision. Nevertheless, in practice this meant that they acquiesced in just so much legislation as

[1] W. S. Jevons, *The State in Relation to Labour* (London, 1882), p. 65.

[2] Thornton's argument was finally 'rediscovered' by Marshall (*Principles*, pp. 695–6).

[3] See Jevons, *The Theory of Political Economy*, 2nd ed. (London, 1879), pp. 63–4, and *Methods of Social Reform and Other Papers* (London, 1883), p. 109.

had already been achieved; at each stage of the debate they warned against further measures. Invariably, notions about the age at which a worker becomes a 'free agent' changed in the wake of legislation, at each turn approving a *fait accompli*.

McCulloch's treatment of the question is typical in this respect. One would hardly describe him as a supporter of the Factory Acts. Senior is another telling example. In his *Letters on the Factory Acts* he agreed that no child of eleven should be employed as much as twelve hours a day; this implied acceptance of Althorp's Act which defined thirteen as the age at which 'the period of childhood, properly so called, ceases'. In 1841 he thought that the 'age of consent' ought to be raised from thirteen to fourteen; in 1847 he urged that it be set at sixteen, that is, two years below the age of consent stipulated in the Ten Hours Bill. Similarly, he now assented to a six and one-half hour day for children, as called for in the Act of 1844. But he never changed his mind about the undesirability of regulating adult labour.[1]

Apart from being wise too often after the event, the classical economists never faced the question whether it was, in fact, possible to protect women and children without interfering with the employment of adult males. Strictly speaking, economists are not concerned with administrative feasibility. Still, the total neglect of the difficulties created by the relay system rendered most of the classical prescriptions for legislation void of practical significance. In addition, the notion of 'free agents' was in itself extremely vague. The whole case against the Factory Acts based on this concept falls to the ground once we consider Mill's argument that the ability of adult operatives to recognize their own self-interests does not prevent them collectively from working longer hours than each alone might

---

[1] Sorenson, op. cit., pp. 260–1. Walker's observation (op. cit.) that 'reputable and orthodox economists like Colonel Robert Torrens, Joseph Hume, Thomas Tooke, Edwin Chadwick, and Leonard Horner, were all favourable to factory legislation as long as it was limited to children' completely begs the question. Not only were some of these 'economists' never regarded, by themselves or others, as spokesmen of economic science, but all public figures after 1820 or thereabouts approved of factory legislation limited to children below some age or other.

E

have found desirable. Although Mill presented this argument in one of the most widely read treatises of the period, he never for one moment succeeded in deflecting the debate from the well-worn theory of free agents. This is all the more surprising since this doctrine is repeatedly attacked in the reports of the factory inspectors.[1]

In the case of Mill and Fawcett the problem of factory reform was complicated by the issue of feminism. They feared that the Ten Hours Bill would encourage the substitution of unprotected adult males for protected female workers.[2] Since the emancipation of women was held to be dependent upon unlimited access to factory employment, they thought it necessary to condemn the Factory Acts in so far as these involved restrictions upon the hours of women workers.

All things considered, the Ten Hours camp was not far wrong in regarding 'political economy' with its slogan of 'free agents' as a major obstacle to factory reform. This is even more true when we consider the arguments based directly upon economic theory. It cannot be doubted that the Ten Hours movement would have met with much less hostility if economists had insisted from the outset, as did John Stuart Mill in 1848, that the wage and employment effects of shorter hours were 'in every particular instance a question of fact, not of principle'. To be sure, economic theory added very little in the way of theoretical analysis to popular thinking about the Factory Acts. The level of formal analysis barely rose above the commonplace: no effort was made to distinguish the short-run and long-run effects of a change in hours, without which distinction any analysis was bound to be naïve. In this sense, it is true to say that 'had there been no classical economic theory, the arguments would have been essentially the same'.[3] Nevertheless, the assumption of a constant productivity of labour

[1] See the citations by K. Marx, *Capital* (New York, 1939), p. 288.

[2] Their fears seem to have been unfounded. Available data covering the period 1835–70 reveal a steady tendency to replace protected children with similarly protected adults and young persons; women above thirteen comprised from 50 to 56 per cent of the labour force throughout the period. See Wood, op. cit., pp. 310–11.

[3] Walker, op. cit., p. 177.

irrespective of the length of the working day had been challenged by at least one economist, William Thornton. On the face of it, there is nothing in classical theory which would have prevented a consideration of this factor; once introduced there is little left of Torrens's *Letter to Ashley*, 'the best tract in opposition to the ten-hours project'.

McCulloch's use of the wages fund doctrine to show that it is fruitless to restrict hours by legislative enactment is simply wrong. He failed to realize that at bottom, and apart from humanitarian motives, the leaders of the Ten Hours movement were trying to restrict the supply of labour in order to maintain the rates of wages in periods of severe unemployment. It is no accident that all the Factory Acts in the first half of the nineteenth century were passed after vigorous working class agitation 'at, or close to, a low point in cyclical fluctuations'.[1] At such times employers were more inclined to accept restrictive legislation, but that is not the point. Only under depressed conditions can workers hope to gain instantly by an elimination of child and female labour; in a boom the immediate effect would be a reduction in real income per family. Needless to say, the wages fund doctrine is quite adequate to show why a reduction in the labour supply does tend to reduce wages. At the same time, it must be said that the doctrine is really inappropriate to a discussion of the Factory Acts: it assumes that the size of the labour force is a constant proportion of the total population, thus ignoring variations in the child and female participation rate.

In a class by itself is Fawcett's contention that pecuniary motives alone bring about the adoption of a work day that optimizes output per man-hour. This argument is open to the objection that it assumes perfect foresight. Contrariwise, Thornton's thesis amounts to a denial of perfect knowledge on the part of the entrepreneur. We should say today that entrepreneurs may have little incentive to reduce hours since the immediate effect, if wages are kept constant, is to increase costs and decrease output; whereas, a simultaneous reduction in wages under these circumstances is bound to affect efficiency

[1] W. W. Rostow, *British Economy of the Nineteenth Century*, p. 118.

adversely. Thus, employers may fail to maximize output per man-hour owing to an excessive emphasis on profit maximization in the short run.[1] Be that as it may, Fawcett's line of reasoning clearly shows where the classical economists' treatment of hours legislation is deficient: they had no theory of the firm.[2]

There is a simple moral in all this: for some purposes a theory of economic growth is not enough.

[1] See J. R. Hicks, *The Theory of Wages*, pp. 104–10. Even on the assumption of perfect foresight, this is a clear case of private costs diverging from social costs. There is no reason why the classical economists could not have considered this possibility; the distinction between private and social costs is implicit in Adam Smith's discussion of public works.

[2] Since Jevons likewise had no theory of the firm he was unable to improve upon classical analysis in this respect.

5 Private versus Public Education, A Classical Economic Dispute

E. G. WEST

[This article was first published in *The Journal of Political Economy*, vol. 72, October 1964.]

This article examines a remarkable division of opinion among the classical economists concerning the applicability of the free-market principle to education. First I offer a brief description of the school and university situation during the time of Adam Smith. Next I shall examine Smith's preference in his own circumstances for the operation of market forces in providing education. I then sketch the development of government policy in education over the subsequent century showing the roles of J. S. Mill, Nassau Senior, and Edwin Chadwick. Finally I contrast the ideas of Robert Lowe, the last true representative of Adam Smith on education, with the dominant ideas of his contemporaries, Mill, Senior, and Chadwick.

In Adam Smith's lifetime it was commonly observed that both in quality and quantity the schools in Scotland were better than those in England, despite the superior material prosperity of the latter. The main explanation of this was to be found in the contrasting legislation in the two countries rather than in any differences in national character. In 1696 an Act of Scotland had ordered schools to be established in every parish and had obliged landlords to build a schoolhouse and a dwelling house for the use of the local master. The salary of this teacher was to come from a small fixed stipend and also from fees payable by pupils or parents. This legislation was so well enforced that by the end of the eighteenth century the majority of children in Scotland were receiving some schooling. Although by that time inflation had substantially reduced the real value of the statutorily fixed part of the masters' salaries, the more efficient ones were managing to survive with incomes deriving largely from fees. Such dependence on direct payments from their customers meant that the teachers' efforts respected more closely the wishes of the pupils and their parents, since teaching incomes conspicuously fluctuated with the numbers on the school register. In many cases the teachers allowed their fees to be divided according to the number or type of subjects taught. Special fees were often paid, for instance, to meet the demand for new lessons in modern subjects. This sort of discriminative pricing developed to such a degree that Robert Lowe observed (approvingly) in the following century: 'In Scotland they sell education like a grocer sells figs.'

Legislation in England had a quite different result from that in Scotland. The Test Act of 1665, by excluding dissenters from the schools and universities, placed a serious brake upon English education that was to last for over a century. While Catholics and Jews were kept out of the universities, grammar-school teachers were restricted by a rigorous system of ecclesiastical licensing. The upshot was that many individuals who were willing to teach were prevented from doing so while those who did were protected against potential competitors. But apart from the legislation, a traditional characteristic of English education was also partly responsible for the reduced competition. This was the typical practice of financing schools and colleges largely from funds bequeathed to them by propertied benefactors, a system which became known as the process of 'endowment'. The more such institutions were endowed, the more they tended to become divorced from the wishes of the parents. Furthermore, with the passage of time, the original objectives of the testators became increasingly re-interpreted in the interests of their administrators. Turgot seems to have been one of the first eighteenth-century econo-mists to make this kind of criticism:

> Endowments, whatever be their utility, carry in them-
> selves an irremediable vice which they derive from their very

nature – the impossibility of maintaining the execution of their purpose. Founders deceive themselves very grossly if they imagine that their zeal will communicate itself from age to age to the person charged with the perpetuation of its effects. . . . There is every ground to presume that an endowment, however useful it may appear, will become one day useless at least, perhaps injurious, and will be so for a long time.[1]

It was the endowment system also which Adam Smith singled out for his strong disapproval when writing about education. It is obvious that Smith's views were deeply influenced by direct experience of both the English endowed institutions and the Scottish method of predominantly fee-paid instruction:

> The endowments of schools and colleges have necessarily diminished more or less the necessity of application in the teachers. Their subsistence, so far as it arises from their salaries, is evidently derived from a fund altogether independent of their success and reputation in their particular professions.[2]

Smith argued that private schools were in an unfortunate minority because the salaries of the public (endowed) school teachers

> put the private teachers who would pretend to come into competition with them, in the same state with a merchant, who attempts to trade without a bounty in competition with those who trade with a considerable one. . . .[3]
>
> The endowments of schools and colleges have, in this manner, not only corrupted the diligence of public teachers, but have rendered it almost impossible to have any good private ones.[4]

[1] Turgot, article on 'Foundations' in the *Encyclopédie*.
[2] Adam Smith, *The Wealth of Nations*, ed. Edwin Cannan, 6th ed. (1950), p. 250. All subsequent references are from this edition and are indicated as *W.N.*
[3] *W.N.*, p. 266.
[4] Ibid.

In his proposals for state intervention in education which appeared in Book V of *The Wealth of Nations*, Adam Smith was especially careful to avoid a state system which would reproduce the errors of endowed schools. His scheme was similar to the Scottish parochial system. State financial aid was intended mainly for school buildings, leaving the masters substantially dependent for their incomes on fees payable even by the poorest parents. When he recommended the encouragement of scientific education 'among all people of middling or more than middling rank and fortune', Smith carefully added the proviso that the State should not do this by giving 'shares' to teachers 'in order to make them negligent and idle'.[1]

Most of the classical economists shared Smith's reasoning. Thus Malthus argued that if each child had to pay a fixed sum, 'the school master would then have a stronger interest to increase the number of his pupils'.[2] Similarly, McCulloch thought that the maintenance of the fee system would

> secure the constant attendance of a person who shall be able to instruct the young, and who shall have the strongest interest to perfect himself in his business, and to attract the greatest number of scholars to his school.[3]

Otherwise if the schoolmaster derived much of his income from his fixed salary he would not have the same interest to exert himself,

> and like all other functionaries, placed in similar situations, he would learn to neglect his business, and to consider it as a drudgery only to be avoided.[4]

When discussing his proposals for state intervention in education, Adam Smith deliberately avoided the provision of a specially selected teaching body. He disliked both state training of teachers and a system of pedagogic licensure operated by a self-governing teaching profession. People were

---

[1] *W.N.*, p. 281.

[2] Malthus, letter to Whitbread, 1807.

[3] Note XXI in McCulloch edition to *The Wealth of Nations* (1828).

[4] Ibid. James Mill also shared such reasoning (see *Westminster Review* article, 1813).

to be left free to choose since 'they would soon find better teachers for themselves than any whom the state could provide for them'.[1] Smith supported his objection to state-provided teachers with historical evidence (mainly from classical Greece) illustrating their general inferiority compared with free-lance practitioners. His objection to teachers licensed by their own profession is to be inferred from his rejection of the principle of occupational licensure in general, a subject upon which Smith best expressed himself when considering the parallel case of the medical profession. Since this context is of particular relevance to subsequent discussion in this article, Smith's argument will be examined here in detail.

In 1778 Dr Cullen, a colleague at Glasgow University, wrote to Adam Smith asking for his opinion on the proposition that the medical profession, in order to protect the interests of patients and also those of properly qualified doctors, should be restricted to graduates of recognized universities. Smith's reply is particularly interesting here since it illustrates the full and extended strength of his desire to remove all obstacles to competition in the professions generally. He told Cullen first that his proposal would strengthen still further the existing monopoly power of the (endowed) universities which granted the examination certificates: 'Monopolists seldom make good work, and a lecture which a certain number of students must attend, whether they profit by it or no, is certainly not very likely to be a good one.'[2]

Secondly, Adam Smith dealt with the objection to the market system that J. S. Mill was later to make with reference to education – the objection that in some cases it failed because the consumer was an incompetent judge. Smith maintained that people were not such children in the choice of their doctors, as the less patronized doctors were fond of believing:

> That Doctors are sometimes fools as well as other people, is not, in the present times, one of those profound secrets

[1] *W.N.*, p. 281.
[2] Adam Smith's letter to Cullen is to be found in John Thomson, *The Life, Lectures and Writings of William Cullen, M.C.*, vol. I (Edinburgh, Blackwood, 1832).

which is known only to the learned. The title is not so very imposing, and it very seldom happens to a man that he trusts his health to another merely because the other is a doctor. The person so trusted has almost always either some knowledge or some craft which would procure him nearly the same trust, though he was not decorated with any such title.[1]

Thus the people did not require such props to their judgement as university degree qualifications, either in the choice of doctor or, presumably, in the selection of teachers and schools.

Smith then pointed out that the holders of degrees comprised a heterogeneous group of practitioners, so that the degree offered no sure guide for choosing among doctors within the group. Some doctors had taken twice as long as others to get their degrees. In other cases, especially at poor universities, the examination was perfunctory and the degree obtained merely by 'doing time' and paying fees at the university. Furthermore, by giving a label of credit worthiness to a person of low competence, the degree title might also have extended his practice 'and consequently his field for doing mischief; it is not improbable, too, that it may increase his presumption, and consequently his disposition to do mischief'.[2]

Finally, Adam Smith argued that the degree licensing system would so strengthen a growing monopoly as to lead to still higher prices. Many of the public would then be deprived of medical attention altogether for want of money.

> Had the Universities of Oxford and Cambridge been able to maintain themselves in the exclusive privilege of graduating all the doctors who could practise in England, the price of feeling a pulse might by this time have risen from two and three guineas, the price which it has now happily arrived at, to double or triple that sum; and English physicians might,

---

[1] It is interesting to observe that J. S. Mill also objected to a teaching profession confined to graduates, but for the 'libertarian' reason given by W. von Humbolt, that this practice would be giving too much power to the government. Apart from this, he could well have agreed to the proposal on the grounds that the consumers were incompetent to judge and needed such protection.

[2] Thomson, op. cit., letter to Cullen.

and probably would, have been at the same time the most ignorant and quackish in the world.[1]

Smith chided the doctors for affecting to champion society's interests when all the time their real purpose was to prevent the erosion of their own incomes:

> Stage doctors, I must observe, do not much excite the indignation of the faculty; more reputable quacks do. The former are too contemptible to be considered as rivals: they only poison the poor people and the copper pence which are thrown up to them in handkerchiefs could never find their way to the pockets of a regular physician. It is otherwise with the latter: they sometimes intercept a part of what perhaps would have been better bestowed in another place. Do not all the old women in the country practise physic without exciting murmur or complaint? And if here and there a graduated doctor should be as ignorant as an old woman where can be the great harm? The beardless old woman takes no fees; the bearded one does, and it is this circumstance, I strongly suspect, which exasperates his brethren so much against him.[2]

In the century that followed the publication of *The Wealth of Nations*, the English educational scene rapidly changed. The French Revolution caused such nervous reaction in England that the means of communication of knowledge of all kinds became suspect. Hostile government actions against the press, the paper tax (referred to by J. R. McCulloch and James Mill as a tax on knowledge), together with the dislike of combinations, corresponding societies, and political pamphlets of the Tom Paine variety, were all symptomatic of the official climate of opinion. The period of 1800–30, which Dicey described as the time of 'Old Toryism' or 'Legislative Quiescence', witnessed the failure both of the movement to repeal the Test Acts and of Samuel Whitbread's 1807 Bill to establish parochial education in England, a Bill which had the particular support of T. R. Malthus.

[1] Ibid., Smith's letter to Cullen.   [2] Ibid.

The Whig victory of 1832 brought a swift reaction in the opposite direction and a period of legislative enthusiasm ensued. J. A. Roebuck, representing the utilitarians, introduced an Education Bill in 1833 that had the effect of getting Parliament to endorse the first of the annual grants to education, which have existed ever since. Roebuck's arguments, and also the later utterances of Edwin Chadwick concerning the educational opportunities and responsibilities facing the new Poor Law Commissioners, drew the special praise of J. S. Mill. All the utilitarians were educationists in a very special sense. It was their enthusiastic adherence to the new psychological Principle of Association which led Bentham and James Mill to attach so much importance to the power of environment upon a child's character. While the vast legislative reform machinery of the Benthamites was openly directed to the cause of individual freedom, they intuitively recognized that education was a political prize of the first order. So confident were they of the superiority of their own special pedagogic ideas that they seized any political chance to impose them in a manner which, however benevolent in intention, was fully authoritarian in reality.

The Benthamite's main chance offered itself with the operation of the new Poor Law, following the celebrated Poor Law Report of 1834 in which the ideas of Senior and Chadwick had predominated. The last page of this Report alleged that there was a widespread failure of privately organized schooling and emphasized the urgent educational duties of government. The election of Edwin Chadwick to the secretaryship of the Poor Law Commissioners was a great tactical triumph for the Utilitarians. Chadwick was the main author of the plan that was embodied in the 1834 Poor Law Amendment Act. This Act appointed three Commissioners with extensive powers vaguely defined and with no representative in Parliament. Its provisions were directed not towards the Malthusian idea of the gradual reduction of poor relief but towards the 'better' administration of this relief. The large-scale central administration beloved by Bentham was now established. A spate of reports to the Secretary of State, mostly inspired by Chadwick, flowed from the Poor Law Office between 1834 and 1841. In 1837 the Commissioners were empowered to combine parishes or unions in order to set up enormous Benthamite schools into which could be drawn all the pauper children of the districts, children who had been separated from the 'evil adult influences' of the old workhouses.

It was from the experience of the 'scientific administration' of such establishments that the zealous and dogmatic Chadwick proceeded to announce to the world the practical success of Benthamite pedagogic principles. Bentham's ideas can be traced to a paper called 'Outline of a Work To Be Called Pauper Management Improved', which was published in Arthur Young's *Annals of Agriculture* in 1797. 'Industry houses' ruled by a central board were to secure contracts for labour, and paupers were to be paid on an incentive method. The industry houses were to offer scope for submitting poor children to the most effective 'plastic power' conceivable. 'The influence of the schoolmaster on the conduct of the pupil in ordinary life, is as nothing compared with the influence exercised by the Company over these its wards.' Bentham also applied to this problem his architectural principle of universal inspection, while the new and controversial monitorial system was accepted with enthusiasm. These were the ideas which his disciple, Edwin Chadwick, was later to help to bring into such confident operation as to claim eventually that the pauper schools were superior to those of the private sector. During this experimental period Chadwick was in constant communication with Nassau Senior and J. S. Mill, both of whom were duly impressed and gave him much encouragement.

It is quite evident that Edwin Chadwick provided an important source of information from which J. S. Mill derived his stereotypes of working-class life. In chapter vii of his *Principles of Political Economy* entitled 'On What Depends the Degree of Productiveness of Productive Agents',[1] Mill was very severe on the 'uneducated' English labouring class and compared them unfavourably with continental workers. His 'evidence' was attributed to the Report of the Poor Law Com-

[1] All references to this work refer to the Ashley edition, 1915.

missioners in 1840 on the training of pauper children. This report had, in fact, been written entirely by Chadwick and it had given an account of a typically amateur piece of sociological investigation. Leading questions had been put by Chadwick to certain 'witnesses', the manner of selection of the latter being unstated. But it was from such dubious evidence that J. S. Mill no doubt formed his general opinion of English popular education:

> even in quantity it is (1848) and is likely to remain, altogether insufficient, while in quality, though with some slight tendency to improvement, it is never good except by some rare accident, and generally so bad as to be little more than nominal.[1]

Nassau Senior's views showed similar superficiality. As a member of the Royal Commission on Popular Education, 1861, he gave Chadwick the task of supplying him with certain evidence. Senior severely opposed the proposal of a fellow commissioner that education was a matter that should be left in the hands of the parents:

> For fifty years they have been managing their own trades unions. There is not one which is not based on folly, tyranny and injustice which would disgrace the rudest savages. They sacrifice their wives', their children's and their own health and strength to the lowest sensuality. The higher the wages the worse seems, in general, to be the condition of the families.[2]

Senior, however, could not refute the statistics of his own commission. It reported that there were 2,535,462 children attending school out of a total of 2,655,767 of school age – a shortfall of only about 4·5 per cent.[3] These figures showed that the growth of voluntary schooling (i.e. schools run by the churches and also private adventure schools) over the previous thirty years had been most remarkable. Furthermore, the figures

---

[1] *Principles of Political Economy*, p. 956.
[2] N. Senior, *Suggestions on Popular Education* (1861), p. 258.
[3] *1861 Schools Inquiry Commission*, vol. I, p. 79.

easily matched those of European countries where, unlike England and Wales, compulsory state education prevailed. Senior's main criticism, therefore, was directed against the quality rather than the quantity of education. To understand the full nature of his criticism it will be necessary to sketch the developing policy problem in education.

The State's contribution to education had been swiftly growing since 1833, but private expenditure had been growing rapidly, too. The annual grant in 1833 was £20,000. By 1858 it had reached £663,435. The 1833 allocation of this grant was supervised by the Committee of Council for Education which was specially established in 1839. The first secretary of this committee was Dr Kay (1804–77), who later became Sir James Kay-Shuttleworth. It was Kay who had drawn public attention to the squalid social conditions in early nineteenth-century Manchester, and it was his strongest conviction that education was the key to reform. Kay was connected with Senior and the Mills, and it was on Senior's recommendation that he had been appointed an assistant Poor Law Commissioner.[1] Kay and Chadwick thought alike on most matters and Kay willingly accepted the delegated task of reorganizing the pauper schools on Benthamite lines.[2] Kay's subsequent experience led him to emphasize the importance of a specially trained teaching body. When he was appointed first secretary of the Committee of Council on Education, the post which eventually was to become that of Minister of Education, he therefore brought to this office the tradition of an authoritarian and utilitarian educational administrator. The parliamentary annual grant to education was made available to any school in the private sector whether it was run by a church or a private body, so long as certain conditions were observed. One of these was that the school receiving the grant should be agreeable to inspection – another Benthamite principle. It is quite obvious that Kay was in a strategic position not only to appoint the 'right' kind of

---

[1] S. E. Finer, *The Life and Times of Edwin Chadwick* (1952), p. 151.
[2] See *The Report to the Secretary of State from the Poor Law Commissioners* (1841), esp. p. 19 (hereinafter cited as *Commissioners Report*). The first chapter of this Report was written by Chadwick; most of the rest was the work of Kay.

inspectors but also to dictate the criteria of their inspection, criteria which naturally reflected the image of the large and 'scientifically' administered pauper schools.

The basis of Nassau Senior's criticism of free parental choice of education is therefore quite clear. In his view, too many people were choosing non-inspected schools, the standards of which, according to his closest official advisors, were very inferior. In pauper schools the administrators had been un-hampered by the irritation of parental free choice. In the private sector where this irritation could not be removed, the problem was that the parents could not be trusted to select the best kind of school, that is, the larger monitorial school of the Benthamite variety. Even though the fees were subsidized by the State, too many parents, according to Senior, thought that these schools were vulgar 'or their boy had been punished there, or he is required to be clean, or to be regular, or the private school is half a street nearer, or is kept by a friend, or by someone who will submit his teaching to their dictation'.[1] Furthermore, in view of Kay-Shuttleworth's ardent struggle to establish special colleges for the training of teachers in every type of school, it was embarrassing to discover how many untrained people were taking advantage of the complete freedom of entry into teach-ing. The Report of Senior's 1861 Commission contained many protests from government inspectors about the freedom of entry into teaching. According to them, a 'mushroom growth' of private schools had occurred since the 1851 census of popu-lation. Dr Hodgson complained, 'when other occupations fail, even for a time, a private school can be opened, with no capital beyond the cost of a ticket in the window'.[2] Another protested that the private teachers had picked up their know-ledge 'promiscuously' and that several combined the trade of school-keeping with another.[3] It was thought that 'none are

[1] N. Senior, op. cit., p. 39.

[2] *Commissioners Report* (1861), p. 94.

[3] Mr Cumins reported from Plymouth: 'Of the private schoolmasters in Devonport, one had been a blacksmith and afterwards an exciseman, another was a journeyman tanner, a third a clerk in a solicitor's office, a fourth (who was very successful in preparing lads for the competitive examination in the dock-yards) keeps an evening school and works as a dockyard labourer, a fifth was a seaman, and others had been engaged in other callings' (ibid., p. 93).

too old, too poor, too ignorant, too feeble, too sickly, too un-qualified in any or every way to regard themselves and to be regarded by others as unfit for school-keeping'.[1]

The above outline of the development of the policy problem in education in the century following Adam Smith, will, I think, help to place Nassau Senior's and J. S. Mill's special treatment of education in perspective.

In his celebrated chapter, 'On the Grounds and Limits of the Laissez-Faire or Non Interference Principle', John Stuart Mill wrote, 'Is the buyer always qualified to judge of the commodity? If not, the presumption in favour of the competi-tion of the market does not apply to this case.'[2]

According to Mill, medicine was an obvious example of this sort of market failure. Even if the patient could be relied upon to purchase some minimum amount at his own expense and from his own free will, this would not necessarily imply 'that the patient will select the *right* medicine without assistance'. (*Italics supplied.*) Similarly with education: 'The uncultivated cannot be competent judges of cultivation.'[3] Long experience was necessary to appreciate education, and therefore the market could not adequately provide for it. Pecuniary speculation could not wait: 'It must succeed rapidly or not at all.'[4] Like Senior, Mill did not trust the average good sense of the parents, and obviously for similar reasons. Mill's opinion is thus shown to have been in striking contrast to Adam Smith's preference for private enterprise in the provision both of education and of medicine. Whereas J. S. Mill thought that the competitive market principle broke down in education because the customer was not a competent judge of his interests, Adam Smith had argued that the competitive market principle had not been allowed to operate properly in the first place due to the hindrance of endowment.

J. S Mill acknowledged that endowments had hindered the development of education but thought that their effects could be improved by wise central administration. Certainly the

---

[1] Ibid.   [2] Op cit., p. 953.   [3] Ibid., p. 953.
[4] Ibid., p. 954. Pushed to its extreme, this argument would preclude the possibility of *any* entirely new product gaining a threshold.

endowment principle could not be abolished because it was one of the attributes of property:

> the ownership of a thing cannot be looked upon as complete without the power of bestowing it, at death or during life, at the owner's pleasure; and all the reasons, which recommend that private property should exist, recommend *pro tanto* this extension of it.[1]

Nevertheless, property in Mill's view was a means to an end and not itself the end. The use of it may conflict with the permanent interests in society so there must be room for some judicious adjustment. Mill thought that a typical abuse of the power of bequest occurred

> when a person who does the meritorious act of leaving property for public uses, attempts to prescribe the details of its application in perpetuity; when founding a place of education (for instance) he dictates, for ever, what doctrines shall be taught. It being impossible that any one should know what doctrines will be fit to be taught after he has been dead for centuries, the law ought not to give effect to such dispositions of property, unless subject to the perpetual revision (after a certain interval has elapsed) of a fitting authority.[2]

It will be observed that Mill's complaint about endowments was not quite the same as Smith's. Smith had placed the main emphasis upon their alleged effect in blunting of competition. Mill's primary anxiety, on the other hand, was that the doctrines taught would become out of date. Smith considered this to be only a subordinate defect since if competition were restored it could be relied upon to see that among other things the 'right' doctrines *were* taught.[3] Although Mill did not stipulate at this point the principle upon which the 'right' doctrines should be selected, there can be no doubt that at the time of writing (1833) it was linked with the idea of some sort of middle class cultural paternalism.

[1] *Commissioners Report* (1861), p. 226.   [2] Ibid.
[3] See Lowe's answer to question 6607 in the *Report of the Schools Inquiry Commission* (1868).

Did the new kind of educational paternalism of Senior, Mill, and Chadwick reflect a natural adjustment of the principles of political economy to suit the changed environment and circumstances of the nineteenth century, or did it derive from the historical chance of personality and the accidents of political opportunity? Such a question in the last resort is unanswerable. Nevertheless, I wish to emphasize that there were several political economists who did persist in reaffirming Adam Smith's views even if it caused them much political unpopularity at the time. The most noticeable example was Robert Lowe, and I propose to conclude this article with a brief outline of the views of this nineteenth-century Gladstonian financier and economist which, so far, do not seem to have had the attention they deserve.[1]

It was to be expected that when such an avowed admirer of Adam Smith as Sir Robert Lowe became, in 1862, the vice-president of the Committee of Council on Education (the office which James Kay had originally held) much friction and controversy was to follow. Lowe's opinions, for instance, followed Smith with especial devotion on the matter of endowed schools. Lowe felt that Smith's presumption that competition was necessary to overcome the natural desire of every man to live as much at his ease as he could, was sincerely intended as a *universal* principle. For Smith's principle was

> true without any limitation of time or place, and can never by any change of circumstances become obsolete or inapplicable. . . . Those therefore who seek to work out education on the basis of endowments, deliberately reject a superior machine in order to avail themselves of an inferior one. There is no occupation more likely to degenerate into lifeless routine and meaningless repetition.[2]

[1] Dicey described Lowe as the last of the genuine Benthamites but this seems not to be the case where education is concerned. Chadwick could best be described as the last Benthamite representative on education while Lowe was the last true disciple of Adam Smith, at least on this subject. Another contemporary supporter of Adam Smith's type of reasoning was Herbert Spencer. Gladstone was impressed with the evidence of average parental behaviour, and he approved only of marginal intervention by the State.

[2] R. Lowe, *Middle Class Education: Endowment or Free Trade?* (1868), pp. 7–8.

One obvious question arose, however. If endowed institutions became inefficient, could not ordinary commercial establishments compete them out of existence? Lowe, following Adam Smith's reasoning about the advantages of a merchant who trades with a bounty, contended that all sects, communities, and districts desired endowments because they were glad that the money of the founder would be employed

> to discharge for them those obligations to their children which they would otherwise have to discharge themselves. ... Their competition with private schools is not which shall provide the best instruction, but which shall give it at the cheapest rate, a contest in which the unendowed schools must always be defeated.[1]

Lowe argued that an endowment, like a patent, appeared to be useful enough at the start. But in fact its monopoly power extended insidiously into the future, so undermining all the apparent good:

> It can always undersell its competitor; and what is still worse, it can by the prospect of a disastrous and unfair competition prevent the existence of any competition at all. ... What they actually do, we see, and for that they get full credit. What they prevent others from doing we do not see, and consequently do not reflect upon; but the agency of endowment is just as real in preventing better teaching than is teaching badly itself.[2]

But it was on the question whether ordinary people were competent to choose education that Lowe, again following Smith, placed himself in the most politically unpopular position at a time when nineteenth-century education was becoming a possession shared between the government departments and the increasingly organized teaching profession. Lowe seems to have been the only witness in the Schools Inquiry Commission of 1868 to have put Smith's argument:

> Chairman: 'Should you have any apprehension that the parents, if left the sole or principal judges of the course of

[1] R. Lowe, op. cit., p. 8.   [2] Ibid., p. 9.

study to be pursued, might, from inadequate knowledge on those subjects, make a mistake; that they would prefer superficial accomplishments to a solid and well-grounded course of education?'

Lowe: 'I think so; they are very liable to make mistakes, and they do constantly now; but I know of nothing else. I know no alternative between that and some minister of education or some educational board which should regulate it, which I think is abhorrent to the feelings and principles of this country. I myself see nothing for it but to make the parents of the children the ministers of education, and to do everything you can to give them the best information as to what is good education, and where their children can be well taught, and to leave it to work itself out.

It was nevertheless John Stuart Mill's argument that triumphed in the Royal Commission's final report, which in its wording showed distinct signs of the direct influence of Mill's reigning treatise, the *Principles of Political Economy*.[1] The report recognized that the principle of supply and demand governed completely those private schools (i.e., uninspected and un-subsidized) which were also secular and unendowed. But it claimed that the principle failed in two respects:

> it fails when the purchasers demand the wrong thing and it fails also when they are incompetent judges of the right thing. The utmost, that it could do in the matter of education, would be to supply, not what is best, but what the parents believe to be best.[2]

The report found the parents wanting in both respects. First, they demanded what was 'showy and transitory' rather than what was 'solid and permanent'. There was nothing to raise the child above 'the traditions of his own home'. 'An un-educated father generally has a low conception of education.'[3]

---

[1] This report dealt with the education of the 'middle class'. The Newcastle Report of 1861, upon which Senior sat, was concerned with popular education. The later Clarendon Report dealt with the 'public' schools: Eton, Winchester, etc.

[2] *Report of the Schools Inquiry Commission* (1868), pp. 306–7.

[3] Ibid., p. 307.

His child would be taken away from school too early and would therefore not rise above his father's tastes. Secondly, the parents were not competent judges:

> Now it is quite certain that it cannot be said that the majority of parents are really good judges of education. They are good judges of certain things and they press these particular things, until the whole teaching is dislocated; but of the best means of training the mind, and of strengthening the faculties, they are no judges at all.[1]

Furthermore, the report complained that the parents pressed unduly those subjects which, for instance, were of practical use in business life, such as commercial arithmetic.

However, the Schools Inquiry Report did admit that the public (i.e. subsidized and inspected) schools were less dynamic and inventive. Lowe was quick to remind them of this:

> It is, in the opinion of the Commissioners, in private schools rather than in public that we are to look for improvements and the discovery of new methods. That is in private schools there is progress, there is power of adaptation to new circumstances.[2]

For the report agreed that unendowed private schools offered a field for enthusiasts who could not work in 'the trammels of the recognized system of the day'. They were the men who most often made improvements and discovered new methods which the state schools could hardly do. Such men were often dogmatic but their enthusiasm made up for this:

> One man holds that natural science ought to be the one subject of instruction; another will teach nothing but algebra and the Bible. Such theories in ordinary hands are grievous blunders. But the enthusiastic believer often succeeds in spite of his theories, and turns out pupils if not already knowing all that is necessary yet capable of rapidly acquiring

---

[1] *Report of the Schools Inquiry Commission* (1868), p. 307.
[2] R. Lowe, op. cit., p. 10.

it, and possessed meanwhile of a passion for learning which is almost worth all knowledge that could have been learnt.[1]

The commission also praised the private schools on another account. Although it thought that the desire of the parents to have each child educated according to his own peculiar needs was 'unreasonably exaggerated', yet it felt that there were undoubtedly some boys who could only be catered for by the 'individual' teaching which the unendowed private system could give.

Robert Lowe also agreed with Adam Smith that the supply of teachers could best be left to the free market. The Schools Inquiry Commission of 1868, which called in Lowe as a witness, informed him that several other witnesses 'of extensive knowledge of the feeling of schoolmasters throughout the country' were suggesting a register of bona fide schoolmasters. This itself indicated that the opinion of the 'orthodox' teachers had already become fully articulate. Their 'evidence' could be much more organized and readily consulted by official Commissions than the scattered opinion of parents. Lowe, again obviously aware that the political tide was against him, relentlessly persisted with his own reasoning. The schoolmaster organizations wanted to have a register of their own members compiled as a first step in the direction of being placed in the same position as surgeons and apothecaries. Accordingly, they advocated also that all recruits to the 'profession' should pass an examination that would license them to teach. The penalty for teaching without a licence was to be similar to that in the case of unqualified surgeons: that they should have no legal mode for recovering payment for their services. Asked his opinion on this, Lowe replied flatly that he was entirely against the suggestion.

> Chairman: 'I suppose you would not consider that the educational profession should be put on the same grounds as the medical profession?'
> Lowe: 'I myself doubt exceedingly the policy of the Medical Act. There are plenty of quacks inside.'[2]

[1] *Report of the Schools Inquiry Commission*, p. 304.   [2] Ibid., Q. 6617.

This reaction was, of course, exactly in accordance with the views of Adam Smith, who, as we have seen, had declared himself in even stronger terms on this same matter of occupational licensure and had used precisely the same example of the medical profession. On this issue, at least, Lowe was supported by another witness to the 1868 Schools Commission, a Mr Frearson. Frearson questioned the ability of an inbred academic teaching profession to make suitable innovations from its protected position within education:

> It is the nature of teachers to recommend that which they know best themselves. To recommend anything else is to impose on themselves the trouble of going to school again. . . . Besides there is nothing in the occupation of a teacher which tends to give that large acquaintance with men and things which enables a man to discover what are the wants of society in respect of instruction, and how those wants may be supplied. Nor has the State any peculiar means of forming a right conclusion on this subject.

The issues which divided the political economists on the subject of education and which have been examined in this article are among the most difficult that any free society has to decide. But they are issues which are only too easily swamped by dogma and political expediency. The duty of a government to protect children from ignorance is a proposition with which most people would agree. But it is easily forgotten that, in so far as such a proposition points towards policy at all, the suggested improvements must be envisaged in the realm of the politically possible. The state is not a disembodied abstraction and its officials are presumably just as fallible as other human beings. The choice of educational supervisors for children must therefore always be regarded as a choice between imperfect mortals. For this reason we conclude this article by giving the last word to Robert Lowe. However much one may disagree with the final value judgement contained in this last pronouncement, the framework of alternatives in which Lowe expresses it can hardly be rejected:

Parents have one great superiority over the Government or the administrators of endowments. Their faults are mainly the corrigible faults of ignorance, not of apathy and prejudice. They have and feel the greatest interest in doing that which is for the real benefit of their children. They are the representatives of the present, the living and acting energy of a nation, which has ever owed its sure and onward progress rather to individual efforts than to public control and direction. They have the wish to arrive at a true conclusion, the data are before them, they must be the judges in the last resort; why should we shrink from making them judges at once?[1]

[1] R. Lowe, op. cit., p. 12.

6 The Classical Economists and the Labourer

A. W. COATS

[This article was first published in E. L. Jones and G. E. Mingay (eds.), *Land, Labour and Population in the Industrial Revolution*, Arnold, 1967.]

In his important study, *The Making of the English Working Class* (1963), E. P. Thompson revived two familiar themes of nineteenth-century romantic and socialist literature – condemnation of the social evils of the Industrial Revolution and bitter criticism of the classical economists, and in his treatment of the latter he went far beyond either the Hammonds or the Webbs. It was Arnold Toynbee who remarked that the protracted debate between the disciples of Ricardo and the human beings had ended with 'the conversion of the economists',[1] and as this caricature of the classical economist as the personification of man's congenital inhumanity to man has long been popular among undergraduates, it is worth re-examining the original with some care.

To sketch the main outlines of the classical economists' attitude to early nineteenth-century conditions is, however, no easy task. Against the humanitarian and socialist indictment can be set an equally polemical liberal defence of classical economics, and distinguished academic authorities fully armed with apt quotations from the writings of the accused can be mustered on both sides. Any student who wishes to make up his own mind on the matter faces a formidable task, for after immersing himself in innumerable books, monographs, pamphlets, magazine articles, reports, minutes of evidence,

---

[1] A. Toynbee, *Lectures on the Industrial Revolution* (1884). Cf. E. P. Thompson, *The Making of the English Working Class* (1963), pp. 224, 265, 313, 341, 543, 552, etc.

speeches, and letters, he must endeavour to condense complex discussions, reconcile inconsistencies, assess successive changes of opinion, and, above all, thread his way through those terminological, conceptual, and factual disagreements that inevitably arise whenever two or three economists are gathered together. The following pages represent a modest attempt to present an impartial summary view of the classical economists' attitude to the labourer.[1] Instead of the familiar questions about the nature and validity of the labour theory of value, the Ricardian theory of production and distribution, the wages fund, etc., which form the staple diet of historians of economic theory, we shall ask what the classical economists knew of the labourer's difficulties, his motives, and his aspirations. Were they hostile, sympathetic, or indifferent? Were they perhaps well intentioned, but blinded by their own values and prejudices? And were their policy recommendations – especially those designed to relieve poverty and to promote economic progress – derived from abstract speculation, totally unrelated to current conditions; or were they based on genuine efforts to obtain trustworthy evidence?

Before commencing this inquiry, however, it is advisable to dispose of an elementary methodological point, one that would hardly be worth mentioning had it not been a fruitful source of serious, sometimes deliberate and wilful, misunderstanding. The classical economists were neither poets nor novelists; they were aspiring social scientists – the first 'professional economists', and therefore we should not expect to find in their writings the kind of insights into the infinite complexity, variety, and subtlety of the human personality that we might legitimately seek in the works of the literary men. As the antithetical terms 'classical' and 'romantic' suggest, the Ricardians and the lakeland poets were interested in different things and asked different kinds of questions; it is, therefore, hardly surprising that they obtained very different, though not always incompatible, answers.[2] The classical economists were deeply

---

[1] See *Note. infra* p. 178, for an account of the sources used in this essay.

[2] The same is often true, *mutatis mutandis*, of the 'optimistic' and 'pessimistic' interpreters of the Industrial Revolution. Cf. W. Woodruff, 'Capitalism and the Historians', *Journal of Economic History*, vol. XVI (1956), *passim*.

concerned about individual freedom and happiness; but, as economists, they dealt with 'man in the aggregate – with states not with families; with general passions and propensities, not with those which occasionally influence the individual'.[1] This preoccupation does not, of course, excuse unsound generalizations, or a neglect of relevant differences – whether sex, age, family, occupational, or regional – in labour conditions. But we are chiefly concerned with the nature and quality of their performance as social scientists, and we must not convict them of failure to perform a task that was no part of their intention.

I

As social scientists, the classical economists endeavoured to formulate general principles, and although they repeatedly used hypothetical 'models' – what Ricardo called 'strong cases' – to illustrate the operation of these principles, they claimed that their generalizations were based on 'fact and experiment', and did not hesitate to cite empirical data in support of their arguments. Thus the widely held notion that classical economics was a tissue of abstractions built on *a priori* assumptions is erroneous; but it is no easy matter to determine the exact relationship between general principles and particular facts in the classical literature.[2] Malthus's *Essay on Population*, for instance, is rightly said to have become longer and longer and duller and duller with successive editions as he incorporated the results of his extensive search for demographic evidence to buttress his central law; but while the younger authors came to the conclusion that the weight of evidence was against Malthus's theory, Malthus himself made only minor changes after his second edition.[3] Much the same is true of McCulloch, whose desire to base political economy on 'fact' rather than

---

[1] J. R. McCulloch, *A Discourse on the Rise, Progress, Peculiar Objects and Importance of Political Economy* (1824).

[2] For a recent disagreement on this point, cf. Mark Blaug, *Ricardian Economics: a Historical Study* (1958), pp. 182–8, and B. A. Corry, *Money, Saving and Investment in English Economics 1800–1850* (1962), pp. 10–12. (On the whole the present writer endorses Dr Corry's view.) See also W. J. Ashley's introduction to J. S. Mill's *Principles of Political Economy* (1920), pp. xviii–xx.

[3] See Blaug, *Ricardian Economics*, chap. 6, for a summary of the changing attitudes to the Malthusian Law of population.

'hypothesis' led him to publish several editions of his massive *Dictionary of Commerce* and his *Statistical Account of the British Empire*. He ridiculed the efforts of those 'intrepid calculators' who 'have amused themselves by framing estimates of the value of plate, furniture, clothes, etc., belonging to individuals', because 'there are no data whatsoever on which to construct such estimates – which are, in fact, good for nothing unless it be to throw discredit on all statistical computations'. As far as the condition of the people was concerned, McCulloch declared that

there is no subject about which so many contradictory assertions are made, by those pretending to be acquainted with it, as the state of the middle and lower classes in all parts of the country. We, in fact, *have no real knowledge of the matter*. There are no authentic accounts of the qualities and current prices of articles in any great market, the rent of houses and lodgings, the rate of wages in proportion to the work done, and a variety of other particulars, indispensable to be known before anyone can pretend to estimate the condition of the bulk of the people, or to compare their state at one period with their state at another . . . Ministers are quite as much in the dark as to these matters as other people. The Secretary for the Home Department is about as well informed respecting the demand for labour, wages, diet, dress and other accommodations of the people of Canton and Manilla, as of those of Manchester and Paisley. Were he questioned on the subject, he would, of course, affirm, and perhaps truly, that the manufacturing labourers in the last-mentioned towns were highly prosperous. . . .[1]

[1] McCulloch (ed.), *A Statistical Account of the British Empire*, II (1839), pp. 507–8; also ibid., I, p. viii. McCulloch, 'State and Defects of British Statistics', *Edinburgh Review*, vol. CXXIII (1835), p. 175. (Hereinafter cited as *Edin. Rev.*) Italics in original. Also McCulloch's evidence before the *Select Committee on Public Documents* (1833), pp. 12–16. He advocated the establishment of a Board of Statistics in London like those in Europe, with agents in the principal manufacturing towns. For an example of a case where McCulloch claimed to have decisively changed his opinion in response to 'consideration of the historical facts with respect to the operation of the principle', see *Select Committee on the State of the Poorer Classes in Ireland* (1830), pp. 590–1. In many other cases the classical economists openly admitted that there were important disagreements among qualified observers with respect both to facts and proposals for reform. For example, Senior, *Letters on the Factory Act*, 2nd ed. (1844), pp. 30 ff.

Nevertheless, despite his ardent desire for more extensive and reliable information, McCulloch's own appraisal of the compatibility between his theories and the facts leaves much to be desired. As is well known, he was a sincere disciple of Ricardo, and his confidence in the validity of Ricardian principles was seldom disturbed by evidence that ran counter to his presuppositions.

Before condemning this attitude, however, we must remember that the evidence was often unreliable, and could not be used to falsify *general theoretical* principles. How, for example, was Torrens to adjust his theory of wages to take account of the earnings of cotton workers employed in 'common mule spinning about No. 36 weft, or 36 hanks to the lb' when his sources indicated that in computing such wages 'much depends upon the quality of cotton, etc., furnished by the master; also upon the state of repair, etc., in which machinery is kept, likewise upon the attention of both manager and operative'?[1] This is, of course, an extreme case, and it is no part of our purpose to offer a blanket defence of the classical economists' use of evidence. As Ricardo wisely observed, 'There are perhaps very few men who are not in some degree biased either by the love of their party or by the love of their favourite system',[2] and his fellow economists were human in this as in other respects. Since their primary objective was to construct a theoretical system, they were naturally reluctant – and often rightly so – to abandon their hard-won generalizations as a result of new and conflicting evidence which could usually be dismissed either as unsound, unrepresentative, or the product of 'disturbing causes' which had been specifically excluded from the theorists' model. As the philosopher Morris Cohen has said, 'It is only as a last resort that we modify (as little as possible) the old ideas. If we did not hold on to our old ideas

[1] Robert Torrens, *The Budget, On Commercial and Colonial Policy* (1844), p. 326. Elsewhere he distinguished between 'speaking statistically' and speaking 'hypothetically upon the principles of political economy'. *Select Committee on the Disposal of Lands in the British Colonies* (1836), p. 140.

[2] In a letter to James Mill, 9 November 1817. Cf. P. Sraffa and M. H. Dobb (eds.), *The Works and Correspondence of David Ricardo* (1952), VII, p. 205. (Subsequently cited as *Ricardo's Works.*)

tenaciously, if we threw them away the moment they encountered difficulties, we could never develop any strong ideas
and our science would have no continuity of development.'[1]

On the other hand, as time passed, the accumulation of
evidence of contemporary economic conditions figured ever
more prominently in the classical economists' writings, and
their individual attitudes towards the problems of poverty,
factory legislation, public health, and so forth underwent
significant modifications as their knowledge of the facts
increased. On matters of fundamental principle they were often
unduly rigid, and their conception of the labourer's predicament was undoubtedly seriously deficient. Yet, as we shall see,
it was neither without empirical foundations nor wholly
irrelevant to the facts of contemporary life. The classical
economists were neither ignorant of nor indifferent to current
evils, for their pages contain innumerable eloquent and detailed
passages about the hardships encountered by such special
groups as the Spitalfields silk workers, the London coal whip-
pers, the Coventry ribbon-makers, the Nottingham lace-
makers, the inevitable hand-loom weavers, and many others.
Their lengthy and impassioned accounts of the degradation of
the Irish peasantry and the English rural paupers were designed
to warn the English working man – who, they believed, was
in a significantly more favourable condition – of the dangers
that accompanied reckless, idle, and improvident conduct. And,
with the benefit of hindsight, we can now see that their hopes
for long-term improvement (and they were mainly concerned
with the long run) were not wholly unjustified.

II

The classical economists' conception of the labourer's predicament and prospects was based on a theory of human nature and
motivation that can broadly be termed utilitarian.[2] From Locke,

---

[1] Morris R. Cohen, *Reason and Nature, An Essay on the Nature of Scientific
Method* (1931), p. 27. For reasons why the economists were reluctant to abandon
their hard-won positions, see my article 'The Role of Authority in the Development of British Economics', *Journal of Law and Economics* (October 1964).

[2] On the intellectual background see Leslie Stephen. *The English Utilitarians*
(1900); and Elie Halévy, *The Growth of Philosophic Radicalism* (1928).

Hume, and Adam Smith, they inherited the notion that all men are fundamentally alike in respect of their native characteristics and potentialities, but since they also believed that environment exerted a profound influence on men's actual habits and customs, their views on specific issues comprised a changing amalgam of long-term and short-term elements which cannot easily be summarized.

On the whole, their middle-class perspective, reinforced by their genuine desire to elevate the lower orders, led the economists to underestimate the difficulties of realizing the labourer's *bourgeois* potentialities – the qualities of self-reliance, thrift, prudence, industriousness, etc., which they believed were latent in every man. According to Senior, the independent labourer was the 'normal type . . . the natural offspring of the Saxon race', whose customary virtues would readily reassert themselves once the 'rash interference' of the State ceased, while the sanguine McCulloch maintained that:

> The poor have, upon plain and practical questions that touch their immediate interests, the same understanding, the same penetration, and the same regard to consequences as those who are rich. It is indeed a contradiction, and an absurdity to pretend, that if the labourers are capable of earning, by an ordinary degree of application, more than is sufficient to support them, they alone, of all the various classes of society, will spend the surplus in riot and debauchery. They have the same common sense, they are actuated by the same passions, feelings, and principles as other men; and when such is the case, it is clear that they cannot generally be guilty of such inconsiderate conduct.[1]

There is, accordingly, an important current of optimism in the classical literature, despite the gloomy shadow cast by the Malthusian law of population. Even Malthus, who held that the labourer's desire for self-improvement was 'perfectly feeble' by comparison with the 'passion between the sexes', allowed

[1] Nassau W. Senior, 'Poor Law Reform', *Edin. Rev.*, vol. CXLIX (1841), reprinted in his *Historical and Philosophical Essays* (1865), pp. 97–8. Cf. McCulloch 'Combination Laws, Restraints on Emigration', *Edin. Rev.*, vol. LXXVIII (1824), p. 334.

himself some cheerful prognostications in the later editions of his *Essay* – provided, of course, that his policy recommendations were adopted.[1] McCulloch and Senior went much further, and resembled Adam Smith in their belief that the diffusion of a spirit of emulation, a desire for respectability, and the opportunity to acquire a taste for the luxuries and conveniences of life, would greatly promote the long-run economic and social improvement of the lower orders. Underlying this attitude was a residue of eighteenth-century faith in progress that persisted throughout the strains and stresses of early nineteenth-century industrialism.[2] When Senior observed approvingly that the gradations of wealth in England were insensible, he was echoing the eighteenth-century view that a nation benefits from 'an easy gradation from rank to rank';[3] and one of the main reasons for the classical economists' stress on the need for education was their conviction that vertical social mobility was both possible and desirable.

Of course there were notable exceptions and qualifications in this as in most other matters. McCulloch, for instance, took a far more hierarchical view of the interrelationships between social classes than most of his fellow economists.

> The distinction of rich and poor, is not as some shallow sophists would seem to suppose, artificial, but real; it is as much a part of the order of Providence as the distinction of the sexes. It depends on the differences of the mental and physical powers and dispositions of different individuals,

[1] William Hazlitt declared that Malthus's excessively 'amorous complexion' led him to suppose that all other men were made of 'the same combustible materials'. Cf. Stephen, op. cit., II, p. 255. Cf. D. E. C. Eversley, *Social Theories of Fertility and the Malthusian Debate* (1959), pp. 250–4, 294. Also Malthus, *An Essay on Population*, Everyman ed. (1914), II, pp. 206, 257–61. For Malthus's attempt to defend his law of population while retaining his optimism, see Senior, *Two Lectures on Population* (1831), pp. 68 ff.

[2] See, for example, S. G. Checkland, 'Growth and Progress: The Nineteenth Century View in Britain', *Econ. Hist. Rev.*, 2nd ser., vol. XII (1959), esp. pp. 49–53.

[3] Senior, 'Ireland', *Edin. Rev.*, vol. CLIX (1844), p. 194. But compare his unpublished lectures of 1849–50 quoted by Leon Levy (ed.), in *Industrial Efficiency and Social Economy* (n.d.), I, p. 322. For a useful background essay on this question see Asa Briggs, 'The Language of "Class" in Early Nineteenth-Century England', in *Essays in Labour History*, Asa Briggs and John Saville (eds.) (1960), pp. 43–73.

F

and of the different circumstances under which they happen to be placed ... [while] riches are evidence of superior good conduct in the vast majority of cases ...[1]

So influential were the standards set by the higher orders of society that the constitutional details of government were unimportant provided that its leaders were men of talent and spirit. As far as the labourer's potentialities were concerned:

> If you would develop all the native resources of a man's mind, if you would bring his every faculty and power into full activity, you must make him aware of his inferiority in relation to others, and inspire him with a determination to rise to a higher level.

But in practice, he regretfully admitted, the desire to attain wealth was much more effective a spur to ambition than the desire to excel in 'learning, benevolence, or integrity'.[2]

In educational matters also, the classical economists did not invariably overrate the possibility of indoctrinating the lower orders. On one occasion J. S. Mill threw up his hands in despair at the difficulties of the task.

> In England, it would hardly be believed to what a degree all that is morally objectionable in the lowest class of the working people is nourished, if not engendered, by the low state of their understandings. The infantine credulity to what they hear, when it is from their own class; their incapacity to observe what is before their eyes; their inability to comprehend or believe purposes in others which they have not been taught to expect, and are not conscious of in themselves – are the known characteristics of persons of low intellectual faculties in all classes. But what would not be equally credible without experience, is an amount of deficiency in the power of reasoning and calculation which

[1] *Ricardo's Works*, VIII, pp. 129, 300 (Ricardo to Malthus, 24 November 1820). For Malthus's views see ibid, VIII, pp. 107–8; also McCulloch, *Observations on the State of the Country, and on the Proper Policy of Administration* (1830), p. 26.

[2] McCulloch, *Outlines of Political Economy*, ed. McVickar (1825), p. 49; *Treatise on the Succession*, pp. 31, 34.

makes them insensible to their own direct personal interests. Few have considered how anyone who could instil into these people the commonest worldly wisdom – who could render them capable of even selfish prudential calculations – would improve their conduct in every relation of life, and clear the soil for the growth of right feelings and worthy propensities.[1]

This outburst was not typical, either of Mill himself or of the group; but, on the other hand, it was not unique, and as time passed there was a growing realization that the process of reforming the labouring classes would be neither quick nor easy. It was recognized that the labourer's habits could not be changed overnight, whether by moral suasion, instruction, or some comparatively straightforward legal or institutional change, and in these circumstances the persistence of optimism reflects the classical economists' faith in the typical English working man's natural virtues. When riots and disorders occurred, they often defended the poor against the calumnies of the rich, and among the multifarious excuses they advanced for such unseemly conduct were the customs and excise laws – which tempted the people to maltreat the enforcement officers; the combination laws – which were both oppressive and ineffectual; the petty despotism of the magistrates, or 'that law for the encouragement of Murder and Robbery' (to cite McCulloch's words) which prohibited the sale of game.[2] Politically speaking, the classical economists occupied a wide spectrum, from the radicalism of James Mill to the High Toryism of De Quincey, and their attitude towards the 'mob' varied accordingly. The case of Peterloo is instructive, for it has often wrongly been regarded as a typical manifestation of early nineteenth-century middle- and upper-class hostility to

---

[1] J. S. Mill, 'The Claims of Labour', *Edin. Rev.*, vol. CLXIV (1845), p. 511. Cf. Senior, *Reviews of the Waverley Novels*, etc. (1821), p. 226. For James Mill's views see 'State of the Nation', *Westminster Review*, vol. VI (1826), p. 263, and Briggs, 'Language of Class', p. 64.

[2] See, for example, McCulloch, 'Comparative Productiveness of High and Low Taxes', *Edin. Rev.*, vol. LXXII (1822), pp. 535–6; 'Impolicy of Increasing the Duties on Spirits', ibid. (1830), pp. 488–9; 'Causes and Cure of Disturbances and Pauperism', ibid., vol. CV (1831), pp. 51, 60.

the poor, and it was the subject of considerable discussion in Ricardo's correspondence. Ricardo himself adopted a middle-of-the-road position, describing the affair in Manchester in 1819 as cruel, illegal, and unjust, and adopting a much more temperate view of the situation than his friend Hutches Trower, who was less tolerant of the poor. Three years earlier, in 1816, Ricardo had denied that the war had degraded the morals of the people.

> The outrages of which they are at present guilty may be sufficiently accounted for from the stagnation in trade which has never failed to produce similar consequences. I am disposed to think that the people are both improved in morals and in knowledge, and therefore that they are less outrageous under these unavoidable reverses than they formerly used to be. I am in hopes too that as they increase in knowledge they will more clearly perceive that the destruction of property aggravates and never relieves their difficulties.[1]

In the specific case of Peterloo, Ricardo disapproved of the magistrates' unwarranted violation of the right of assembly, and he opposed the Six Acts for similar reasons. However, mob violence presented the middle-class intellectual with a dilemma which was epitomized in Malthus's belief that although the demands of the mob 'should not be regarded', the pressure of public opinion should not be ignored.[2] James Mill and Ricardo agreed that the real test of a reformer was his willingness to allow the people to have genuinely independent representation in Parliament, and by this criterion Ricardo comes out quite well, for although he disapproved of universal suffrage, he maintained that 'it is always unwise for a Government to set itself against the declared opinion of a very large class of the people', especially in important matters! There was, however, no consensus of opinion on the question, for Malthus and McCulloch strongly opposed universal suffrage.[3]

[1] Ricardo to Trower, 15 July 1916, in Sraffa, *Ricardo's Works*, VII, p. 49.

[2] Ibid., VIII, p. 80; III, p. 146; VI, p. 183 (Malthus to Ricardo, 10 March 1815).

[3] Ibid., VIII, pp. 129, 300 (Ricardo to Malthus, 24 November 1820). Malthus believed that to concede universal suffrage and annual parliaments as a result of

Although the classical literature contains few instances of unqualified class hostility towards the poor, the economists viewed the development of an urban industrial society with certain misgivings. Adam Smith had commented extensively on the differences in social outlook between rural and urban labourers, and his successors were fully aware that energetic and independent-minded workers would not submit to injustice or economic adversity without a struggle. McCulloch, for instance, conceded that the English populace was turbulent, inflammable, and easily led astray by radical demagogues, but he regarded these characteristics as inevitable concomitants of the social conditions existing in manufacturing communities, and believed that as time passed the workers' violence would diminish as their intelligence grew.[1] On several occasions, especially in times of acute crisis, individual members of the classical school expressed grave, even hysterical anxiety at the restlessness of the people; in the summer of 1841, for instance, Senior wondered whether, if the depression of the hand-loom weavers became widespread, 'the Peerage, or the Church, or even the Monarchy, could resist the storm'?[2] Yet these gloomy and fearful observations were made without bitterness or hostility, and it has recently been suggested that James Mill regarded the turbulence of the people as an effective way of forcing concessions from an unwilling governing class. Ideally, he believed, the people 'should appear to be ready and im-

---

intimidation by mass meetings would be to invite a 'bloody revolution' (VIII, pp. 107-8), while McCulloch, for all his generosity towards the labouring class, predicted 'nothing but insecurity, revolution and rapine' if universal suffrage were to be adopted. Cf. *Observations on the State of the Country, and on the Proper Policy of Administration* (1830), p. 26.

[1] McCulloch, 'Rise, Progress, Present State, and Prospects of the British Cotton Manufacture', *Edin. Rev.*, vol. XCI (1827), pp. 37-8. J. S. Mill concurred; see his *Principles*, pp. 756-7. For Smith's views see also Nathan Rosenberg, 'Adam Smith on The Division of Labour: Two Views or One?', *Economica* N.S. vol. XXXII (1965), pp. 127-39.

[2] Senior, 'Grounds and Objects of the Budget', *Edin. Rev.*, vol. CXLVIII (1841), pp. 506-11, 518. Cf. Torrens, *Address to the Farmers of the United Kingdom on the Low Rates of Profit in Agriculture and in Trade* (1831), p. 13; and 'A Paper on the Means of Reducing the Poor's Rates', *The Pamphleteer*, vol. X (1817), p. 524. Also McCulloch, 'Causes and Cure of Disturbances', pp. 62-3.

patient to break out into outrage *without* actually breaking out'.[1]

The classical economists were not, of course, invariably optimistic, even though they believed that English workers were generally more highly paid, more industrious, and enjoyed better living conditions than their Continental counterparts. They were aware that unfavourable environmental conditions – whether natural, institutional, or psychological – could easily undermine the labourer's virtues and reduce him to that 'degraded stratum' which was 'so low intellectually as to be almost without providence, and so low morally as to be almost without self-respect'.[2] Recognition of the importance of the psychological climate is evident in Malthus's insistence that poverty ought to be held disgraceful, and in the Benthamite principle that a pauper ought to be 'less eligible' than an independent labourer. If pauperism ever became as commonplace in England as in Ireland – where a beggar was not merely regarded as an equal, but was even welcomed at a peasant's fireside – the English labourer's cherished sense of self-reliance would be crushed.[3] Socio-psychological influences could, of course, work in either direction, for even the Irish had been known to develop sound morals and industrious habits after settling in England and coming into daily contact with native workers; but it would be folly to take undue risks – hence the classical economists' almost obsessive hostility to the so-called Speenhamland system, which so dangerously blurred the crucial distinction between the pauper and the independent labourer.

At times this distinction seems to have been treated as if it defined a point of unstable equilibrium, above or below which there were prospects of continuous improvement or deteriora-

---

[1] Cf. Joseph Hamberger, *James Mill and the Art of Revolution* (1964), p. 115. Italics in original. A severe critic of the aristocracy, Mill was nevertheless no uncritical admirer of the populace. See his 'State of the Nation', pp. 263–7.

[2] Senior, quoted from unpublished lectures 1849–50 by Levy, *Industrial Efficiency*, I, p. 305.

[3] Senior, 'The Poor Law in Ireland', *Edin. Rev.*, vol. CLVI (1843), pp. 400–1. Cf. James Mill, *Elements of Political Economy* (1826), p. 58; and 'State of the Nation', p. 263.

tion in the labourer's condition.[1] Certainly, in their policy recommendations the classical economists were anxious to find the right psychological balance between the stick of necessity and the carrot of incentives. In fiscal matters, for example, McCulloch accepted Hume's view that while moderate taxes would encourage effort, exorbitant taxes would engender hopelessness and despair; but only J. S. Mill among the later classical economists recognized Hume's subtle distinction between 'active' and 'passive' habits of work, for they almost exclusively emphasized the disutility of labour.[2] Similarly, Malthus repeatedly stated that although 'fear of want' (combined with the hope of bettering his condition) was necessary to keep the independent labourer industrious, 'actual want' was wholly destructive because indigence 'palsies every virtue'.[3] As McCulloch observed, in characteristically confident tones:

> It would, however, be a most detestable policy, waiving the question of practicability, to attempt to reduce the labouring classes to a scanty supply of the mere necessities of life. The experience of all ages has shown that a needy and starving populace lose a sense of their dignity and rights as men, and become depraved and enslaved. It is vain to expect industry where it does not meet with a suitable reward; men will not submit to privations and labour, but in the hope of securing corresponding comforts.[4]

This theme was repeatedly illustrated by reference to the Irish labourers, whose predicament was variously attributed to oppressive government by the English, insecurity, the prevalence of poverty in their midst, and concomitant defects of

[1] J. S. Mill emphasized the obstacles to improvement, *Principles*, pp. 348-9, and note, while Malthus identified a 'wretchedly poor' substratum incapable of reproducing themselves. *Essay*, II, pp. 143-4, 209, 214-15.

[2] McCulloch, *An Article on Taxation*, p. 5. Also 'Progress of the National Debt, Best Method of Funding', *Edin. Rev.*, vol. XCIII (1828), p. 82. Cf. E. Rotwein (ed.), *David Hume, Writings on Economics* (1955), xiii; J. S. Mill, *Principles*, p. 286.

[3] Malthus, *Essay*, II, pp. 143, 177. For Senior's opposing view see Levy *Industrial Efficiency*, I, p. 12.

[4] McCulloch, *An Essay on the Question of Reducing the Interest on the National Debt* (1816), pp. 132-3.

character such as idleness, dissipation, improvidence, inefficiency, recklessness, cruelty, violence, vindictiveness, and
ignorance (a point on which there was some disagreement).
Despite their belief in the influence of environment on character, the classical economists could not agree about the prospects
of reforming the Irish. Some feared that Irish immigrants
would contaminate the English labour force, and favoured
immigration restrictions; but Senior, who had first-hand
knowledge of Irish conditions, and a less favourable view of
the English labourer than McCulloch, was shocked by this
suggestion. As 'an inhabitant of the British Empire' he
declared himself

> inexpressibly disgusted at the wish to deprive the Irish
> labourer of his resort to England. . . . The evidence is full of
> the improvement in habits, of feelings introduced into
> Ireland by those who have visited England.

And he endeavoured to buttress his argument by the (somewhat dubious) assertion that in counties like Lancashire,
Cumberland, and Westmorland, where the Irish were very
numerous, wage rates were among the highest and the proportion of poor rates to population among the lowest of any part
of the country.[1]

The question of the influence of insecurity on the labourers'
incentives provides yet another illustration of the need for an
appropriate psychological climate, and reveals the dangers of
simple generalizations about the classical outlook. Fluctuations
of prices and wages, like irregularities of employment, were
generally believed to discourage thrift and steady industry. By
comparison with the British worker, Senior observed,

---

[1] Senior, *A Letter to Lord Howick, On a Legal Provision for the Irish Poor* (1831),
pp. 46–8, 50. In *An Outline of the Science of Political Economy* (1836), p. 134, he
hinted that in London and its environs, Irish competition was pushing English
labourers up the socio-economic ladder. For contrary views see Malthus, *Select
Committee on Emigration* (1827), pp. 312–13; McCulloch, 'Ireland', *Edin. Rev.*, vol.
LXXIII (1822), p. 62, and *Statistical Account*, I, p. 397; Torrens, *On Wages and
Combination* (1834), pp. 31–2, and *The Budget*, p. 117; T. De Quincey, *The Logic
of Political Economy* (1844), p. 145 n., 147–8 n. On immigration restrictions see
James Mill, 'State of the Nation', p. 246; McCulloch *Select Committee on the State
of the Poorer Classes in Ireland* (1830), pp. 584–5.

foreign labour is ill-fed, ill-clothed, ill-lodged . . . it is at least secure of employment. The only accidents to which it is subject are accidents of the seasons. Such a population necessarily acquires habits of economy and prudence.[1]

The earnings of casual workers should, therefore, not only be sufficient to support them in periods of enforced idleness; their wages 'ought also to afford them', as Adam Smith remarked, 'some compensation for those anxious and desponding moments which the thought of so precarious a situation must sometimes occasion'.[2] In dangerous trades like mining and grinding, however, recklessness was observed to be a discernible occupational trait, and this might be attributable either to the influence of occupation on character or to the fact that such occupations attracted certain types of individuals. Senior seems to have taken the latter view, for he remarked that the general dislike of 'steady, regular labour' was so strong 'that the opportunities of idleness afforded by an occupation of irregular employment are so much more than an equivalent for its anxiety as to reduce the annual wages of such occupations below the common average'.[3]

But while insecurity was harmful, security was not an unmitigated advantage. Apart from the pernicious consequences of guaranteeing a pauper his income irrespective of his efforts, even the security of property could be harmful, unless it was coupled with opportunities of self-improvement. The peasant proprietor, said McCulloch, was believed to be 'exempted from those painful anxieties that embitter the existence of day labourers, and of occupiers liable to be turned out of their holdings'; but in practice, the independence and security conferred by a patch of land is

> uniformly associated with poverty, frequently degenerating into destitution; it gives rise to the most revolting of all

[1] Senior, 'Grounds and Objects of the Budget', p. 504. He believed that improvidence was the British workman's greatest weakness.

[2] McCulloch, *Principles of Political Economy* (1870), p. 129. Similarly J. S. Mill's evidence on savings among building workers, *Select Committee on Investment for the Savings of the Middle and Working Classes* (1850), p. 89.

[3] Senior, *Outline of Political Economy*, p. 208. Cf. McCulloch, *Treatise on Wages*, p. 55.

combinations, that of penury, pride, and laziness; and instead
of expanding, contracts and benumbs every faculty . . . the
happiness of peasant proprietors seems very much akin to
that of the oyster – they are ignorant and satisfied.[1]

III

Industriousness and efficiency were among the English
labourer's greatest merits, and in general the classical economists
believed that the high average wages of labour in Britain represented a just reward for high productivity. 'To complain of our
high wages', Senior caustically observed,

> is to complain that our labour is productive – to complain
> that our workpeople are diligent and skilful. To act on such
> complaints is as wise as to enact that all men should labour
> with only one hand, or stand idle four days in every week. . . .
> The well-directed labour of an Englishman is worth twice as
> much as that of any inhabitant of Europe; it is worth four or
> five times as much as the labour of the less advantaged
> European districts; and it is worth twelve or fifteen times as
> much as the labour of the most civilized Asiatic nations.[2]

However, Senior went far beyond his fellow economists in
extolling the benefits of hard work, although he himself defined
employment as 'toil, trouble, exposure, and fatigue', all of
which were evils *per se*.

> The poor and half-employed Irish labourer, or the still
> poorer and less industrious savage is as inferior in happiness
> as he is in income to the hard-worked English artisan. The
> Englishman's industry may sometimes be excessive, his
> desire to better his condition may sometimes drive him to
> toils productive of disease ill recompensed by the increase of
> his wages,

---

[1] McCulloch, *A Treatise on the Succession*, pp. 89–90. J. S. Mill took exactly the
opposite view. Cf. *Principles*, bk. II, chaps. VI and VIII.
[2] Senior, *Three Lectures on the Cost of Obtaining Money* (1830), p. 28; *Three
Lectures on the Transmission of the Precious Metals* (1830), pp. 93–4. Cf. Malthus,
Essay, II, p. 174.

but such an outcome is unusual, despite 'the apparent un-healthiness of many of their occupations [and] the atmosphere of smoke and steam in which they labour for seventy-two hours a week', as is shown by the fact that the expectation of life in England is above that of the 'lightly-toiled inhabitants of the most favoured soils and climates', and still rising. This striking inconsistency is probably due to Senior's concern at the English labourers' propensity to dissipate their surplus earnings on idleness and debauchery.

> When wages are high, they work fewer hours and inhabit better houses; and, if there still remain a superfluity the women and girls waste it in dress, and the men in drink or luxurious living. When wages fall, they endeavour to in-crease their earnings by more assiduous labour, and to econo-mize, first in house-rent, then in dress, then in fuel, and ultimately in food. When their earnings become insufficient for a maintenance, they throw themselves on the parish. The virtue of which they possess the least is providence.[1]

Neither Malthus nor James Mill, nor yet Ricardo, was an un-qualified advocate of high wages, though in general they assumed that slowly rising wages would be accompanied by improved habits and higher productivity. McCulloch, however, unhesitatingly denounced the 'common and hackneyed com-plaint, which the interested views of the master manufacturers, and fanatical declamation, have contributed to make too much believed' that high wages encouraged riot and debauchery, and were therefore harmful to the workers and to the State. On the contrary, he declared, in words reminiscent of the eighteenth-century economist, Malachy Postlethwayt:

> High wages are only advantageous because of the increased comforts they bring along with them; and of these, an addi-

[1] Senior, *Three Lectures on the Rate of Wages* (1830), pp. 52, 16–17; 'Grounds and Objects of the Budget', p. 505; 'Poor Law Reform', *Edin. Rev.*, vol. CXLIX (1841), p. 3; *Introductory Lecture on Political Economy* (1827), p. 12. For inconsistent statements by Senior, cf., *Outline of . . . Political Economy*, p. 55, and Levy, *Industrial Efficiency*, II, p. 298.

tion to the time which may be devoted to the purposes of amusement, is certainly not one of the least. Whenever wages are high, and little subject to fluctuation, the labourers are found to be active, intelligent and industrious. But they do not prosecute their employment with the same intensity as those who are obliged, by the pressure of the severest necessity, to strain every nerve to the utmost. They are enabled to enjoy their intervals of ease and relaxation; and they would be censurable if they did not enjoy them.[1]

Malthus, too, agreed that indolence might be advantageous under certain circumstances if, by restricting labour productivity when the demand for labour was ample, it checked an incipient tendency for wages to fall, while Ricardo on one occasion undermined the general classical attitude towards industriousness by admitting that the indolent labourer might be happier than his hard-working counterpart, provided that he had enough to eat.[2]

Whatever the effect of high wages on the effort of labour, the classical economists fully appreciated that high money wages did not necessarily mean high labour costs per unit of output. Senior contended that the Englishman's superior productivity was due to the growth of our population, the variety of wants, and our greater 'powers of production', while Torrens drew attention to our mechanical inventions, our superior manual dexterity and skill, and our more productive coal-mines. In the 1840s, however, Torrens painted a gloomy picture of the decline of our comparative advantages owing to diminishing returns in agriculture, the Corn Laws, and the tendency of the powers of production to outgrow 'the field of employment' – presenting a kind of stagnation thesis associated with his advocacy of colonization.[3] De Quincey also feared for the

---

[1] McCulloch, *Principles*, pp. 93–4; *Essay on Reducing the Interest*, pp. 133–4; cf., 'Effects of Machinery on Accumulation', *Edin. Rev.*, vol. LXIX (1821), pp. 105–6. Also Malthus, *Essay*, II, pp. 45, 215, 255; and *Ricardo's Works*, VI, p. 225; James Mill, *Elements*, pp. 242–3, 245.

[2] Malthus, 'Newenham and Others on the State of Ireland', *Edin. Rev.*, vol. XXIV (1808), p. 341; Sraffa, *Ricardo's Works*, VIII, p. 185.

[3] Torrens, *The Budget*, pp. 234, 288.

English labourer who, he argued, was facing the triple threat of Irish competition, machinery, and child labour. Only a determined adherence to 'the high standard of comfort inherited from his English ancestors' could protect him from experiencing 'the very basest human degradation ever witnessed amongst oriental slaves'.[1]

Before about 1830 the tendency of population to outstrip the means of subsistence seemed to be the most serious threat to the labourer's standard of living, and against this threat the economists had little better to offer than the removal of impediments to capital accumulation and the advocacy of moral restraint on the part of the labouring classes. No part of classical doctrine has aroused more hostility (either at the time or since) than the advocacy of moral restraint, and it is therefore important to recognize that Malthus, who introduced the concept, distinguished carefully between moral restraint and prudence. While both entailed the postponement of marriage until the parties concerned could afford to support a family, the former also required chastity before marriage and was an ideal – one that has aptly been said to belong more to a sermon than to political economy.[2]

As Malthus himself recognized, moral restraint was unlikely to be achieved in practice. Prudence, on the other hand, was not only attainable: at home it was the main cause of 'a degree of happiness, superior to what could be expected from the soil and climate', while in Europe it was both increasing and likely to continue to increase in the future. Habits of prudential restraint were usually due to the custom of enjoying conveniences and comforts, although liberty, security of property, and the diffusion of knowledge played a contributory role.[3] Given a decent standard of living, the labourer was unlikely to propagate his species without regard to the consequences, which helps to explain the classical economists' desire to prevent real wages from falling. But here, too, apart from the level of real income,

---

[1] De Quincey, *Logic of Political Economy*, pp. 147–8.
[2] Kenneth Smith, *The Malthusian Controversy* (1951), p. 42. Cf. Malthus, 'Godwin on Malthus', *Edin. Rev.*, vol. LXX (1821), p. 373.
[3] Malthus, *Essay*, I, pp. 236, 315; II, pp. 168, 175, 208, 257.

social considerations such as 'the desire to be thought respectable' played an important role. According to Senior:

> Want of actual necessaries is seldom apprehended by any except the poorest classes in any country. And in England, though it is sometimes felt, it probably is anticipated by none. When an Englishman stands hesitating between love and prudence, a family really starving is not among his terrors. Against actual want he knows that he has the fence of the poor laws. But, however humble his desires, he cannot contemplate, without anxiety, a probability that the income which supported his social rank while single, may be insufficient to maintain that when he is married; that he may be unable to give his children the advantages of education which he enjoys himself; in short, that he may lose his caste.[1]

Underlying their reliance on the prudential check was the classical economists' dedication to the principle of individual freedom, their firm belief in the labourer's capacity for self-improvement without the intervention of any external agency – whether autocratic, paternalistic, or philanthropic, and their conviction that co-operation between the various social classes and ranks was both possible and desirable. The future of the labouring classes, and of society in general, depended on a kind of co-partnership between the well-to-do and the poor, in which the former provided an appropriate framework of laws and a rate of savings and capital accumulation sufficient to ensure a high demand for labour, and the latter – being the more numerous class – exercised a proper degree of restraint over the growth of numbers.[2] However unjust it might seem, postponement of marriage was less necessary among the middle and upper classes, who could afford to bear the costs of their own imprudence. But it is worth mentioning that Ricardo, Malthus, and James Mill had between them a total of twenty children, and the joy with which each new arrival was recorded in

---

[1] Senior, *Lectures on Population*, pp. 26–7; *Outline of Political Economy*, p. 38. Cf. Malthus, *Essay*, I, pp. 12–13.

[2] But while population pressure was an immediate problem, capital accumulation was viewed as a slow process. See R. D. Collison Black, *Economic Thought and the Irish Question 1817–1870* (1960), p. 86 n.

Ricardo's correspondence was not unmixed with feelings of irresponsibility – even though it never produced a response like that of Francis Place, who said of a group of his utilitarian friends: 'mustering among us no less, I believe, than 36 children, rare fellows we to teach moral restraint'.[1]

Despite the grave shortcomings of Malthus's proposals, they were well intentioned, for he ardently wished to protect domestic happiness from the misery of poverty caused by overpopulation. Similarly, his stern opposition to parochial aid stemmed from his conviction that it would destroy the precious ties of parental affection and responsibility. But as he insisted that the labourer should normally support his own children, the wisdom and timing of the labourer's decision to marry became matters of great importance, and this decision was presumed to depend on the bridegroom's estimate that 'he is in a capacity to support the children that he may reasonably expect from his marriage'.[2] Even if the labourer possessed what a modern economist has called an irrational passion for dispassionate calculation, the task of estimating his probable family income and expenditure in the foreseeable future would tax the ingenuity of a trained economic forecaster, if only because of the irregularity of his prospective employment and earnings. Beyond this, however, the labourer would need to calculate his prospective progenitiveness, for Malthus ruled out contraception, and evidently assumed that the happy couple would abandon all restraint once the period of pre-marital abstinence was over.[3]

Malthus was not entirely unaware of the difficulties facing those 'who had a greater number of children than they could be

---

[1] Cited by James Arthur Field, *Essays on Population* (1931), pp. 110–11.

[2] Malthus, *Essay*, II, pp. 169, 243; on domestic happiness and parental responsibility, ibid., pp. 204–6. Malthus believed that restraint increased the force of the 'passion between the sexes', but also raised its quality and hence represented a civilizing influence. Ibid., p. 156.

[3] McCulloch ridiculed Sismondi's proposal that all classes should marry freely, but live in a state of continence after producing two or three children. McCulloch to Ricardo, 18 April 1819; *Ricardo's Works*, VIII, p. 25. On contraception see James Mill, 'Colony' in *Encyclopaedia Britannica* (1818), pp. 12–13; also Eversley, *Social Theories of Fertility*, pp. 156–7; Field, *Essays on Population*, pp. 94, 125–6. Only James Mill seriously contemplated contraception as a possible solution.

expected to foresee', and in the second and subsequent editions of his *Essay*, he advocated the payment of allowances for every child in excess of six, a concession that stands as a notable exception to his usual hostility to State aid for the imprudent.[1] Senior also acknowledged that it was virtually impossible in practice to demonstrate that any given marriage was improvident, because of the potential earning power of wives and children.

A girl of 18 can attend to a power loom as well as a full-grown man; a child of 13 is more valuable as a piecer than an adult – its touch is more sensitive, and its sight is more acute. A factory lad of 18 who marries a factory girl of the same age, finds himself immediately richer; and although he may be pinched during some of the following years, yet as each child attains the age of 9 years it can earn more than its support; and the earnings of 3 children between the ages of 9 and 16 can, in prosperous times, support the whole family. It was under the influence of this enormous stimulus, with some assistance from immigration, that the population of our manufacturing districts increased during the thirty years that elapsed between 1801 and 1831 – the last period for which returns are published – at a rate equalled only in some portions of America.[2]

Thus, despite their serious lack of insight into the labourer's mind and situation, the classical economists were not wholly unconscious of the practical difficulties facing a labourer who endeavoured to decide when he was able to support a family, although they clearly underestimated them. As time passed and their fears of the effects of population growth diminished, the matter came to occupy a less prominent place in their writings, although they never abandoned their insistence on the virtues of prudence.

[1] Malthus, *Essay*, II, pp. 254–5.
[2] Senior, 'Grounds and Objects of the Budget', p. 506.

IV

Having considered some of the psychological determinants of the economists' view of the labourer's position and prospects, we must now examine the economic determinants, and although we are not interested in theory as such, the classical theory of wages is the most suitable starting-point. This much-misunderstood theory comprised two elements: a long-term equilibrium 'natural' or 'necessary' wage rate, and a series of short-term oscillations of actual or 'market' wages. The equilibrium level was believed to alter slowly from time to time and place to place according to changes in the supply and demand for labour; but for the sake of analytical simplicity it was usually treated as a minimum governed by 'the absolutely necessary subsistence, demanded by the customs of the people for the maintenance of their life and the propagation of the race'.[1] The classical economists had no illusions about the adequacy of this long-term wage rate; though significantly higher in England than in Ireland or on the Continent, it was variously described as 'a miserable pittance', a sum insufficient to permit the labourer 'to economize to any extent', and an amount 'everywhere much too low for human happiness and dignity' – to select a few typical statements.[2] It is, however, essential to appreciate that this minimum was defined not in physiological terms, as a sum just sufficient for survival, but in *social* terms, as a customary or habitual minimum; and as Schumpeter observed, this 'social minimum of existence theorem' virtually amounted to accepting customary wages as an institutional datum, and abandoning the attempt at a purely *economic* explanation of the

[1] Michael Theodore Wermel, *The Evolution of the Classical Wage Theory* (1939), p. 162. The minimum equilibrium wage rate represented the base of a structure of wage rates that varied according to skill, length of training, unpleasantness, etc. Torrens also specified a 'moral and necessary maximum of wages'. See *On Wages and Combination*, p. 8; *The Budget*, pp. 107–8.

[2] For passing references to factors encouraging increased productivity, which usually conflicted with the customary assumption that habits changed only slowly, see McCulloch, *Outlines of Political Economy*, p. 64, and *Historical Sketch of the Bank of England* (1831), p. 40; Senior, 'Report on the State of Agriculture', *Quarterly Review*, vol. XXV (1821), p. 485, and *Introductory Lecture on Political Economy*, p. 12.

wage level.[1] Non-economic factors, such as liberty, security of property, and a taste for the comforts and conveniences of life, contributed to raise this level, while despotism and ignorance lowered it; and the object of policy should be to encourage a spirit of independence, pride, and a taste for cleanliness and comfort among the poor.[2] Beyond this, however, the classical economists made few constructive proposals designed to increase labour incentives or to create wants[3] – largely because they assumed that wants were virtually unlimited among non-pauperized labourers in advanced economies, and that given a minimum standard of living the labourer's desire to better his condition would more than counteract his distaste for hard work. Although the labourers as a class could not directly influence the demand for their services – which was governed mainly by the rate of profit and the quantity of capital – they could protect their accustomed living standards whenever wages fell temporarily by restricting the labour supply by postponement of marriage. This, of course, explains the importance which the classical economists attached to the prudential check. But this remedy obviously had grave limitations: its effects were delayed, it was no help at all to a married man with a large family, and self-restraint on the part of a couple contemplating marriage could make no perceptible difference to the aggregate labour supply. But the classical economists could offer no better solution, for they were desperately anxious to preserve the

---

[1] Joseph A. Schumpeter, *History of Economic Analysis* (1954), pp. 664–5.

[2] Malthus, *Essay*, II, p. 215.

[3] For example, McCulloch remarked that once the practice of exchange is introduced 'a spirit of industry is universally diffused, and the apathy and languor of the rude state of society disappears'. *Outlines of Political Economy*, p. 64. Senior maintained that an increase in the supply of corn 'will produce immediately an improvement of habits and, if permanent, an increase of numbers of the labouring part of the population', 'Report on the State of Agriculture', *Quarterly Review*, vol. XXV (1821), p. 485; and elsewhere Senior claimed that 'as soon as he begins to save, a labourer becomes sober and industrious, attentive to his health and to his character . . . no institution could be more beneficial to the morals of the lower orders, i.e. to at least nine-tenths of the whole body of any people, than one that should increase their power and their wish to accumulate', *Introductory Lecture on Political Economy*, p. 12. Cf. McCulloch, *Historical Sketch of the Bank of England* (1831), p. 40. These quotations conflict with the usual classical view that the labourer's habits changed only slowly.

labourer's sense of independence and personal responsibility, and so they flatly opposed legal restraints or taxes on marriage such as existed in other European countries.

The prospects of control over the ratio between population and subsistence obviously depended on the speed with which population responded to changes in the demand for labour. If population increased rapidly when real wages rose, the numbers seeking employment would increase and money wage rates would fall as the competition for jobs became more intense. On the other hand, if the workers readily acquired a taste for additional comforts and conveniences when real wages rose, and if population changed only after a considerable time-lag, then the labourers' conception of the socially acceptable minimum standard would rise and a new and higher equilibrium level of real wages would be established. Unfortunately the classical economists were neither unanimous nor individually consistent in their treatment of this possibility, and it is all too easy to judge them by casual remarks divorced from their context. On the whole, Malthus, Ricardo, Torrens, and the two Mills regarded population growth as a serious obstacle to any permanent rise in real wages. Yet Malthus, for instance, denied that changes in real wages were the principal determinants of population change, acknowledged that there was a considerable time-lag between a rise in marriage rates and an increase in the labour supply, and in the later editions of his *Essay* placed considerable emphasis on the effectiveness of the prudential check.[1] Senior, De Quincey, and McCulloch (who periodically protested at what he called Malthus's 'mechanical theorem') also regarded the adjustment of population to changes in real wage rates as a protracted process, and considered that Malthus had exaggerated the dangers of population growth.[2] Senior 'utterly

---

[1] Malthus, *Essay*, II, pp. 139, 257; *Principles of Political Economy* (1836), pp. 257, 280. On the other hand, Malthus's discussion of emigration schemes reveals his conviction that the 'population vacuum' would rapidly be refilled. See R. N. Ghosh, 'Malthus on Emigration and Colonization', *Economica*, N.S. vol. XXX (1963), esp. pp. 53–4.

[2] For example, Senior, *Outline of Political Economy*, pp. 43–8; and *Two Lectures on Population*, pp. 68–90; but cf. his earlier opinion, 'Report on the State of Agriculture', p. 484. McCulloch, *Principles*, p. 182; 'Chalmers on Political

repudiated' the view that the natural rate of wages would be held down to the minimum level of subsistence, and denied that in every trade there was a stratum of workers whose ordinary wages were only equal to their necessary expenses.[1] Most of the classical economists assumed that the habits of the labouring classes changed only slowly over time, and they regarded this as both an obstacle to the reform of an impoverished and imprudent people such as the Irish and a safeguard against a deterioration of the customary standard in England when a temporary fall in real wages occurred. On the other hand, variations in the labour supply were not solely determined by changes in the number of marriages and births, for irregularity of the seasons also played a part. Despite evidence produced before the House of Commons, McCulloch insisted that money wages tended to fall in years of high prices because

> an increased number of females, and such poor children of both sexes as are fit to work, are obliged to quit their homes, or to engage in some species of employment; while those labourers who work by the piece, endeavour, by increasing the quantity of their work, to obtain the means of purchasing a greater quantity of food. It is natural, therefore, that the *immediate* effect of a rise of prices, should be to lower, not to raise the rate of wages.[2]

One important source of misunderstanding of the classical view of wages is the term 'subsistence', which was rarely defined with precision. Senior, for example, carefully distinguished between 'necessaries', 'conveniences', and 'luxuries', but admitted that the components of each category were liable to change, and added that the classification of any given commodity depended on the time, the place, the habits, and the

---

Economy', *Edin. Rev.*, vol. CXI (1832), p. 56; and *An Article . . . On Taxation*, pp. 13–14; De Quincey, *Logic of Political Economy*, p. 150. Torrens, *On Wages and Combination*, p. 28. It was recognized that the effects of sudden changes in real income differed from those of more gradual changes, and this is a further reason why it is risky to summarize the classical view.

[1] Letter to Archbishop Whately, 20 March 1845, cited by Levy, *Industrial Efficiency*, II, p. 26.

[2] McCulloch, *Principles*, p. 180.

social rank of the individual consumer.[1] James Mill included 'something for enjoyment' in the category of 'necessities', and it was invariably assumed that the English labourer's normal subsistence included some non-essentials.[2] The terms 'corn' and 'subsistence' were often used interchangeably, partly because theoretical analysis was greatly simplified by ignoring price variations between different commodities. But the distinction had important policy implications, as noted by De Quincey, who complained in 1844 that the 'corn law incendiaries' endeavoured to win converts to the anti-corn-law camp by claiming that a 10 per cent change in wheat prices was equivalent to a 10 per cent change in wages, though in other parts of their writings they denied that wages 'at all sympathize with the price of food'. Ricardo himself, whom De Quincey warmly admired, was responsible for this error.

Yet if Ricardo were right in supposing a labourer to spend half his wages upon wheat only, then his beer, bacon, cheese, milk, butter, tea, and sugar, must proportionably cost, at the very least, all the rest of his wages; so that for clothes, lodging, fuel, to say nothing of other miscellanies, he would have no provision at all. But these are romantic estimates, and pardonable in Ricardo from his city life, which had denied him, until his latest years, all opportunities of studying the life of labourers.[3]

Although they were unable to make reliable general statistical estimates of the prices and quantities of goods consumed by the labourer and his family, the economists were well aware of the variety of components of the labourer's budget. Wheat, bread, cheese, beer, porter, sugar, tea, beef, and bacon were

---

[1] Senior, *Two Lectures on Population*, pp. 3–6; *Outline of Political Economy*, pp. 36–7. He believed that fear of losing the 'decencies' of life was an effective check to population growth, whereas fear of losing 'necessaries' was not, at least in England. Cf. Eversley, op. cit., p. 93.

[2] James Mill, *Elements*, p. 220. Torrens and James Mill believed that the labourers could not afford to pay taxes on 'necessaries', as they had no surplus income; but McCulloch, Senior, and J. S. Mill disagreed. For Ricardo's position see Carl S. Shoup, *Ricardo on Taxation* (1960), pp. 65–77.

[3] De Quincey, *Logic of Political Economy*, p. 153.

among the foodstuffs most commonly mentioned as the English labourer's 'necessaries', while garden vegetables, fresh butter, veal, and lamb were included among the 'agricultural luxuries'.[1] Inter-regional and international dietary comparisons were common, and it was persistently emphasized that any tendency to substitute inferior for superior foodstuffs, such as potatoes for bread, would be highly undesirable, because the inferior goods allowed less scope for retrenchment in time of dearth and because an inferior diet might become 'congenial from habit' and would then be accompanied by a fall in the labourer's economic and social aspirations, his capacity and his desire for work.[2] The importance of expenditure on non-foodstuffs was recognized, but was never subjected to systematic study.[3]

Among the principal short-term influences on the labourer's earnings, the classical economists listed irregularity of the seasons, the caprices of fashion, domestic commotions, and policy changes at home and abroad. They recognized that time-lags occurred between price changes and movements of wages, and that in the interim some labourers and their families might either be thrown on the parish or, alternatively, might dissipate any windfall gains in idleness and luxury. The relationship between wages and 'subsistence' – i.e. the prices of those commodities that constituted the labourer's customary purchases – was held to be close, but neither direct nor exact, and Senior aptly depicted the classical view by describing the belief that wages were determined by the price of corn as a 'falsism', since it was either true or false according to the circumstances.[4] The differential effects on mortality of a *series* of bad harvests as against a particular year of dearth were fully acknowledged, and in times of extreme distress the classical economists dis-

---

[1] For example, Torrens, *The Budget*, pp. 183–4.

[2] McCulloch even suggested that the workers' taste for gin and tobacco helped to elevate their conception of an appropriate standard of living, and that without it their wages would fall. *Treatise on Wages*, pp. 40–1.

[3] See W. D. Grampp, 'Malthus on Money Wages and Welfare', *American Economic Review*, vol. XLVI (1956), pp. 924–36; and Eversley, op. cit., p. 211, for interesting comments on this matter.

[4] Senior, 'The Budget of 1842', *Edin. Rev.*, vol. CLI (1842), p. 197. Cf. Grampp, op. cit., *passim*.

played a surprising readiness to waive their usual objections to State aid for the needy. On the whole, they regarded stable or slowly rising real wages as the optimum state of affairs, arguing that the equilibrium level should be high enough to provide an incentive to effort and to enable the labourer to accumulate a reserve for unforeseen contingencies.[1]

Although their theoretical reasoning was based on the assumption that factors of production were highly mobile and that wage differentials in any given place or occupation would be speedily eliminated by the process of competition, unless checked by monopolistic action or legal restraint, the classical economists frequently discussed wage differentials between occupations, places, skills, and sexes. McCulloch claimed that 'the difference of a half or more, between the price of labour, etc. in the remote counties, and London and its vicinity' which had been noted by Adam Smith, had largely disappeared by 1820; but Senior regarded ignorance and inertia as significant obstacles to mobility, and asserted that between town and country, and between different regions, the differences 'in occupations, in wages, in habits, in wants, and in morals' were as great as between Paris and Berlin – a view that was fully echoed in McCulloch's writings.[2] More interesting, perhaps, was their disagreement about occupational mobility within the more advanced sectors of the economy. According to McCulloch,

a person who has been trained to habits of industry and application, can easily be moved from one employment to another. The various subordinate branches of all the great departments of industry have so many things in common, that an individual who has attained to any considerable proficiency in one, has seldom much difficulty in attaining to a like proficiency in any other;

---

[1] Although Ricardo disapproved of the Gloucestershire practice of maintaining wage rates in periods of slack business (*Ricardo's Works*, VIII, p. 316), several of the classical economists supported State aid or intervention in times of acute distress to protect the labourer from a fall in his customary living standards.

[2] McCulloch, *Essay on Reducing the Interest*, pp. 9–10; Senior, 'Poor Law Reform', p. 40; also *Three Lectures on the Rate of Wages*, p. 14.

whereas Senior held that

> British workmen, and more especially the most numerous
> classes, those employed in manufactures, resemble the com-
> ponent parts of the vast machine which they direct. Separately
> taken, they are as useless as a single wheel or a single roller.
> Combined with many hundreds or many thousands of others,
> each helpless when alone, a hundred families can produce
> results which could not have been obtained by the individual
> labour of a thousand.

Consequently, once the motive power animating this great
machine ceased, the component parts lost their value–'the engine
becomes old iron, the spinners and weavers become paupers'.[1]

The workers' readiness to emigrate, given unfavourable
conditions at home and a modest subsidy or other inducement
to move, was the subject of extensive debate,[2] while the
differential between the real incomes of single and married
labourers was repeatedly referred to in discussions of the poor
relief system. Ricardo, who assumed that the average current
wage rate was too low to enable the married labourer to pay
taxes without public assistance, denied that the single man
enjoyed a surplus that encouraged him to live in an extravagant
manner. According to Torrens, the unmarried labourer in an
old and settled country had sufficient income 'to purchase the
finer manufactured goods, and the articles of convenience and
luxury, which have fallen in value as compared with the necessaries of life'; but added that a large family 'deprives the working man of the ease, the comfort, and independence which he
enjoys in the single state' – and consequently the marriage rate
tended to fall as a country approached the limit of its resources.[3]
In general, however, the earnings of women and children were
believed to encourage improvident marriages and large families.
Married women were described as good earners but bad

---

[1] McCulloch, 'Effects of Machinery on Accumulation', p. 115; Senior,
'Grounds and Objects of the Budget', pp. 504–5.

[2] Donald Winch, *Classical Political Economy and Colonies* (1965), chap. 5.

[3] *Ricardo's Works*, VIII, pp. 117–18, 124. Torrens, *On Wages and Combination*,
pp. 29–30. The implications of this remark for the Malthusian view need not be
stressed.

mothers, and children's employment was said to undercut the wages of adults, preventing them from obtaining education, and even diminishing the parents' industriousness.[1] But it was appreciated that the opportunities for family earnings were by no means uniform.

> The earnings of the wife and child of many a Manchester weaver or spinner exceed, or equal, those of himself. Those of the wife and children of an agricultural labourer, or of a carpenter, or coalheaver, are generally unimportant – while the husbands, in each case, receive 15 shillings a week, the weekly income of the one family may be 40 shillings, and that of the other only 17 shillings or 18 shillings.[2]

As might be expected from their insistence on the need to provide incentives to effort, there were occasional references to the desirability of piece-rate payments, a system which, McCulloch claimed, had been 'generally adopted' in Great Britain wherever practicable, because it

> gives the workmen an interest in being industrious; and makes them exert themselves to execute the greatest quantity of work in the least space of time. And in consequence of its prevalence, this practice materially influences even the day labourers, who, to avoid invidious comparisons, make exertions unknown in other countries.

The introduction of piece-rate payments in agriculture, he remarked a few years earlier, had emancipated the agricultural labourers from their former dependence on the farmer under the traditional hiring system.[3]

V

Both conceptually and chronologically, the classical economists represent an intermediate stage between the eighteenth-century

---

[1] McCulloch, *Treatises and Essays on Money, Exchange, Interest, etc.* (1859), pp. 457–8; *Treatise on Wages*, p. 96; 'Taxation and the Corn Laws', *Edin. Rev.*, vol. LXV (1820), p. 169; Malthus, 'Godwin on Malthus', p. 373.

[2] Senior, *Outline of Political Economy*, p. 148.

[3] McCulloch, *Statistical Account*, I, p. 619; *Observations on the State of the Country*, p. 9.

belief in the harmony of interests and the Marxian idea of class conflict, and they left it to others to draw socialistic conclusions from Ricardo's doctrine, because they broadly accepted the social system of their day, and were under the influence of inherited ideas of economic and social progress. During the early years of the century, it is true, the omnipresent fear of rising population darkened future prospects; but as time passed the once inexorable Malthusian 'law' was translated into a 'tendency' that was being counteracted by the advance of wealth, prudence, and civilization. The strain of optimism was never unqualified, for it was still true at the mid-century that the Malthusian doctrine conflicted with 'those plans of easy beneficence which accord so well with the inclination of man, but so ill with the arrangements of nature'.[1] Pouring cold water on revolutionary or utopian proposals for reform was part of the classical economists' essential function as social scientists, and whenever they argued that the removal of long-established evils could not be accomplished without considerable suffering, their warnings stemmed from realism rather than from hard-heartedness. Senior may have been tragically wrong when he maintained that 'what are called severity and hardness in the administration of relief are by far the best things for the welfare of the labouring classes';[2] but, like his eighteenth-century predecessors, he was anxious to discourage misplaced sentimentalism and ill-judged philanthropy which had long bedevilled the efforts of Poor Law reformers. As it transpired, for all their shortcomings, Senior and his ardent Benthamite collaborator Edwin Chadwick helped to lay the foundations of an administrative revolution which provided an essential starting-point for subsequent social services;[3] and although the classical economists undoubtedly carried their belief in uniform-

---

[1] J. S. Mill, 'The Claims of Labour', pp. 501–2.

[2] Senior, *House of Lords Select Committee on the Burdens Affecting Real Property* (1846), p. 470. There is an almost exact parallel between the economists' desire to protect the pecuniary capital of the rich and their concern for the 'intellectual and moral capital' of the poor. In this respect they anticipate recent interest in the role of 'human capital' in economic development.

[3] See, for example, S. E. Finer, *The Life and Times of Sir Edwin Chadwick* (1952), *passim*; and Marian Bowley, *Nassau Senior and Classical Economics* (1937), part II.

ity and system too far, historians have generally undervalued this aspect of their influence while exaggerating the rigidity with which they adhered to their fundamental economic principles.

As the preceding pages have shown, the classical principles were capable of considerable modification and adaptation to changing circumstances – so much so, indeed, that the presentation of a brief summary of classical opinion on any important question is a hazardous undertaking. The influence of popularizers like Jane Marcet, Harriet Martineau, and James Wilson of the London *Economist*,[1] who drew their authority from Ricardo and his followers, was so pervasive that it has taken a generation of scholarship to dispel the widespread view that the classical economists were dogmatic proponents of laissez-faire. They were, of course, generally sceptical of the value of State interference – albeit with substantial justification, considering the governmental and financial facts of contemporary life – and their influence was, in a number of specific instances, distinctly obstructive. But no serious historian will nowadays argue that either they or their ideas presented 'a solid obstacle to all plans of social reform',[2] for they were themselves essentially reformers of a piecemeal and moderate type, and were increasingly prepared to grant exceptions to the principle of non-intervention in response to the changing facts of economic and social life.

As far as the labourer was concerned, they firmly believed that his lot could and should be improved; and when Torrens claimed that political economy merited

> the peculiar attention of the benevolent and good, mainly because it explains the causes which depress and elevate wages, and thereby points out the means by which we may mitigate the distress, and improve the condition of the great majority of mankind,[3]

he was merely stating in unusually naïve terms a belief that was generally accepted by members of his group.

[1] See especially, Blaug, *Ricardian Economics,* chap. VII; and Scott Gordon, 'The London *Economist* and the High Tide of Laissez-Faire', *Journal of Political Economy*, vol. LXIII (1955), pp. 461–88.

[2] J. L. and Barbara Hammond, *The Town Labourer, 1760–1832* (1925), p. 196.

[3] Torrens, *On Wages and Combination*, pp. 1–2.

By themselves, good intentions count for little, and the classical economists' belief in the natural operation of economic forces and their insistence on the values of individual freedom and the rights of private property undoubtedly prevented them from seriously considering some feasible proposals for reform. No twentieth-century student of industrialization will argue that they possessed either an adequate knowledge of the facts or a sufficient understanding of the labourer's needs and desires. All too often their analysis was influenced by their middle-class preconceptions and prejudices, while their policy proposals as often reflected their aspirations as the practical possibilities of reform. But if their attitude to the lower orders was deficient in subtlety and sensitivity, it was neither hostile nor unsympathetic. They did not fully appreciate the richness and variety of the individuals and groups that comprised the labouring classes; but neither did they homogenize the masses into a conceptual monolith – 'the working class', as some overenthusiastic labour historians are inclined to do. They certainly failed to enter into the minds of the unskilled and casual labourers, who formed a large proportion of the wage-earning population, or, at least in the short run, to win the intellectual support of a majority of workers.[1]

Nevertheless, for the most part, they endeavoured to enlist the workers as accessories to reform.[2] Taking nineteenth-century British history as a whole, the classical economists were not far wrong when they assumed that the labouring classes would readily seize any opportunities to adopt middle-class attitudes, standards, and patterns of behaviour.

A note on sources

For the purposes of this essay, 'classical economics' means the economic writings, speeches, official evidence, and correspondence of A. Smith, J. Bentham, T. R. Malthus, D. Ricardo, J. Mill, R. Torrens, E. West, T. De Quincey, J. R. McCulloch, N. W. Senior, and J. S. Mill. The article deals only with the

---

[1] Cf. R. K. Webb, *The British Working Class Reader, 1790–1848* (1955), pp. 97 ff.
[2] Thompson, *The Making of the English Working Class*, p. 139, with special reference to Francis Place.

period 1800–48, because Smith's ideas are well known (see, for example, my articles in the *Economic History Review*, 2nd ser., vol. XI, 1958–9, and vol. XIII, 1960–1, and *Renaissance and Modern Studies* (Nottingham, 1962) and because there are few comments on the labourer in *Bentham's Economic Writings*, ed. W. Stark (1952–4). J. S. Mill's views changed so significantly after 1848, and in ways so intimately bound up with his opinions on non-economic issues, that they merit separate treatment. There is indeed some justice in Marx's jibe that he was 'perfectly at home in the domain of flat contradiction'.

Attention has been concentrated on published material, but this represents a large portion of the total extant, and within the selected period the coverage has been wide, though incomplete. For authorship of the numerous unsigned reviews see F. W. Fetter's articles in the *Journal of Political Economy*, 1953, 1958, and 1962; and the *Scottish Journal of Political Economy*, 1960. Dr Donald Winch generously lent me, in advance of publication, his edition of *James Mill, Selected Economic Writings* (1966), and I am also grateful for comments on an earlier draft by Mr M. Caplan, Dr D. P. O'Brien, and Professor S. Pollard.

7 The Ideology of Laissez-Faire[1]

H. SCOTT GORDON

I ECONOMIC POLICY IN THE AGE OF CLASSICAL POLITICAL ECONOMY

During the hey-day of Classical Political Economy, was there a laissez-faire ideology at work which guided the policy decisions of Parliament and government? Certainly there is no doubt that a strong current of liberalization of economic activity was in motion even by the time Adam Smith published *The Wealth of Nations*. Wesley C. Mitchell pointed out[2] as a notable fact that this trend was not reversed even by the national crisis of the Napoleonic wars. Britain did not revert to a policy of mercantilistic regulation under the stress of what was, for the time, 'total' war, but allowed economic activity to operate under the degree of freedom from economic regulation it had acquired. This might be viewed as evidence of the strength of laissez-faire ideology, but no one who writes of the existence of such a doctrine of economic policy dates it as established as early as this and, moreover, it is implausible that any abstract doctrine could have stood in the way of state mobilization of the economy in the service of national survival under the conditions of intense fear of the French which prevailed at the time. It is more plausible to interpret the policy stance of the British Government in this period as indicating that, by this time, few men of influence viewed the older types of intervention as efficient. These interventions, as Adam Smith had intended, had become typed as special-interest legislation which, if anything, must needs be sacrificed for the national cause in time of war.

With the onset of peace, the current of liberalization resumed

---

[2] W. C. Mitchell, *Types of Economic Theory* (New York, Kelley, 1967), vol. I, p. 180.

and quickened. The second and third decades of the century witnessed a great and almost continuous freeing of economic activity from state regulation.[1] Clearly Britain was now embarked upon a new approach in her economic policy. But this trend does not, in itself, prove the existence of a guiding economic ideology, such as laissez-faire is supposed to have been. It is evidence to be sure, but only prima facie, not conclusive – sufficient to justify an indictment, but not a verdict. To reiterate the terms of reference of this essay: the acts of policy necessary to demonstrate a functioning ideology of laissez-faire are acts which sprang from and were justified by laissez-faire as a first principle.

Again, there is no lack of accusers, both contemporary and retrospective, giving witness to the dominance of ideology over reason and humanity in the economic policies of Westminster and Whitehall in the Victorian Age. But, again, upon examination the issue becomes replete with ambiguity. To illustrate this, I would like to draw attention here to passages from two notable contemporary authors, Charles Kingsley and Samuel Smiles, two men whose political philosophy and reactions to the florescent industrial and commercial capitalism of their time could not have been more divergent.

Kingsley was one of the founders of the school of 'Christian Socialism', the first radical movement to penetrate significantly into one of the established estates of the realm, the Church of England. He was a radical activist both inside the Church itself and outside in workingmen's movements and associations. He wrote voluminously on social questions in essays, letters, poetry, and fiction. Literary scholars remember him more today as the one who goaded John Henry Newman, upon the latter's apostasy, into writing his great *Apologia pro Vita Sua*, than for his own creations. But he was an exceedingly popular author in his own day and some of his fiction is still read for enjoyment by young people. His most important social novel *Alton Locke* (1850) is now forgotten by all but scholars, but it was a best seller (in both England and America) when first published. As

---

[1] S. G. Checkland, *The Rise of Industrial Society in England, 1815–1885* (London, Longmans, 1964), chap. 9.

a story, it was a real Victorian tear-jerker. Alton Locke is a poor lad, apprenticed to a sweatshop tailor, but he thirsts for learning and beauty and begins to read books. He is befriended by an old Scots bookseller of radical views who guides his education. He writes poetry, which brings him to the notice of some members of the upper classes and clergy who aid in the publication of his poems, though not without some political expurgation, as he later deeply regrets. Of course he falls in love with a beautiful girl of this class, and equally 'of course' it is impossible that his love should be requited. He becomes a Chartist, is involved in a riot, and is imprisoned. Later he takes part in the great Chartist agitation of 1848 but emerges disillusioned. Physically ill and sick at heart, he takes a ship to America, but dies *en route*.

In the process of taking Alton Locke through this stereotyped romance, Kingsley gives some horrifying descriptions of the working conditions of the poor, and preaches the need for workingmen's associations, and the mission of the Anglican clergy to guide and spearhead the movement for social and political reform. As one might guess from the narrative skeleton of *Alton Locke*, Kingsley's democratic sympathies were, to say the least, uncertain. Miscegenation between the upper and lower classes was nearly as unthinkable as between white and black. When that great test of democratic pretensions, the trial of Governor Eyre for the judicial murder of the Negro Jamaican leader, William Gordon, came about in the 1860s, he, along with most of the other literati of the day, failed with flying colours.[1]

Kingsley was equally ambiguous towards Political Economy. He liked to regard himself as a man of scientific attitude and advanced thought; to think well of and be thought well of by the new intelligentsia. But there was much in Political Economy and the idea of laws of nature in the social sphere that he deplored. In the course of discussing the miseries of the labouring poor in *Alton Locke*, Kingsley puts these words into the mouth of Crossthwaite, a sweated needleworker:

[1] See Bernard Semmel, *The Governor Eyre Controversy* (London, McGibbon & Kee, 1962).

But you can recollect as well as I can, when a deputation of us went up to a member of Parliament – one that was reputed to be a philosopher and a political economist, and a liberal – and set before him the ever increasing penury and misery of our trade, and of those connected with it; you recollect his answer – that, however glad he would be to help us, it was impossible – he could not alter the laws of nature – that wages were regulated by the amount of competition among the men themselves, and that it was no business of government, or anyone else, to interfere in contracts between the employer and the employed, that those things regulated themselves by the laws of political economy, which it was madness and suicide to oppose.[1]

Now that seems to be plain enough, and it is a double-barrelled shot; it identifies Political Economy as the intellectual basis of laissez-faire ideology and it certifies the effective penetration of that ideology into Westminster. But if we use such a passage as an indicator of Kingsley's own view of the responsibilities of the State, we are on treacherous ground. A few years later, when bread rose in price during the Crimean War and there was threat of rioting, we find him taking a different stance. At a meeting of one of the workingmen's associations in which he was active, a member asked why the government did not adopt what he called 'Joseph's plan' – buy up grain to prevent speculation and provide fair distribution – to which Kingsley replied: 'Yes, and why ain't you and I flying about with wings and dewdrops hanging to our tails? Joseph's plan won't do for us. What minister could we trust with money enough to buy corn for the people, power to buy where he chose?' and went on to give the questioner an orthodox lecture on Political Economy.[2] The fact is, even those who castigated the State for insensitivity and inaction and deplored the theory they thought it was based upon, quailed at the prospects of intervention, when they reflected upon the character of the instrument that was to do the intervening.

[1] Charles Kingsley, *Alton Locke* (London, Macmillan, 1886), p. 112.
[2] M. Kaufmann, *Charles Kingsley* (London, Methuen, 1892), p. 181.

G

Samuel Smiles has achieved historical immortality as the very symbol of Victorian individualism. He celebrated the Calvinist bourgeois virtues in books devoted to *Self-Help* (1859), *Character* (1871), *Thrift* (1875), and *Duty* (1887). The first of these sold an astounding 20,000 copies in its first year and was translated into all the major languages of the world. (F. L. Mott's *Golden Multitudes* lists all four among 'better sellers' in the United States, meaning that not quite one American in ten bought copies.) A whole series of other books sang the praises of the great men of business and industry who, by practising these virtues had created the economic greatness which made Victoria's Britain first among the nations of the world. He even practised the virtues himself, sometimes to the despair of his family. If there is any author of the Victorian Age in which we should expect to find the government carefully examined on the question whether it was promoting self-reliance or dependence, it is in Samuel Smiles, and so we do, but note this passage from one of the books in the four virtues series:

> When typhus or cholera breaks out, they tell us that nobody is to blame.
> That terrible Nobody! How much he has to answer for! More mischief is done by Nobody than by all the world besides. Nobody adulterates our food. Nobody poisons us with bad drink. Nobody supplies us with foul water. Nobody spreads fever in blind alleys and unswept lanes. Nobody leaves towns undrained. Nobody fills jails, penitentiaries and convict stations. Nobody makes poachers, thieves and drunkards.
> Nobody has a theory, too – a dreadful theory. It is embodied in two words: Laissez-faire – Let alone. When people are poisoned by plaster of Paris mixed with flour, 'Let alone' is the remedy. When *Cocculus Indicus* is used instead of hops, and men die prematurely, it is easy to say, 'Nobody did it'. Let those who can, find out when they are cheated: *Caveat emptor*. When people live in foul dwellings, let them alone. Let wretchedness do its work; do not interfere with death.[1]

[1] Samuel Smiles, *Thrift* (Chicago, Belford Clark, 1889), pp. 358–9.

This is the most powerful anti-laissez-faire passage I have encountered in the literature of the Victorian age. It surpasses anything in Carlyle or Dickens. 'Let wretchedness do its work; do not interfere with death.' Who would not shudder to read that indictment of his social philosophy? Its date is 1875 and it *could* be pointed at Darwinism and the 'Social Darwinism' that was the monstrous offspring of the new biology. But it wasn't – its point of focus was the presumed theory of Classical Political Economy, and its presumed dominance over social and economic policy. Following this passage, we find Samuel Smiles urging that there ought to be a law, indeed a whole series of laws, about drainage, water, paving, ventilation, etc. And this from the leading apostle of Victorian self-reliance! There is no doubt that the self-help doctrine was a fundamental constituent of nineteenth-century liberalism. It is ubiquitous in the social literature of the period, regardless of the political colour of the author. There is no doubt either that the appeal of such ideas was a ready-made lever for laissez-faire propaganda.[1] But when we find the St Paul of the liberal faith exclaiming so bitterly that its tenets are excessively held and applied, we have to pause and consider whether the faith was quite as simple and straightforward and doctrinaire as we have been led to believe.

I have quoted these passages from Kingsley and Smiles because they could be used so effectively in a simpliste way if one chooses to disregard the complexities introduced by further knowledge of their sources. Read by themselves, they say that an obtuse and insensitive doctrine had entrenched itself in the bosom of the State, that government had chained itself to laissez-faire. But read with an eye to the surrounding ambiguities, passages of this sort mean something else. They testify to the inactivity of government in a purely *relative* sense – relative to the growing needs of the time. The world was changing very rapidly and the arts and acts of government were lagging behind the developments in industry and commerce. In such a situation even Samuel Smiles was urging the State to be up and doing.

[1] See J. F. C. Harrison, 'The Victorian Gospel of Success', *Victorian Studies*, vol. I (December 1957).

And, indeed, the Victorian State *was* up and doing. Its seeming sluggishness was only relative to the problems which economic change was presenting with such rapidity, and it is this gap that contemporary and retrospective observers have mistaken for ideology or torpor. But relative to what preceded it, the Victorian State was full of energy and innovation and was continuously straining against the practical boundaries set by its political and administrative capacity. W. L. Burn, in his beautiful book on the mid-century decades, remarks that some of the legislation of the period 'contained startling exceptions to the laissez-faire doctrine' over a wide field of concern.[1] But it is startling only because of the stereotype that has come down to us. If we think of Britain as the first society in the history of the world to experience the impact of industrialization, urbanization, and the replacement of communal social organization by the proletarianization of labour, our interpretation changes and we see her struggling to cope with large and novel problems. Kitson Clark has pointed out[2] that in dealing with the complex problems of a society such as Britain was becoming, the coercive powers of the State must be wielded by experts, and in ways which the general mass of the public cannot understand. The science of Political Economy sometimes yields conclusions that are astonishing to the common-sense mind, even one freed from conventional wisdoms, and the art of Public Administration is frequently arcane. The rise of a new class of professional public servants who could understand what was occurring and apply effective measures, was one of the most remarkable and most momentous developments of the Victorian age. The fact that they achieved so much, even before the movement to excise corruption and nepotism from the civil service got well under way, testifies against the existence of a controlling ideology of laissez-faire.

Among other things, the new problems required the growth of central administration. Today, especially in America, we

---

[1] W. L. Burn, *The Age of Equipoise: A Study of the Mid-Victorian Generation* (London, Allen & Unwin, 1964), p. 153.

[2] G. Kitson Clark, *The Making of Victorian England* (London, Methuen, 1962), p. 280–1.

think of local governments as the classical loci of corruption
and inefficiency, but it was otherwise in the early period of
English industrialization. Britain entered upon these great
economic changes with a maldistribution as well as a general
under-supply of governmental talent. It was the administrative
resources of Whitehall that had to be expanded, at the expense
of the traditional responsibilities of local authorities. Much of
the debate over the role of government was a jurisdictional
dispute rather than a debate over the philosophy or political
economy of intervention as such. De Tocqueville, in 1833,
quoted John Bowring as remarking that 'England is a country
of decentralization. We have got a government, but we have
not got a central administration. Each county, each town, each
parish looks after its own interests.' And this is as it should be:
'It is not in the nature of things that a central government
should be able to watch over all the needs of a great nation. . . .
Centralization is too good a bait for the greed of the rulers.'[1]
But despite such views, which were widespread, and despite
the entrenchment of vested interests in local government, the
need for centralized intervention forced a rapid growth in this
sphere of government. In the twenty years after de Tocqueville's
visit, some sixteen central government agencies were created
in the field of welfare alone, with powers to supervise local
authorities and private philanthropic institutions.[2] The centralized administration recommended by the Poor Law Commission of 1834 was hotly disputed, but decentralization as a
principle acted as only a small brake upon the growth of
London as the locus of administrative power during the next
two decades. By the time the issue became important again, in
the Board of Health debate of the 1850s, the full apparatus of a
central administrative State had come into being.[3]

As one surveys the legislative and administrative activity of
the Victorian period it seems impossible, except by Procrustean
foolishness, to draw a general principle which would define

[1] Alexis de Tocqueville, *Journeys to England and Ireland* (London, Faber, 1958)
pp. 61–2.
[2] David Roberts, *Victorian Origins of the British Welfare State* (New Haven,
Yale, 1960), pp. 106 n., 315–16.
[3] Ibid.

what the State found it legitimate to do and what to leave alone. Some inconsistencies are almost incredible. For example, the government did practically nothing to regulate the operations of railway companies, despite the large number of accidents and the clear evidence of elementary negligence; yet, at the same time, it enacted many measures to control the operation of passenger ships. One might think that laissez-faire and *caveat emptor* were regarded as the right rules for continuing British residents, but those who voyaged or emigrated abroad would have to risk the moral dangers of a regulated trade. W. L. Burn, surveying the legislation of the mid-century decades, comes to the conclusion that 'As "evils" came to light they were dealt with, but it is very difficult to see any principle of selection behind the dealing.'[1] If we go further and try to discover how the 'evils' came to light, we will often discover a Samuel Plimsoll or an Edwin Chadwick; men dedicated, even obsessed, not by a principle, but by the need for pragmatic improvement. Granted there were those who deplored such a loose and *ad hoc* attitude on the part of government, who wished to see the general principles of State policy clearly defined and rigorously applied. And granted also, there were those among them who argued that practical problems would be best solved by the free play of the market, and the unconstrained exercise of self-interest. But those who regarded this as the *vade-mecum* of the legislator were few and, I think, unimportant, except in some very specific cases, which will be noted below.

There is a companion stereotype in the literature, that the ideology of laissez-faire was reflected in practical politics, in the debates over the tariff, factory and health legislation, the poor laws, and other specific issues. In the days before the existence of disciplined political parties, there is supposed to have been a distinct division in the House of Commons reflecting the predispositions of Members towards intervention by the State. A recent study by W. O. Aydelotte[2] requires us to abandon this view. He compares how Members voted on measures which are

---

[1] Burn, op. cit., pp. 160 ff.
[2] William O. Aydelotte, 'The Conservative and Radical Interpretations of Early Victorian Social Legislation', *Victorian Studies*, vol. II (December 1967).

supposed to have been clear 'radical' or 'conservative' issues in the 1840s – whether to receive the Chartist petition, income-tax Bills, the Corn Laws and the Factory Acts. He finds no correlation in the pattern of voting on such issues. Members who voted 'radical' on one were as likely as not to vote 'conservative' on another. We find no evidence in the voting patterns of Members of Parliament that would indicate the existence of any firmly fixed ideology concerning the role of the State in social and economic matters. What we find instead is, again, the ideological inconsistency of pragmatism.

Nevertheless, there were certain issues of State policy which were invested with ideological content of the sort we are seeking. The distinction one must make here is essential to an understanding of the history of laissez-faire. We do not find that an ideology ruled men's minds and thus determined the thrust of policy. But we do find that in some notable cases an ideological type of laissez-faire argument was a constituent of the public debate. Laissez-faire was not a maxim which determined the issue in any instance, but it played a notable role in the contemporary lobbying and propaganda. It was the peacock's tail not its skeleton; it had much to do with the amount and kind of attention it attracted but little importance otherwise. W. L. Burn has noted that 'although the idea of a coherent and dominant laissez-faire philosophy cannot be maintained, there was a well-used set of *laissez-faire clichés* which possessed emotional appeal'.[1] The clichés emerged in the political debate on specific issues. For this reason I wish to discuss those issues not as evidence of a controlling laissez-faire ideology, but as an aspect of public opinion and political propaganda.

II POPULAR POLITICAL ECONOMY AND PUBLIC DEBATE

Anyone who has been squeezed reluctantly through a high school course in 'modern economics' with its emphasis upon the Gross National Product and the leading industries of Brazil, or a college course with its recondite graphs and diagrams, will

---

[1] Burn, op. cit., p. 289.

find it hard to believe that it was ever a popular subject. But in the second quarter of the nineteenth century it was popular in England, even to the point of being a fad in some quarters. Young ladies of 'accomplishment' were admired if they could prattle Political Economy just as they were if they could play the pianoforte or sing parts. 'It has now become high fashion with blue ladies', wrote Maria Edgeworth to her aunt in 1822, 'to talk political economy. . . . Fine ladies now require that their daughters' governesses should teach political economy. "Pray Ma'am," said a fine Mamma to one who came to offer herself as governess, "Do you teach political economy?" The governess who thought she had provided herself well with French, Italian, music, drawing, dancing, etc., was quite astounded by this unexpected requisition she hesitatingly answered – "No, Ma'am, I cannot say I teach political economy, but I would if you think proper try to learn it." – "Oh dear no, Ma'am – if you don't teach it you won't do for me." '[1]

Instruction in Political Economy for the working classes was a rather more serious business. The middle and upper class sponsors of working class education held it as essential that the true principles of Political Economy should be taught to the lower orders. And it was never too early to begin – in the Birkbeck and other schools, a working class child was catechized on economic 'laws' as soon as he could read, or even before. When Charles Dickens created the immortal and fatuous Gradgrind in *Hard Times* in the 1850s, his satire was not entirely a work of imagination; it was an extravagance modelled upon real teachers, real schools and real books.[2]

The modern academic intellectual must remember that not everyone takes 'education' to mean that the student is assisted to think and to investigate and to form opinions for himself. The idea that an educated person is one with a permanently open mind is a monstrous impertinence to a wide spectrum of even a highly civilized people. One has only to read the current

---

[1] P. Sraffa (ed.), *Works and Correspondence of David Ricardo* (Cambridge, University, Press, 1955), vol. X, p. 172.

[2] Robin Gilmour, 'The Gradgrind School: Political Economy in the Classroom', *Victorian Studies*, vol. II (December 1967).

editorial pages of a middle-western American newspaper to see that the task of the schools and universities is conceived to be that of opening students' minds only for the purpose of filling them up with revered verities, and securely bolting them down again. Even when the modern 'liberal' speaks of education as the solvent of social ills he usually means by it the inculcation of particular attitudes and codes of behaviour.

It was even more so in the Victorian age. The schooling of the working classes knew no distinction between education and indoctrination. For that matter, neither did the schooling of the comfortable and the wealthy. But whereas in the latter case the objective was the simple social acculturation of the young, in working class schools the indoctrination had a more significant purpose – the production of political quietude.

Robin Gilmour, in his examination of the Victorian passion to teach Political Economy to the working classes, comes to the conclusion that the didactic political economists 'were engaged in what was, in effect, a campaign of containment. The end of their labours was to give the working class child an education which stressed as its dominant principle not the potentialities of life but its inevitable limitations: every object-lesson, every "useful" book and economic cautionary tale, every exhortation to prudence and parental forethought, combined to impress upon the poor the impossibility of escaping from the rigours of their social position.'[1] This judgement is, I think, a little warped. The advocates and practitioners of popular education in Political Economy did not preach a doctrine of resignation; they were in fact full of advice as to how one might improve oneself. Moreover, they did not even advocate that class lines should be rigid; on the contrary, many held the view that permanent improvement was most assured for those labourers who had adopted middle class standards of behaviour, personal habits, and aspirations.

What Gilmour refers to as the 'campaign of containment' is a correct description of this didactic literature if we see it as an effort to induce the working classes to forswear violence and collective action of a class nature. It was not working class

[1] Ibid., p. 223.

hopes for a better life that made the 'establishment' uneasy, it was fear that these yearnings might be channelled into political directions. The message of the economic teachers and preachers to the working class was 'Do not be led into the ways of wickedness by political and labour agitators. These are false friends. Your true friends are the laws of nature, including the laws of Political Economy. Properly understood and properly heeded, they point to improvement and happiness for all. Have faith in an economic system of enterprise and competition, and in the qualities of thrift, hard work, and self-reliance which inevitably lead to personal success in such a system.' It is but a step from this to the doctrine that the beneficent action of nature will be maximized if she is left entirely unfettered, and many popular writers make this 'small' extension. In the eyes of Carlyle, Political Economy, middle class apologetics, mammonism, capitalism, and laissez-faire were all of one piece and should be flung into Hell in a clean sweep. But one did not have to be as corybantic and distraught as Carlyle to make equations and judgements of this sort. It is not difficult to see how a calm and rational reader of mid-nineteenth-century popular Political Economy could have reached the same conclusions.

So far as the working classes themselves were concerned, there is little evidence that these efforts were very effective. Their leaders, for the most part, were able to see the Political Economy instruction for what it mainly was – an attack upon their growing political strength by the entrenched and *arriviste* classes, different in form but not in essentials from the repressive measures by which working class radicalism had been combated in the disturbed years after Waterloo.[1] Francis Place noted that the radical Rotundanists of the 1830s used the term 'Political Economist' as an expletive for all who were regarded as enemies of the working class.[2] There was more to this than Ricardo's wage-fund theory or the Malthusian explanation of poverty; there was the fact that Political Economy was being

---

[1] See R. K. Webb, *The British Working-Class Reader, 1790–1848* (London, Allen & Unwin, 1955), chaps. III and IV.

[2] Graham Wallas, *The Life of Francis Place* (London, Allen & Unwin, 1951), p. 273.

cited as a condemnation of the exercise of political power. Britain was becoming more civilized, and the grosser forms of coercion were giving way to more subtle and urbane ones; propaganda was only an infant, but it was a real brawny lad, with champion lungs.

It is not possible here to pass in review all the various efforts at working class propagandization by means of Political Economy, but in order to give the foregoing general statements some concreteness, I would like to pay some attention to the most notable of these. This was, of course, Harriet Martineau's series of novelettes published under the general title of *Illustrations of Political Economy* in 1832–4. At first, Harriet Martineau had difficulty in finding a publisher for her plan to write stories which would exemplify and illustrate the principles of Political Economy and in fact she had finally to make a contract wherein she herself bore all the risks of loss should they not sell. But her intense conviction that the lower orders desperately needed her instruction proved to be in correlation with the market. The stories were, from the first, an immense success. Charles Fox, her publisher, made a fortune, and Harriet Martineau herself was launched upon a career as novelist, journalist, essayist, travel writer, popular philosopher, and pundit so outstanding that she even finds a place today in the history of feminism, as one of those remarkable nineteenth-century women who first breached the established male enclaves of status and power.

The stories, it must be said at once, were not immortal literature. They were a cut above the penny-dreadfuls to be sure, but there is little in them in the way of character creation, narrative development, description, or any of the other aspects of the literary art that would serve to explain their great popularity without reference to their didactic intention. The largest part of the explanation must be found in the contemporaneous passion for improving, instructional, and inspirational reading, upon which was superimposed an intense interest in the vitally important new science of Political Economy. In the tales themselves, there was no direct instruction in Political Economy, and if the author had not appended a 'Summary of Principles Illustrated in This Volume' at the end of each, the didactic point of many of them would have remained an enigmatic puzzle to the reader.

It is difficult to say how important these summary appendages were to the success of the novels, or to use them to chart their influence upon contemporary thought. I myself cannot recall a single instance of seeing them quoted in contemporaneous literature. It is possible that the general title of the series and the summaries acted primarily as certificates of indulgence – in an era when novel reading was regarded as a wasteful and possibly dangerous use of time, one could read Harriet Martineau without feeling wicked. One has the impression that it was an age when anything that would permit one to take pleasure and leisure without a sense of guilt would enjoy a strong demand.

There are mysteries enough, then, in Harriet Martineau's popularity as a novelist, but there is no mystery in the message she wished to convey. All twenty-five of the 'Summaries of Principles' are worth reading *in toto*, but the purpose of this essay will be sufficiently served by a briefer series of quotations from them:

> As the materials of nature appear to be inexhaustible, and as the supply of labour is continually progressive, no other limits can be assigned to the operations of labour than those of human intelligence. And where are the limits of human intelligence? (No. I)

> The interests of the two classes of producers, Labourers and Capitalists, are therefore the same; the prosperity of both depending on the accumulation of CAPITAL. (No. II)

> The interests of the manufacturing and agricultural classes are therefore not opposed to each other but closely allied. (No. III)

> A free trade in sugar would banish slavery altogether since competition must induce an economy of labour and capital; i.e., a substitution of free for slave labour. (No. IV)

> Nothing can permanently affect the rate of wages which does not affect the proportion of population to capital.

Legislative interference does not affect this proportion and is therefore useless. Strikes affect it only by wasting capital and are therefore worse than worthless. . . . Whether reasonable or not, combinations [of workmen] are not subjects of legislative interference; the law having no cognizance of their causes. (No. VII)

The number of consumers must be proportional to the subsistence-fund. To this end, all encouragements to the increase in population should be withdrawn, and every sanction given to the preventive check, i.e., charity must be directed to the enlightenment of the mind, instead of the relief of bodily wants. (No. VIII)

Whatever affects the security of property, or intercepts the due reward of labour, impairs the subsistence-fund by discouraging industry and forethought. (No. IX)

By universal and free [international] exchange . . . an absolutely perfect system of economy of resources is established. As the general interest of each nation requires that there should be perfect liberty in the exchange of commodities, any restriction on such liberty, for the sake of benefiting any particular class or classes, is a sacrifice of a larger interest to a smaller – that is, a sin in government. (No. XVII)

Free competition cannot fail to benefit all parties: – Consumers, by securing the greatest practicable improvement and cheapness of the article; Producers by the consequent perpetual extension of demand; – and Society at large, by determining capital to its proper channels. (No. XVIII)

The duty of government being to render secure the property of its subjects, and their industry being their most undeniable property, all interference of government with the direction of the rewards of industry is a violation of its duty towards its subjects. (No. XXI)

A general glut is impossible. A partial glut is an evil which induces its own remedy. All interference [by government] which perplexes the calculations of producers, and thus causes the danger of a glut, is also a social crime. (No. XXII)

As public expenditure, though necessary, is unproductive, it must be limited. . . . That expenditure alone which is necessary to defence, order, and social improvement, is justifiable. (No. XXIII)

A just taxation must leave all the members of society in precisely the same relation in which it found them. (No. XXIV)

Here we have the whole doctrine of laissez-faire, bag and baggage: the perfection of the competitive system; the harmony of interests that reigns within a society so organized; the illegitimacy and perverse consequences of governmental interference. It is not a *Panglossian* picture. It does not urge the reader to resign himself to a vile and miserable world because it is the best possible; it promises eternal progress – if only the laws of nature are allowed to work. We would even look in vain in Harriet Martineau's sun-drenched landscape for that little cloud upon the horizon which made orthodox Political Economy a 'dismal science' and turned some of its believers to socialism – the Ricardian theory of rent. Nature is as generous with her gifts (see No. I above) as she is beneficient in her laws.

In Harriet Martineau's tales, we find the true fusion of ideas and confusion of understanding that is the essence of the doctrine of laissez-faire. She could not distinguish between the 'laws of Political Economy' as a simple abstract model whose focus is the heuristic one of assisting one to analyse the complex processes of the real economy; 'laws' which are the findings of such an analysis; and 'laws' which are ethical precepts. Notice in the above quotations how the same air of certainty, indeed necessity, is given alike to statements that are logical deductions, empirical predictions, and moral exhortations. 'Principle' was one of her favourite words, but she could not distinguish the difference between saying that a person is a 'man of principle' and that if $a = b$ and $b = c$, then $a = c$ is a 'principle' of mathematics. Nor could she accept the fact that scientific knowledge is partial and tentative; for her this too was a matter of 'principle'.[1]

But let us regain perspective. Is it possible to believe that the great myth of Victorian laissez-faire was the independent creation of myopic popularizers of classical Political Economy in the abstract, such as Harriet Martineau? I think not. A much larger part of the explanation must be traced to the use made of such versions of Political Economy in public debate on concrete political issues. Another series of Harriet Martineau's didactic stories entitled *Poor Laws and Paupers*, which she wrote at the request of Lord Brougham and the Society for the Diffusion of Useful Knowledge to drum up support for the recommendations of the Poor Law Commission of 1832, was probably more important. They did not sell well and this time Charles Fox lost money, but they identified the laws of Political Economy with one side of a political issue on which interest and feelings ran high. Discussion of Poor Law policy was so intense and general that one did not actually have to read the stories to be aware of the fact that Political Economy had spoken. As scholars now know, the leading economists of the day were not simple-minded Malthusians and laissez-faireists on the poverty question. Moreover, the Commission's recommendations and the resulting legislation were, if anything, the opposite of laissez-faire ideology in the type of poor relief and the degree of central government administration envisaged. Nevertheless, in the popular mind, it became a debate between hard-hearted and tight-fisted individualism on the one side and compassionate generosity and concern for communal values on the other. The oracular Miss Martineau left no doubt that Political Economy was wholly on the former side.

Political Economy got a bad name in the 1830s, in large part because of its putative stand on the poverty and trade union issues, but the label of laissez-faire was not firmly riveted upon it until the 1840s, as a result largely of the great debate over the Corn Laws. Here was a controversy that penetrated, and for a

---

[1] I have been assisted in my understanding of this characteristic of Harriet Martineau's thought by the work of Mrs Sara Kreider Hartzler, a graduate student in one of my classes in 1967–8.

time dominated, the whole range of English political life: the newspapers, journals, pamphlets, tracts and books, the speakers' platform, the political club, the pub, the shop and factory, Parliament, the hustings, the farmer's cottage, the working-man's kitchen, the middle-class parlour, the upper-class drawing-room. This was a debate like a civil war, and it left a mark upon politics comparable only to the political controversy accompanying the acute civil war of the seventeenth century. The seventeenth century established the importance of political *theory* in Britain's political life; the nineteenth, the power of its modern vulgarizations: propaganda and 'public opinion'.

The Corn Laws were not merely a tariff, they were a *symbol*, an emblem of the old constitutional order. The attack upon them was nothing less than an attack upon the established order of privilege.[1] The fact that the controversy focused on an economic question is, in certain respects, fortuitous, but at all events, it exerted a great impact on the history of economic thought and the interpretation of that history. The character of the controversy, and the fact that it resulted in a 'Great Victory' that dominated the political life of subsequent decades, invested with special significance and qualities all that had been involved in it. The Corn Law controversy was a prodigious political foundry, full of noise and heat, in which was cast some of the most distinctive moulds of Victorian stereotype. Such moulds do not mirror the variegated truth of social life. They are smooth and simple vessels, and their products bear only a stylized resemblance to the original material. The facts of the case provide little ground for interpreting the Corn Law controversy as a debate over the general issue of laissez-faire rather than the specific and much more limited one of free trade, and less for the view that the leading economists were unambiguously ranged on one side of the issue. Like all generic groups, the economists had mixed opinions, some of them, like Malthus, even opposing Repeal outright. Even the 'Manchester School' free traders who spearheaded the fight for Repeal and financed the massive attack, were not a homogeneous sect.

[1] See Betty Kemp, 'Reflections on the Repeal of the Corn Laws', *Victorian Studies*, vol. V (March 1962).

William Grampp, in his study of the School, finds that it contained a number of diverse groups, each with its own ideas about free trade and reasons for advocating it. The idea that the School were doctrinaire exponents of a general laissez-faire is a legend that enjoys widespread currency, but has a shallow foundation.[1] Later economists themselves contributed to the legend, motivated, one suspects, by a desire to fix blame for the ideology upon a source other than their own scientific progenitors.[2]

Whatever laissez-faire ideology there may have been in the Repeal campaign, it was not powerful enough nor appealing enough to penetrate through to the House of Commons where the issue had finally to be decided. Macgregor's examination of the great final Parliamentary debate of 1846 which occupies 1,500 double-columned pages of *Hansard*, disclosed that 'the phrase "laissez-faire" never occurs, and no important speakers referred to this expression as a principle'.[3] Sir Robert Peel later recalled that at this time there were no more than half a dozen members of Parliament who believed in applying a laissez-faire principle to economic questions generally, and Grampp gives it as his opinion that even this estimate was probably too high.[4]

There is some evidence that a free trade view, widened and hardened to the point of being a general laissez-faire doctrine, had penetrated into high levels of the bureaucracy. Lucy Brown's study of the Board of Trade indicates this.[5] G. R. Porter, who was joint secretary of the Board at the time of Repeal, displayed an adequately doctrinaire laissez-faire ideology in his own writings, and there is no reason to believe that he shed these private beliefs when engaged in official duties. In her study of the Irish famine, the event which actually

[1] William Grampp, *The Manchester School of Economics* (Oxford University Press, 1960).

[2] See, for example, Francis A. Walker, *The Wages Question* (New York, Holt, 1876), p. 161, and J. Tinbergen, *On the Theory of Economic Policy* (Amsterdam, North Holland, 1952), p. 3.

[3] D. H. Macgregor, *Economic Thought and Policy* (Oxford University Press, 1949), p. 56.

[4] Op. cit., p. 61.

[5] Lucy Brown, *The Board of Trade and the Free Trade Movement* (Oxford University Press, 1958).

precipitated Repeal, Cecil Woodham-Smith traces the inaction of the British government in substantial part to the grip of laissez-faire dogma upon C. E. Trevelyan, permanent head of the Treasury, and other senior officials.[1] Walter Bagehot, whose powers of trenchant observation were unique, testified in 1848 that opposition to Irish aid during the famine had stemmed in part from the 'sentiment' of laissez-faire, which he felt to be 'very susceptible of hurtful exaggeration'.[2] The searching study by Black[3] corroborates the view that economic policy towards Ireland in these dreadful years was an exhibition of laissez-faire doctrinairism at work.

Recall Samuel Smiles's characterization of laissez-faire: 'Let wretchedness do its work; do not interfere with death.' What could stand as a better example of this than the Irish policy? For a moment one might be tempted to locate the seat of laissez-faire ideology in the bureaucracy. But it will not work. The bureaucracy was extending the arm of the estate in too many directions at this time to be characterized as laissez-faire. Moreover, it is rarely (or never) possible to make generalizations about English opinion or politics on the basis of her attitude to Ireland. The English were struck into a catatonic trance by their inability to understand Ireland and its people. I cannot believe that the great myth of a pervasive laissez-faire ideology in Victorian England is founded on the rock of Ireland, though one must grant that the Irish policy was a notable instance.

The largest part of the explanation of the growth of a laissez-faire myth has to be traced to the character of the Anti-Corn Law campaign, and to the psychological significance of the eventual Repeal. The campaign was evangelical. The free traders attacked the Corn Laws with a zeal born of utter conviction in the moral and economic correctness of their cause. Those who have interpreted them as acting from the simple motivations of class interest overrate the power of greed. The

[1] C. Woodham-Smith, *The Great Hunger* (London, Hamilton, 1962).

[2] E. Barrington (ed.), *The Works and Life of Walter Bagehot* (London, Longmans, Green, & Co., 1915), vol. VIII, pp. 147–8.

[3] R. D. Collison Black, *Economic Thought and the Irish Question, 1817–1870* (Cambridge University Press, 1960).

campaign was a crusade against evil, not a commercial manoeuvre. Halévy remarked that it fused Political Economy and theology together.[1] John Bright, speaking before the League at Covent Garden Theatre, averred that free trade was more than a mere policy designed by political man; it was 'a plan laid down by the Creator of man when man was first created'.[2]

In considering the relationship between the Anti-Corn Law campaign and the ideology of laissez-faire, the most essential thing to recognize is that, for the great bulk of free trade advocates, it was free trade itself that was the basic faith. The leading orators and publicists of the League were willing to employ almost any instrument that would aid their cause, and sometimes they spoke fervently of the harmony of an economic universe left free to revolve according to the laws of nature. But an examination of their thought discloses no profound Leibnitzian metaphysics. A case study of the relationship between their arguments and their rhetoric leads one, in my view, to conclude that the occasional bit of laissez-faire harmony in their expressions served merely as oratorical rococo which the Leaguers found congenial and useful. They had a faith, to be sure, but its bedrock and skeleton was the unqualified merit and constructive power of an international policy of free trade.

There are, however, some notable cases of free trade advocacy which were clearly derivative from a general doctrine of laissez-faire, the most striking being the weekly commercial magazine *The Economist* of London. It was created, in 1843, to promote the Anti-Corn Law cause, but its founder and editor, James Wilson, earlier had become a convinced laissez-faire doctrinaire. In the pages of *The Economist* during the first dozen years of its life, one will find a laissez-faire ideology that was fully developed as a theory and consistently applied as a *vademecum* to all issues of contemporary policy. Next to the writings of Herbert Spencer (whose sociological-philosophical theory of extreme individualism was worked out while he was an

---

[1] Elie Halévy, *A History of the English People* (New York, Peter Smith, 1951), vol. IV, p. 89.
[2] *The Economist* (London, 22 February 1845), p. 174.

employee of *The Economist*), the pages of this magazine contain the most elaborated and consistent laissez-faire ideology I have encountered in the English literature of the Victorian Age.[1] The case of *The Economist* is evidence against the general thesis of this essay – until one remembers how unique it was.

In accounting for the impact of the Corn Law struggle on English opinion, some considerable weight has to be given to the dramatic nature of the eventual victory. Peel's sudden and unexpected decision to repeal the corn tariff was like the capitulation of a citadel, which not only gave victory to the insurgents on this specific field of battle, but disclosed the general weakness of the entrenched establishment. For the quiet revolution which England was undergoing, it was like the fall of the Bastille for the French, and it became the symbol for the shift in political power that was taking place. The Great Exhibition of 1851 was, as intended, a celebration of industrialism and material progress, but it was far more than this – it solemnized a new political legitimacy whose cardinal tenet was free trade. One can best appreciate this when one examines the revival of tariff controversy in the 1880s and after the Boer War It was not possible, even half a century after the great Repeal victory, for a respectable Englishman to advocate tariff protection plainly; it was necessary for him to speak in the dissembling terms of 'Fair Trade' or 'Tariff Reform'.

A widespread development of free trade ideology developed in mid-nineteenth-century England, but a similar laissez-faire ideology did not. A large part of the error which the historiography contains in its categorization of the period as one of laissez-faire is due to a false identification of laissez-faire and free trade. It is striking how often one finds the two phrases used synonymously by later writers. Even today, one sometimes finds the same identification in the writing of historians who have steeped themselves deeply in the literature of the mid-Victorian age. More than anything else, it is responsible for the fact that the myth continues to draw fitful breath despite the blows that scholarship has rained upon it in recent years.

[1] See my article, 'The London *Economist* and the High Tide of Laissez-Faire', *Journal of Political Economy*, vol. LXIII (December 1955), pp. 461–88.

Free trade = laissez-faire is a false equation, but this is not to deny that free trade was a policy of non-intervention. Moreover, it was a policy of non-intervention in an area of national concern that was far from minor. The point is that, however important it was, international trade was nevertheless a particular area of economic activity and therefore free trade was a particular policy; whereas laissez-faire is a general theory of economic policy applicable, as *The Economist* exemplified, to all particular cases. I have argued here that international trade was the most important particular area of policy in which a philosophy of non-intervention was victorious. Was it the only one? One other such area of major importance can be identified – finance and banking.

When the Bank of England suspended the redemption of its notes for gold in 1797, a period of intense monetary controversy was inaugurated which continued for three-quarters of a century. The issues involved are surprisingly little reflected in the great treatises of Political Economy, but anyone who has examined the periodical and pamphlet literature or the Parliamentary papers and debates of the period cannot be doubtful of their practical importance. One of these issues (perhaps, in retrospect, the central one) was whether Britain should have a regulated or a 'self-regulated' currency and banking system. This issue was largely determined by Peel's Bank Charter Act of 1844 which, in effect, established an automatic system of money supply regulation. Those who argued at this time that the Bank of England should be given discretionary power to alter its note issue and should therefore assume responsibility for monetary regulation, were defeated. 'Central banking' and 'monetary policy' of the sort we have today was rejected in favour of the free play of market forces operating under the rules of the gold standard system.

Frank Fetter, in his definitive study of the monetary controversy,[1] attributes this decisive act of policy in part to the existence of a general laissez-faire sentiment. Much as I hesitate to quarrel with this superb work of scholarship, I cannot agree

[1] Frank Whitson Fetter, *Development of British Monetary Orthodoxy, 1797–1875* (Cambridge, Harvard University Press, 1965).

with Fetter on this point. There was no such general sentiment in a position of commanding influence at this time. The evidence suggests rather that the choice of an automatic system of regulation was dictated by a strong sense of the incapacity of government to manage by deliberate acts of policy an area of the economy as complex and as mysterious as the monetary system. It was the result of a fearful awareness of the grave consequences of mismanagement in this area and an assessment of the limits of administrative competence, rather than a positive choice of an abstract optimum. The fact that the gold standard became one of the great idols of nineteenth-century economic thought does not testify to laissez-faire origins so much as it reflects the continuing sense of mystery that was widespread concerning the functioning of monetary processes. Positive policy can be undertaken only when one is convinced (whether validly or not) that one understands what one is doing. Monetary policy was impossible in the nineteenth century because, in this area, unlike many others, such an assuring conviction was lacking.

The same can be said for fiscal policy as well. There is some identification in the literature of 'Gladstonian finance' with laissez-faire. Gladstone himself held a general predilection to non-intervention and one could build a case for doctrinairism around Robert Lowe, his first Chancellor, but it would have to be rather forced. The power of the great fisc was growing, but not until the 1930s, with the rise of Keynesian economics, did the idea begin to gain ground that the fiscal balance itself – the surplus or deficit of the overall budget – could be an instrument of economic policy. As long as the view was general that government exerted its influences only via particular acts of taxation and expenditure, there was nothing really that could be said against the propositions of 'sound finance' that budgets should be at least balanced and, if possible, a surplus should be provided for reduction of the national debt. Gladstone might not have believed Keynesian economics if it had been available to him, but in his own day, economists were not saying anything that suggested that the government should view its finances differently from those of a prudent businessman. The lack of a fiscal policy of the modern type does not have to be explained as a derivative from the principle of laissez-faire.

A contention which I have not here investigated is that laissez-faire ideology was a strong force among those who unsuccessfully opposed the welfare-oriented (and other types of) intervention of the State in the nineteenth century. The argument is made by Ruth Hodgkinson,[1] for example, that the progressive improvement of health services for the poor and indigent was opposed by many on such ideological grounds. That may be, and it would be a contribution to the history of laissez-faire thought to examine such cases with a view to determining whether the ideology was in fact the basic reason for such opposition or whether it was merely argumentative or hypocritical. I have not made such a direct examination myself and there is not as yet enough secondary literature bearing on the point to permit one to draw general conclusions. However, even if it should be demonstrated that a substantial body of sincere laissez-faire theory is to be found in this location, it would identify laissez-faire only as an ideology of those fighting a rear-guard action against the overwhelming forces of intervention, and would therefore not act as support for the contention, with which this essay is concerned, that the ideology exerted a controlling force upon economic policy in the nineteenth century. It would be evidence of its existence to be sure, but, more significantly, evidence of its weakness.

[1] Ruth Hodgkinson, *The Origins of the National Health Service* (Berkeley, University of California Press, 1967).

Select Bibliography

This bibliography does not include the items reprinted in this volume or the writings of the classical economists. The latter are listed in the biographical articles in the *International Encyclopedia of the Social Sciences* (see Section 8, below). The critical and historical literature on the classical economists and economic policy is vast, and this bibliography is therefore restricted to those items most likely to be useful to students. Items on the colonies have been excluded as they appear in another volume in this series: A. G. L. Shaw, *Great Britain and the Colonies 1815–1865*. The place of publication is London, unless otherwise stated.

1. *General*

BLAUG, MARK, *Ricardian Economics, A Historical Study* (New Haven, 1958) (esp. chap. 7, 'Political Economy to be Read as Literature', and chap. 10, 'Matters of Economic Policy').

BRYSON, GLADYS, *Man and Society: The Scottish Inquiry of the 18th Century* (Oxford, 1945; reprinted New York, 1970).

CHECKLAND, S. G., 'The Prescriptions of the Classical Economists', *Economica*, N.S. vol. XX (February 1953), pp. 61–72. (A review of L. C. Robbins, *Theory of Economic Policy in Classical Political Economy*.)

COATS, A. W., 'The Role of Authority in the Development of British Economics', *The Journal of Law and Economics*, vol. 7 (October 1964), pp. 85–106.

GRAMPP, W. D., *Economic Liberalism* (New York, 1965), vol. 2.

GRAMPP, W. D., 'On the History of Thought and Policy', *Papers and Proceedings of the American Economic Association*, vol. 55 (May 1965), pp. 128–42.

HALÉVY, ELIE, *The Growth of Philosophic Radicalism* (1928; reprinted Boston, Mass., 1955).

HUTCHISON, T. W., *'Positive' Economics and Policy Objectives* (1964).

KNIGHT, FRANK H., 'Theory of Economic Policy and the History of Economic Doctrine', *Ethics*, vol. 63 (July 1953), pp. 276–92. (A review of L. C. Robbins, *The Theory of Economic Policy in Classical Political Economy*.)

MITCHELL, WESLEY C., *Types of Economic Theory from Mercantilism to Institutionalism*, ed. Joseph Dorfman, vol. 1 (New York, 1967).

ROBBINS, L. C., *The Theory of Economic Policy in English Classical Political Economy* (1952).

SAMUELS, WARREN J., *The Classical Theory of Economic Policy* (New York, 1966).

SCHUMPETER, JOSEPH A., *History of Economic Analysis* (Oxford, 1964).

STIGLER, GEORGE J., *Five Lectures on Economic Problems* (1949). (Lecture 1 considers 'The Economists and Equality'. Lecture 3, 'The Classical Economists: An Alternative View', examines the report of the Commissioners on the Hand-Loom Weavers, 1841, as an example of the classical economists' 'working technique'.)

VINER, JACOB, 'Bentham and J. S. Mill: the Utilitarian Background', *The American Economic Review*, vol. 39 (March 1949), pp. 360–82; reprinted in *The Long View and the Short* (Glencoe, Ill., 1958), pp. 306–31.

WILSON, CHARLES, 'Government Policy and Private Interest in Modern Economic History', in Charles Wilson, *Economic History and the Historian, Collected Essays* (1969).

2. *Laissez-Faire*

BREBNER, J. B., 'Laissez-Faire and State Intervention in Nineteenth Century Britain', *Journal of Economic History* (December 1948), reprinted in E. M. Carus-Wilson (ed.), *Essays in Economic History*, vol. 3 (1962).

CROUCH, R. L., 'Laissez-Faire in Nineteenth-Century Britain: Myth or Reality', *The Manchester School*, vol. 35 (September 1967), pp. 199–215.

MACGREGOR, D. H., *Economic Thought and Policy* (1949),chap. 3.

SCHWARTZ, P., 'John Stuart Mill and Laissez-Faire: London Water', *Economica*, N.S. vol. XXXIII (February 1966), pp. 71–83.

SCOTT GORDON, H., 'Laissez-Faire', *International Encyclopedia of the Social Sciences* (New York, 1968), vol. 8, pp. 546–9.

STIGLER, G. J., 'The Economist and the State', *The American Economic Review*, vol. 55 (March 1965), pp. 1–18.

VINER, JACOB, 'Adam Smith and Laissez-Faire', *The Journal of Political Economy*, vol. 35 (April 1927), pp. 198–232; reprinted in *The Long View and the Short*, op. cit., pp. 213–45.

VINER, JACOB, 'The Intellectual History of Laissez-Faire', *The Journal of Law and Economics*, vol. 3 (October 1960), pp. 45–69.

3. Free Trade

BROWN, LUCY, *The Board of Trade and the Free Trade Movement, 1830–42* (Oxford, 1958). (A penetrating study of the behind-the-scenes influence of economic ideas on trade and budgetary policy.)

COATS, A. W., 'Political Economy and the Tariff Reform Campaign of 1903', *The Journal of Law and Economics*, vol. 2 (April 1968), pp. 181–229. (Examines the early twentieth-century survival of classical free trade ideas.)

GRAMPP, W. D., *The Manchester School of Economics* (Oxford, 1960).

MCCORD, NORMAN, *The Anti-Corn Law League 1838–1946* (1958).

PROUTY, R. W., *The Transformation of the Board of Trade, 1830–55* (1957).

SEMMEL, BERNARD, *The Rise of Free Trade Imperialism, Classical Political Economy and The Empire of Free Trade and Imperialism, 1750–1850* (Cambridge, 1970).

4. Money, Banking, and Fiscal Policy

FETTER, FRANK WHITSON, 'The Bullion Report Re-examined', *The Quarterly Journal of Economics* (August 1942); reprinted in *Papers in English Monetary History*, T. S.

Ashton and R. S. Sayers (eds.) (Oxford, 1953), pp. 66–75. (A reappraisal of Ricardo's contribution to the Report of the Select Committee on the High Price of Bullion, 1810.)

FETTER, FRANK WHITSON, *Development of British Monetary Orthodoxy 1797–1875* (Harvard, 1965). (An outstanding survey of personalities and ideas that far transcends the conventional limits of the history of economics.)

HORSEFIELD, J. K., 'The Origins of the Bank Charter Act, 1844', *Economica* (November 1944); reprinted in Ashton and Sayers, op. cit., pp. 109–25.

ROSEVEARE, HENRY, *The Treasury, The Evolution of a British Institution* (1969), especially pp. 139–50, 192–7. (Discusses the connections between classical economics, Gladstonian economic liberalism, and the orthodox 'Treasury View'.)

SHOUP, CARL S., *Ricardo on Taxation* (New York, 1960), chaps. 15 and 16.

VINER, JACOB, *The Theory of International Trade* (1937). (Chapters 3–5 contain a classic account of early nineteenth-century monetary controversy.)

5. *Factory Acts*

SORENSON, L. R., 'Some Classical Economists, Laissez-Faire, and the Factory Acts', *The Journal of Economic History*, vol. 12 (Summer 1952), pp. 247–62.

WALKER, KENNETH O., 'The Classical Economists and the Factory Acts', *The Journal of Economic History*, vol. 1 (November 1941), pp. 168–77.

6. *Poor Law, Labour, and Employment Policy*

BLAUG, MARK, 'The Myth of the Old Poor Law and the Making of the New', *The Journal of Economic History*, vol. 23 (June 1963), pp. 151–84; and 'The Poor Law Report Re-examined', *The Journal of Economic History*, vol. 24 (June 1964), pp. 229–45.

CORRY, B. A., *Money, Saving and Investment in English Economics 1800–1850* (1962). (Chapter 4, on 'The Policy Implications of Classical Economics', is especially concerned with employment policy.)

FINER, S. E., *The Life and Times of Edwin Chadwick* (1952).

TAUSSIG, F. W., *Wages and Capital* (1896; reprinted 1932 and 1935). (A classic study of the 'wages fund' theory.)

7. *Education*

GILMOUR, ROBIN, 'The Gradgrind School: Political Economy in the Classroom', *Victorian Studies*, vol. 11 (December 1967), pp. 207–24.

GOLDSTROM, J. M., 'Richard Whately and Political Economy in School Books', *Irish Historical Studies*, vol. XV (September 1966), pp. 131–46.

GOLDSTROM, J. M., *The Social Content of Education, 1808–1870. A Study of the Working Class School Reader in England and Ireland* (Irish University Press, 1970).

HOLLANDER, SAMUEL, 'The Role of the State in Vocational Training: The Classical Economists' View', *Southern Economic Journal*, vol. 34 (April 1968), pp. 513–25.

MILLER, WILLIAM L., 'The Economics of Education in English Classical Economics', *Southern Economic Journal*, vol. 32 (January 1966), pp. 294–309.

TYRRELL, A., 'Political Economy, Whiggism and the Education of Working-class Adults in Scotland 1817–40', *The Scottish Historical Review*, vol. 48 (October 1969), pp. 151–65.

WEST, E. G., 'The Role of Education in Nineteenth-Century Doctrines of Political Economy', *British Journal of Educational Studies*, vol. XII, No. 2 (May 1964), pp. 161–72.

8. *Individual Economists*

COATS, A. W., 'Adam Smith, The Modern Re-Appraisal', *Renaissance and Modern Studies*, vol. VI (1962), pp. 25–48.

CROPSEY, JOSEPH, *Polity and Economy, An Interpretation of the Principles of Adam Smith* (The Hague, 1957).

HUTCHISON, T. W., 'Bentham as an Economist', *The Economic Journal*, vol. 66 (June 1956), pp. 66–74.

International Encyclopedia of the Social Sciences (New York, 1968); articles on:

  'Jeremy Bentham', by MARY PETER MACK in vol. 2;

'Robert Thomas Malthus', by MARK BLAUG in vol. 9;

'John Stuart Mill', by JOHN C. REES and V. W. BLADEN in vol. 10;

'David Ricardo', by MARK BLAUG in vol. 13;

'Nassau William Senior', by MARIAN BOWLEY in vol. 14;

'Adam Smith', by JACOB VINER in vol. 14;

'Robert Torrens', by BERNARD CORRY in vol. 16.

LEVY, S. LEON, *Nassau W. Senior 1790–1864; Critical Essayist, Classical Economist and Adviser of Governments* (Newton Abbot, 1970).

MACFIE, A. L., *The Individual and Society, Papers on Adam Smith* (1967).

O'BRIEN, D. P., *J. R. McCulloch, A Study in Classical Economics* (London, 1970).

ROBSON, J. M., *The Improvement of Mankind: The Social and Political Thought of John Stuart Mill* (Toronto, 1968).

ROSENBERG, NATHAN, 'Some Institutional Aspects of the *Wealth of Nations*', *The Journal of Political Economy*, vol. 68 (December 1960), pp. 557–70.

9. *Miscellaneous*

(including the dissemination of classical ideas)

AYDELOTTE, WILLIAM O., 'The Conservative and Radical Interpretations of Early Victorian Social Legislation', *Victorian Studies*, vol. 11 (December 1967), pp. 224–36.

BLACK, R. D. COLLISON, 'Economic Policy in Ireland and India in the Time of J. S. Mill', *Economic History Review*, 2nd series, vol. 21 (August 1968), pp. 321–36.

CHECKLAND, S. G., 'The Propagation of Ricardian Economics in England', *Economica*, N.S. vol. XVI (February 1949), pp. 40–52.

CROMWELL, VALERIE, 'Interpretations of Nineteenth-Century Administration: An Analysis', *Victorian Studies*, vol. 9 (March 1966), pp. 245–55. (A review of the recent controversy about the influence of Benthamism on the expansion of government activity.)

FETTER, FRANK W., 'Economic Controversy in the British Reviews, 1802–1850', *Economica*, N.S. vol. 32 (November 1965), pp. 424–37.

FETTER, FRANK W., 'The Rise and Decline of Ricardian Economics', *History of Political Economy*, vol. 1 (Spring 1969), pp. 67–84.

HART, JENNIFER, 'Nineteenth-Century Social Reform: A Tory Interpretation of History', *Past and Present*, no. 31 (July 1965), pp. 39–61.

HUME, L. J., 'Jeremy Bentham and the Nineteenth-Century Revolution in Government', *The Historical Journal*, vol. 10 (1967), pp. 361–75.

MACDONAGH, O., *A Pattern of Government Growth, 1800–60; The Passenger Acts and their Enforcement* (1961).

MACDONAGH, O., 'The Nineteenth-Century Revolution in Government: A Reapprisal', *The Historical Journal*, vol. 1 (1958), pp. 52–67.

MEEK, R. L., 'The Decline of Ricardian Economics in England', *Economica*, N.S. vol. XVII (February 1950), pp. 43–62.

ROBERTS, DAVID, 'Jeremy Bentham and the Victorian Administrative State', *Victorian Studies*, vol. 11 (March 1959), pp. 193–210.

ROBERTS, DAVID, *Victorian Origins of the British Welfare State* (Yale, 1960).

SCOTT GORDON, H., 'The London *Economist* and the High Tide of Laissez-Faire', *The Journal of Political Economy*, vol. 63 (December 1955), pp. 461–88.

WEBB, R. K., *The British Working Class Reader, 1790–1848* (1955). (A study of the diffusion of classical economics.)